Hardscrabble Diamonds

Hardscrabble Diamonds

*Postwar Baseball in New England
and the Maritimes, 1945–1960*

COLIN HOWELL

McFarland & Company, Inc., Publishers
Jefferson, North Carolina

Library of Congress Cataloguing-in-Publication Data

Names: Howell, Colin D., 1944– author.
Title: Hardscrabble diamonds : postwar baseball in New England and the Maritimes, 1945-1960 / Colin Howell.
Description: Jefferson, North Carolina : McFarland & Company, Inc., 2023 | Includes bibliographical references and index.
Identifiers: LCCN 2023015938 | ISBN 9781476690711 (paperback : acid free paper) ∞
ISBN 9781476648736 (ebook)
Subjects: LCSH: Baseball—New England—History—20th century. | Baseball—Maritime Provinces—History—20th century. | Baseball—Social aspects—New England—History—20th century. | Baseball—Social aspects—Maritime Provinces—History—20th century. | New England—Social life and customs—20th century. | Maritime Provinces—Social life and customs—20th century. | BISAC: SPORTS & RECREATION / Baseball / History | HISTORY / Canada / General
Classification: LCC GV863.N45 H68 2023 | DDC 796.3570974/0904—dc23/eng/20230411
LC record available at https://lccn.loc.gov/2023015938

British Library cataloguing data are available
ISBN (print) 978-1-4766-9071-1
ISBN (ebook) 978-1-4766-4873-6

© 2023 Colin Howell. All rights reserved

No part of this book may be reproduced or transmitted in any form or by any means, electronic or mechanical, including photocopying or recording, or by any information storage and retrieval system, without permission in writing from the publisher.

Front cover: William "Buddy" Condy (right) of the Halifax Capitals crossing the plate after hitting a home run in 1947 (Halifax Municipal Archives)

Printed in the United States of America

*McFarland & Company, Inc., Publishers
Box 611, Jefferson, North Carolina 28640
www.mcfarlandpub.com*

Contents

Preface: Baseball, Memory and History	1
ONE. The Postwar Flourishing of Baseball in the Maritimes	13
TWO. Home Diamonds: Local Stars of Postwar Maritime Baseball	25
THREE. The Barnstorming Era: American Baseball's Northward Glance, 1948–50	44
FOUR. Tipping the Balance: The American Influence and the Marginalization of Local Players	59
FIVE. Bill Brooks, Art Hoch and the Carolinian Connection	69
SIX. "NCAA North": CWS Champions, Bonus Babies and All-Americans	82
SEVEN. Playing in "Color Bar Limbo": Black Players in the Maritimes, 1946–60	98
EIGHT. Borderlands Baseball: New Brunswick and Maine	110
NINE. Troublesome Times: 1955–57	126
TEN. Playing Out the String: 1957–59	141
ELEVEN. Post-Game Reminiscences	155
TWELVE. Great Performers, Great Performances: A Statistical Retrospective	163
Appendix 1: Career Batting and Major League Equivalencies: Maritimes and Maine	189
Appendix 2: Single-Season Batting and Major League Equivalencies: Maritimes and Maine	191

Appendix 3: Career Pitching	193
Appendix 4: Players from Major NCAA Programs	194
Essay on Sources	197
Chapter Notes	203
Bibliography	209
Index	211

Preface

Baseball, Memory and History

Hardscrabble Diamonds: Postwar Baseball in the Maritimes and New England, 1945–1960 is part baseball history, part memoir and part sabermetric analysis. In addition to telling the story of my growing up with baseball in Canada's Maritime provinces in the 1940s and '50s, it offers an in-depth look at how a peripheral region in the northeastern corner of North America became a baseball hotbed, a summer training ground for elite players from leading American college programs—including three different College World Series champions—and a haven for veteran players attracted by salaries higher than those in the contracting minor-league system south of the border. High-level college programs from New England, New York, and the mid–Atlantic states, and from the Carolinas to Michigan, supplied players. So did major league organizations interested in assessing the talent of young blue-chip prospects and eventual "bonus babies" who would head directly to the major leagues without a minor league stop along the way. In this competitive environment, only the most talented local players were able to crack the rosters of town teams in Nova Scotia, New Brunswick and Maine. How the northeastern borderlands of the Maritimes and New England—and more particularly leagues such as the Halifax and District (H&D) League operating from 1946 to 1959 and the Maine–New Brunswick League (1950–55)—would evolve into "NCAA North" is a remarkable and largely forgotten story. Moreover, recapturing that history provides a contribution to the larger effort to write the story of Atlantic Canada into the larger Canadian historical narrative. (The "northeastern borderlands" refers to a particular transnational region which is characterized by continuing socio-cultural, demographic and economic interaction and a sense of shared identity. Although borderland regions are not precisely defined by state or provincial boundaries, in this study the term refers to the three Maritime Provinces, Nova Scotia, New Brunswick and Prince Edward Island, as well as Massachusetts, New Hampshire, Maine and Vermont in the United States and their interconnected baseball history.)

My decision to connect my personal recollections of the H&D League to an extensively researched history of baseball in small Maritime communities and the northeastern borderlands during the 1940s and 1950s is intentional. Indeed, much of what follows is derived from extensive interviews and interactions over the years with players, scouts, fans, sport historians, journalists and other observers who offer a nuanced and colorful dimension to what otherwise might be a dry, matter-of-fact account of on-the-field performances. It also allows me to bring into focus the voluminous material that I have collected over the years and that fills the shelves of my office at home and to present in a concluding chapter a statistical analysis of individual performances and quality-of-competition indexes for various leagues in the Maritimes and Maine in the postwar era. How could this project not reflect my enduring interest in baseball research, my professional career as a sport and Atlantic Provinces historian, and my personal love of the sport?

Of course, no other North American sport generates more popular reminiscences, collectible memorabilia, and literary reflections than baseball does, although some may think the same is true of hockey in Canada. Many think that baseball embodies and reveals the American character and that the proverbial "field of dreams" has become a civil religion. "I believe in the Church of Baseball," says Susan Sarandon's character in the movie *Bull Durham*. "The only church that feeds the soul, day-in and day-out, is the Church of Baseball." On a secular level the game of catch between fathers and sons has come to represent hopes for a less contentious world and enshrines cherished values. This simple pastime transfers skills from one generation to the next, recognizes the importance of parental responsibilities, and promotes inter-generational bonding as the ball tracks back and forth. Author David McGimpsey contends that "the emotions that the image elicits are not easily dismissed—and that is what makes it such a reliable cliché."[1]

The mythologizing in the writings of William Kinsella and in the movie *Field of Dreams* provides perhaps the most powerful endorsement of the game's redemptive and spiritual character.[2] In Kinsella's world, baseball has a timeless quality, stretching across generations and serving as a comforting and socially interactive practice. Spiritual allusions abound as well, as a baseball diamond hewn out of an Iowa cornfield takes on a heavenly character. By contrast, in the movie

Independence Day, Pulitzer Prize–winning novelist Richard Ford tests the limits of baseball's ability to heal the deep divisions that exist across the generational divide as well as across the economic, social and racial landscape of contemporary America. Rejecting the gushes of sentimentality that often abound in baseball literature, Ford describes a father's attempt to bridge the divide with his son by taking him on an Independence Day holiday visit to Cooperstown and to the Basketball Hall of Fame in Springfield, Massachusetts. Rather than being an elixir, the trip ends with the son being hit in the head by a pitch from a pitching machine, leaving the relationship of father and son as strained as it had been earlier.[3]

This recovery of Maritime baseball in the fifties is likewise connected to my adolescence and coming of age. Of course, writing about baseball and the broader social environment of the time involves a temptation to romanticize growing up, remembering fondly the family's first car or first TV set while avoiding darker judgments about the era's McCarthyism, misogyny and racism. For many of my generation, rock 'n' roll, the Beatles, Marilyn Monroe, '55 Chevies, Elvis and, of course, Mickey Mantle crowd out images of postwar intolerance. It was not until the sixties that I shed the naïveté of my childhood and reflected more deeply upon the reality of social injustice and divisiveness. Simon and Garfunkel brought popular culture, the loss of youthful innocence and baseball together in elegant harmony. "Where have you gone, Joe DiMaggio?" they crooned on the soundtrack of the 1967 film classic *The Graduate*. "Our nation turns its lonely eyes to you."

I first saw *The Graduate* in Cincinnati in January of 1968 while in grad school working on a doctorate in American history. I was blown away by Dustin Hoffman's character Benjamin Braddock and his bewilderment, cynicism and dissatisfaction with the "second-hand world" that our parents' generation left us as we moved beyond childhood. As children of the sixties we envisioned, perhaps naively, a much better outcome from our generation than the one before. What were we going to do with our lives and what kind of world did we hope to create? How would we avoid being drawn down into a life of mindless consumption and suburban complacency?

Having left my small-town experiences of Nova Scotia behind me, I cut my political teeth amid the turbulent struggles and protests around Civil Rights, the Vietnam War and the assassinations of Martin Luther King and Bobby Kennedy. Not only had "Joltin'" Joe gone away as the song told us, but so had "Abraham, Martin and John." "Can you tell me where he's gone?" Dion sang, plaintively affirming the importance of lives of sacrifice and those who had made a difference while dying too soon. It was as though a generation longed to remember its history. It was a moment when history escaped the drab and soul-less study that many had come to associate with high-school narratives of national triumph, and I was convinced that there could be nothing more important to study than the past, whose weight we always carry. Discussions of slavery, women's struggles, and the Cold War were as contentious, energetic, and engaging as the exploits of the NL Champion Cincinnati Reds as they made their way to the 1970 World Series before losing in five games to the Baltimore Orioles.

I left Cincinnati in June 1970, so my memories are of the Reds at old Crosley Field. This was the time of Cincinnati's Big Red Machine led by bullet-armed catcher Johnny Bench, hustling Pete Rose, and pitchers Jim Merritt, Clay Carroll and Jim Maloney. It was also the time of the Montreal Expos experiment. Montreal was awarded a major league franchise in 1968, and the Expos took the field the following year. Whenever they came to town, I would head to Crosley, waving an Expos pennant amid the swirling red towels of the Cincinnati crowd and feeling more Canadian than I had ever felt before. This was important since having gone to the States in the summer of 1967, I missed much of the Centennial experience and the excitement surrounding Pierre Elliott Trudeau. The Expos became for me a nationalist substitute for "Trudeaumania."

As an expansion club the Expos were not much of a challenge to the mighty Reds, and the spectators around me always treated me in a somewhat bemused fashion. I remember one game especially. It was early in the 1970 season, and I was sitting next to a beefy-armed guy with a Reds jersey that wouldn't fully close across his prominent belly. He was a friendly guy and started asking me about the Expos. Balor Moore, a young Texan who had been the first choice of the Expos in the 1969 amateur draft, was starting his first game in the majors, and I remember saying that he was a real prospect. He threw hard but had little control. Even some of his warm-up pitches were bouncing ten feet in front of the plate. Moore lasted two innings that day, giving up five hits and three runs while striking out and walking three batters. My seatmate was unimpressed, of course, but in an olive branch gesture said he liked third baseman "Coco" Laboy. "That Laboy," he said, "he ain't half bad for a Frenchman." I didn't have the heart to correct him. Laboy was a native of Puerto Rico.

The Expos that year had two players who had been stars in Eastern Canada in the 1950s, first baseman and outfielder Ty Cline and right-handed relief specialist Claude Raymond. Born in Hampton, South Carolina, and a college star at Clemson University, Cline played two seasons for the Dartmouth Arrows of the Halifax and District League in 1958 and '59 before signing with the Cleveland Indians and making it to the majors a year later. A twelve-year veteran of major league baseball, Cline spent two years as a back-up centerfielder to Willie Mays in San Francisco before moving to the Expos in the expansion draft. Ironically, he would end his career with the Reds in 1971, having been traded by the Expos the year before in exchange for outfielder Clyde Mashore.

I caught up with Cline a few years after his retirement in his stately home in Charleston, South Carolina. Then a successful businessman with the first Baskin-Robbins Ice Cream franchise in the city, Cline remembered his days in Nova Scotia as important in the transition from college to pro ball. It was his first time away from home, and the sixty-game season meant that he was playing five or six times a week, unlike in college. In addition, playing under the lights and against the best college players from along the eastern seaboard was more like professional baseball than college ball. After two years with the Arrows, Cline moved quickly up the minor league ranks, starting at Double-A Mobile in 1960, where he hit .311 with nine homers and an OPS (on-base percentage plus slugging) of .836. He broke into the majors that same season as a September call-up, hitting .308 over seven games. "I loved playing those two years in Nova Scotia," he recalled. Over his two seasons with Dartmouth, his stats were consistent with those in 1960 in Mobile and Cleveland, hitting .301 with seven homers. He also made an occasional appearance on the mound for the Arrows with respectable but not outstanding results.

Claude Raymond burst onto the baseball scene in Quebec as a teenager, starring in junior ball before signing a contract with the Milwaukee Braves in 1955. With the Braves he played alongside players signed out of the Maritimes and northern Maine by Braves scout Jeff Jones. Among them were fellow big leaguers Ken MacKenzie, Joe Morgan, Mike Roarke, Charley Lau, Al Spangler and Carlton Willey and minor leaguers Ron Liptak, Ernie Christoff, Roger Clapp, Sid Goldfader, Fred Vogel, Charley Wrinn, and Jack Sanford. The first Quebec-born player to play in a major-league All-Star game, Raymond broke into the majors with the White Sox in 1960 and eventually joined the Expos late in the 1969 season. He had a lengthy twelve-year big league career, with a 46–53 won-lost record and a career ERA of 3.66.

I became acquainted with Claude during the 1990s when we both were serving on the Canadian Baseball Hall of Fame's selection committee, an interesting gig for a baseball historian and a chance to swap opinions with people like Tom Valke (then executive director of the Hall), Canadian baseball historian Bill Humber, Cooperstown Hall of Fame broadcaster Bob Elliott, and others. Claude joined me at that time

Twelve-year major league veteran with the Indians, Giants and Expos, Ty Cline, seen here at his home in Charleston, South Carolina, April 16, 1991, played two years in the H&D League with the Dartmouth Arrows. With the Giants he was Willie Mays' backup in center field (author's collection).

in arguing for the selection of New Brunswick–born pitcher Billy Harris, who had a strong minor league career including a number of seasons with the Montreal Royals and a couple of stints with the mighty Brooklyn Dodgers in the 1950s. Before turning pro, he played for the Moncton Cubs in the New Brunswick League and pitched a few exhibition games against teams in the H&D League. Along with Tommy Lasorda, Harris had been stuck in the Dodgers organization behind pitching greats Don Newcombe, Don Drysdale, Carl Erskine, Clem Labine and Sandy Koufax, a starting staff almost impossible to crack. Raymond testified to how good Billy was and thought he should be honored. I remember Elliott's comment at the time: "anyone that Claude Raymond thinks is worthy of induction also has my vote." Billy Harris was inducted in 2008: "I swear to God, this is the greatest thrill of my life," he said. He passed away in 2011.[4]

After my years at the University of Cincinnati, I returned to Nova Scotia in the summer of 1970 to take up a job in the history department at Saint Mary's University in Halifax. With a new family including beautiful daughter Heather, not to mention writing lectures and working to complete my dissertation, I found that there was less time than ever to focus on baseball. However, it was a rewarding time. I had turned to focus on the history of Atlantic Canada as a member of what is now called the "Acadiensis Generation." For too long, the predominant narrative in Canadian history had been the story of how Quebec and Ontario struggled to get along. The place of Atlantic Canada and the West in Confederation was rendered largely peripheral to the story of nation-building. The journal *Acadiensis*, which began publishing in 1971, intended to remedy that.

My first published article, "Nova Scotia's Protest Tradition and the Search for a Meaningful Federalism," appeared in a collection of essays focusing on the West and the Maritimes, edited by David Bercuson and titled *Canada and the Burden of Unity*.[5] The intention was to demonstrate how viewing Canada from the perspective of the regions offered a more complete rendering of national history than that emanating from the metropolitan heartland. Over the next couple of decades, regional scholars published powerful pieces intended to bring the history of Atlantic Canada more fully into the story of the Canadian past and beyond the metropolitan contempt that accompanied social critic Frank Underhill's comment that "as for the Maritimes, nothing much ever happens down there."[6] Since then, I have written extensively in the field of sport history from a perspective of the borderlands rather than the metropole. With respect to baseball, that involved transnational sporting connections in a northeastern borderland region that included the Maritimes, Quebec and New England.

Of course, in life as in baseball, there are sharp, breaking curves. One of those was a major fire that demolished my home in 1991. Out of the ashes, however, good things emerged. My graduate students were wonderful, sorting through sooty remains to see if anything could be salvaged and providing my wife Sandi and me with much appreciated support. While I had lost most of my research from the previous few years, there was quite a bit of material, water-stained and often in blurry ink—this was before computers were completely in vogue—that remained usable. Most of it related to baseball. This was fortuitous and had important effects upon my life. One was to rekindle my interest in baseball and to link it to my work as a professional historian. I put aside another book project and began working in earnest on *Northern Sandlots: A Social History of Maritime Baseball*, subsequently published by the University of Toronto Press in 1995.[7]

All of this might seem an unnecessary digression in a book that will focus on the history of baseball in the postwar Maritimes and northeastern borderlands. But there is a point to all of this. While novelists are encouraged to write about what they know, and musicians to play from the soul and with feeling, historians are at their best when writing about what is part of them. This book is about what is part of me. At the same time, it draws upon my training in the canons of historical scholarship and respect for the patient collection of evidence and takes seriously the responsibility to avoid mythical pleasantries that come at the expense of accuracy. Recapturing the history of baseball in the northeastern borderlands is thus part of a broader historical project that started decades ago, seeking to rediscover what has been lost or devalued in our remembrances of the Atlantic Canadian past.

The baseball story begins with the postwar transition from wartime to peacetime baseball. Given its location on the east coast, the port of Halifax in particular played a major role in the housing and debarkation of soldiers on their way to battlefields overseas. In many cases Canada's most prominent ballplayers ended up playing for teams in the wartime Halifax Defense League while awaiting passage overseas. While doing so, they suited up against the region's best athletes. After the war, local players faced an increasing cadre of college prospects and minor league veterans from the United States, and players of interest to major league organizations and some talented homebrews were unnecessarily pushed aside. The Yankees, Dodgers, Giants, Braves, Red Sox, Cubs and Phillies were particularly active in recommending players to come north. The Dodgers assigned players and coaches to Edmundston in the New Brunswick-Maine League, Amherst in the Central League, and Kentville in the H&D League. They sent regional scout and Saint John native Oakie O'Conner to Edmundston, they sent Northern State University coach Ed Pesaresi to Amherst, and they developed a working arrangement with former major leaguer Emerson Dickman and Hank Swasey of the University of New Hampshire to keep tabs on players with the Wildcats. New York's Giants followed their prospects through a connection to Halifax manager Lou "Crip" Polli, a veteran right-hander who appeared in nineteen games for the National League club in 1944, while the Yankees relied on veteran minor leaguer and playing coach Bob Decker in Dartmouth and later Halifax to look after their interests. Decker remained in the Maritimes until the mid–1950s and was instrumental in sending future major leaguers John "Zeke" Bella, Tommy Carroll and Bob Davis to the big-league club. As for the Red Sox, scouting director Neil Mahoney and director of minor league operations Johnny Murphy were frequent visitors to the province and maintained close connections with the Wildcats and Liverpool Larrupers through a number of their regional scouts and team managers.

As the region's reputation strengthened in baseball circles south of the border, barnstorming teams from New York and New England, including the Brooklyn Junior Dodgers, the 1948 and 1949 U.S. Amateur champion New York Equitable Life, and the Birdie Tebbetts Major League All-Stars as well as various aggregations from the so-called Negro Leagues turned the postwar Maritimes into a burned-over baseball district. These visits, outlined in Chapter Three, both testified to and strengthened the reputation of Maritime baseball in baseball circles south of the border and offered the possibility for smaller towns to field local all-star teams to test their abilities against acknowledged—often big-league—talent. Along the way, many young players from the region were offered the chance to play professional baseball in the United States.

The growing sophistication of regional baseball came at a price, however. The increasing reliance on players from south of the border narrowed opportunities for local stars who had demonstrated in earlier years their ability to play and play well. For a few seasons, clubs in the postwar years maintained a healthy balance between locals and imports, but by the end of the decade the import model was ascendant everywhere. More and more clubs in the Maritimes began assigning roster construction and coaching responsibilities to college coaches, scouting directors of major league organizations, or journeymen pros—many of them with major-league experience—from the United States.

After 1950 the story turns to a Carolinian connection that began when the Stellarton Albions hired Bill Brooks, a veteran minor leaguer from Wilson, North Carolina, as its playing coach. Soon, players from college teams in the Atlantic Coast Conference and elsewhere brought a Southern flair to "NCAA North." Given full rein to fill the roster with players from the Carolinas, Brooks was a graduate of Wake Forest, a baseball powerhouse that finished as runner-up in the 1949 College

World Series and national champion in 1955. Included among the Wake Forest recruits in 1951 was former All-American shortstop Art Hoch, who after graduating in 1950 had been hired to oversee the baseball program at the University of North Carolina. Between them, Brooks and Hoch would play and coach for twelve years in the H&D League, recruiting blue-chip prospects from across the Southern states.

Maritime baseball's outward reach also extended westward after the war. Strong connections emerged with baseball in the Detroit-Windsor area that began during the war. The Middleton Cardinals of the H&D League in the forties, for example, had more than a dozen players with experience in the Detroit-Windsor Baseball Federation. Some of them, like pitcher Jimmy Dumeah and infielder Bernie Parent, would take up permanent residence in the province. The Great Lakes connection became even stronger when University of Michigan baseball legend Ray Fisher signed to coach Blacks Harbour of the Southern New Brunswick League in 1951 and for two summers after that. Fisher's talented Wolverines captured the College World Series in 1953. In 1954 he moved to the H&D League, bringing two first-team All-Americans, infielders Ken Tippery and Bruce Haynam, and a number of others along with him to Truro. His best player with the Bearcats that year, however, was a local boy named Stan "Chook" Maxwell, who led the club in batting and ranged across the outfield with the physical grace of a natural athlete.

In addition to these connections, a pipeline of players from northeastern and mid–Atlantic states nourished clubs across the region. The 1952 NCAA champion Holy Cross Crusaders played a notable role, of course, but players from Harvard, Yale, Princeton, Dartmouth, Cornell, Fordham, Providence College, Penn State, Temple, Saint John's and other colleges throughout the east eagerly joined the northward exodus. Harvard baseball coach John Phalen "Stuffy" McInnis spent two years coaching in Stellarton, while George Owen, a sporting legend at the same school, piloted the Truro Bearcats. Archie Allen, a former Yankees farmhand and baseball coach at Springfield College, spent two summers in Kentville, and Jack Kaiser, the architect of New York's Saint John's University Redmen baseball and basketball program for decades, spent four years as playing coach in Liverpool.

Beginning in 1953, new bonus regulations introduced by MLB required any player signing a bonus contract in excess of $4,000 to be added to the club's 25-man roster for two full years. Chapter Six, "'NCAA North': CWS Champions, Bonus Babies and All-Americans," deals with players from the Maritimes affected by this foolhardy experiment. It addresses the experience of shortstop Tom Carroll of the Yankees, Moe

Drabowsky of the Chicago Cubs, Tommy Gastall of the Baltimore Orioles and a half-dozen other players in considerable detail.

Another chapter addresses baseball's other "great experiment." The postwar weakening of the color bar that accompanied Jackie Robinson's 1945 signing of a minor league contract (with Branch Rickey of the Brooklyn Dodgers) to play for the Montreal Royals, of course, had an important influence upon young players of color in Canada, as it did in the United States. The Robinson story is well known to Canadians, especially since he began his career as a member of the 1946 Montreal Royals. The Dodgers signed other players at the time, including Johnny Wright and Roy Partlow, who were sent to Trois-Rivières of the Canadian-American League. What is often overlooked even by Canadians is the story of the first black Canadian to play in Organized Baseball after World War I. (The term "Organized Baseball" refers to Major League Baseball and its associated minor leagues. It does not include amateur, semipro or independent leagues such as the H&D League, the Maine–New Brunswick League and others that are the focus of this study.) After beginning the 1946 season with Middleton in the H&D League, Vincent "Manny" McIntyre joined the Sherbrooke club in Organized Baseball's Class C Border League. A New Brunswick native, McIntyre had a brief stint with the Negro Leagues' Cuban Giants the year before. After thirty games with Sherbrooke, McIntyre left the club because of the racism he was encountering and returned to finish the season in Nova Scotia. Chapter Seven, "Playing in 'Color Bar Limbo': Black Players in the Maritimes, 1946–60," follows his career and that of a number of other black players, both locals and imports, who played across the Maritimes.

Black players at the time were trapped in "color bar limbo." While it was now possible for them to sign a professional contract, it was nonetheless impossible to escape the obvious constraints of racism that pervaded all of North America at the time. For Maritime natives like McIntyre, Willie O'Ree, Stan "Chook" Maxwell, Art Dorrington, and Johnny Mentis, all of whom had the ability to play professional baseball, hockey provided an alternative opportunity to demonstrate their athletic talent. Even after O'Ree broke into the NHL in 1958, an informal color bar continued to operate for another decade. For African Americans Don Eaddy, Dave Ricketts and Grover "Deacon" Jones, all of whom began their semipro careers in the Maritimes, the road to the major leagues was equally difficult. Their struggles in the inhospitable climate of the time deserve special recognition.

Later chapters address the final years of the import era, the forces at work that brought the experiment to an end, and the legacy it left for baseball in the region. Given my two teenage summers in Kentville in 1958 and 1959, and my subsequent return to Nova Scotia in 1962 to start a degree in history at Dalhousie University, this period evokes my most powerful memories of H&D league baseball and its aftermath. In its last three seasons the H&D League had shrunk to four teams and was the only league in the Maritimes that continued to adhere to the import model. By then the emphasis was almost exclusively on developing college prospects for big league teams like the Red Sox, White Sox, Phillies, Yankees, Cubs, Pirates and Braves. Many players went on to successful major league careers. What I failed to realize was how vulnerable the league had become, given that the Maritimes in the 1950s became increasingly dependent upon a system of federal transfers that attempted to counter regional underdevelopment and iniquitous national policies operating to the advantage of Central Canada and the West. Indeed, sport cannot be fully understood outside of the prevailing economic and social context that it is part of.

Two concluding chapters serve as a postscript. One employs a statistical analysis which focuses on the most important performers and performances over the fifteen-year history of the league. The other addresses the legacy that the H&D League and other leagues had on baseball in the Maritimes in the postwar era. It is fair to say that there was no other time in the history of the region when baseball was as prominent, nor was there a time that matched the level of talent that congregated then throughout the small communities of Nova Scotia and New Brunswick and the northeastern borderlands. That is not to disparage the abilities of those who since then have demonstrated their ability to play with and against the best. Matt Stairs, Jason Dickson, Paul Hodgson, Rheal Cormier, and Vince Horsman are among the players from the Maritimes that made it all the way to the big-time in the years that followed.

ONE

The Postwar Flourishing of Baseball in the Maritimes

A few years back, while sifting through a box of memorabilia, I came across an item that marks the beginnings of my lifetime love affair with baseball. Staring back at me was a three-by-five-inch black-and-white postcard commemorating the 1948 Kentville Wildcats of Nova Scotia's Halifax and District (H&D) League. On the back of the card and addressed to me were autographs of my childhood idols, Dick Gernert, Jack Kaiser, Socrates "Soc" Bobotas, Johnny Watterson and others, who led the Wildcats to the league pennant before falling to Halifax in the first round of post-season play. The front of the card sported individual pictures of all the players. At the center was Wildcats manager Hank Swasey, a coaching legend at the University of New Hampshire (UNH) for over four decades and part-time scout for the Brooklyn Dodgers and Boston Red Sox. Swasey would lead UNH to a fifth-place finish in the College World Series in 1956. To the left was New Waterford native Eddie Gillis, a veteran of the minor league Cape Breton Colliery League during the 1930s and later a scout for the St. Louis Cardinals. A wonderful mentor and highly respected baseball coach across Canada, Gillis would reside in the Nova Scotia Valley town for many years, schooling young players, myself included, in the fundamentals of the game.

For a youngster like me, born in Middleton in 1944 and living my early childhood years in Kentville, the Annapolis Valley in the 1940s and '50s seemed an idyllic place, a paradise of apple blossoms and baseball diamonds bathed in warm summer sunshine. Although my family moved around a bit—first to Dartmouth and then west to Victoria, British Columbia—I spent many summers at my grandparents' house directly across the street from Kentville's immaculately groomed Memorial Park. Adjacent to the big diamond was a complex of

First baseman Dick Gernert of the Kentville Wildcats is greeted at the plate in 1948 by teammates Jack Kaiser (*Varsity Magazine*'s 1949 college player of the year, with his hand extended to Gernert), playing coach Soc Bobotas (behind Kaiser), Don Mackenzie (behind Bobotas) and veteran minor league catcher in the Dodgers organization Paul O'Neil (right). The bat boy may be Billy Wade (Halifax Municipal Archives, CR67-5-975.01.533).

baseball and softball grounds for Little League, Pony League and Babe Ruth League baseball. Most mornings and afternoons the fields were open and kids swarmed the grounds, playing pick-up ball and teaching each other the basics of the game. Although as Brian Pulsifer, who still resides in town, reminded me, "we were basically self-taught," there were always those more knowledgeable, like Gillis and volunteers Frank Fillmore, George "Peanuts" Mahaney, Burton Russell and others, who helped organize teams, set lineups, umpire games, sponsor teams and provide the uniforms that made us want to perform at the top of our game.

At that time, Kentville was an important railway hub busily engaged in exporting apples destined for the British market. As headquarters of the Dominion Atlantic Railway, it had played an important role during the war by moving troops stationed at nearby Camp Aldershot to other parts of the province and eventually overseas. The

One. The Postwar Flourishing of Baseball in the Maritimes 15

shiretown for King's County, Kentville was also home to a regional TB hospital (the Nova Scotia Sanatorium) and a federal experimental farm (the Kentville Research and Development Centre), established in 1911. Although the town's population numbered slightly less than 5000 souls in the decades following the war, the nearby towns of New Minas, Canning, Wolfville and Berwick added substantially to that number and helped sustain the semipro Wildcats until the collapse of the H&D League at the end of the fifties. By the time of the league's demise in the spring of 1960, however, the apple industry was contracting, Camp Aldershot had become largely focused on cadet training, and the railway—the town's largest employer—faced serious competition from automobile and truck travel. With opportunities for future employment increasingly limited, many young men and women would eventually leave in search of a better future elsewhere.

My uncle Bev, who pitched for the Wildcats in 1946 and 1947, was one of those. Growing up in a baseball family—my grandfather "Reg" Buckler had been a player and coach for Annapolis Royal town teams in the twenties—Bev starred in high-school hockey and baseball at King's County Academy and became a low-handicap golfer while caddying at the Ken-Wo Golf Club. After joining the Canadian Army in 1944, he was assigned to Halifax, where he worked out regularly with the vaunted Halifax Shipyards of the Halifax Defense League and awaited deployment overseas. Playing with a Canadian Army all-star squad in Holland in 1945, he posted a 4–1 record, competing against a number of high-profile players with professional experience in the United States. At war's end he was offered a tryout by the Philadelphia Athletics, but my grandfather wouldn't let him go, emphasizing the need for a college education. "Baseball is not a career," he said. Instead, Bev enrolled at Acadia University and played for the hometown Wildcats. Later he would follow in the footsteps of many Maritimers who left the region in search of employment, landing first at the Chalk River nuclear plant in Ontario and later embarking on a lifelong teaching career in New York. He played some semipro baseball in the Chalk River–Pembroke area, but in his estimation the level of play didn't compare to the H&D League. "Up there they couldn't touch my sinker," he recalled. "It was like taking candy from babies." Occasionally he would come back to Kentville for his summer holidays, playing at times for Middleton in a local valley league.

For myself and my cousins John, Jim and Bev Frizzle, Kentville was our summer home, and we were happily thrown together in a couple of rooms in my grandparents' large west end house. To say that our young lives revolved around baseball would be an understatement. Since few entertainment options were available except for the local movie theater, listening to the radio, or playing records, we played ball from dawn to dusk. Now and then if it was raining, I would sit with my grandfather listening to a Red Sox daytime game on the big living room radio console. The reception from Boston was scratchy at best, and we would take turns holding an antenna wire between thumb and forefinger to make it come in a little clearer and louder. Even at the end of the fifties, television sets were just beginning to appear in Valley homes, and the town's location halfway between Halifax and Saint John meant that only a couple of snowy channels were accessible. It goes without saying that electronic amusements available to kids today were nonexistent then. Even transistor radios came later. We made our own fun, which usually meant playing baseball all day and watching the Wildcats whenever they took to the field. I can't recall ever feeling deprived.

Every year, my grandparents billeted visiting players—most of them American boys in their late teens and early twenties. So did the Pulsifer, White, Buchanan, Cochrane, Buckler and Hale families in west end homes within spitting distance of the park. In many cases the young athletes became like members of the family and served as role models for younger kids. Cyril White, who like Brian Pulsifer remained in Kentville over the years and for decades operated the largest funeral home in the Valley, tells the following story. In 1953 Bill Kearns, a veteran of the AA Texas League with a lengthy minor league career in the Dodgers' organization, was hired as playing manager of the Wildcats, boarding with the Whites for the summer. Cyril was only nine years old at the time and, much to the chagrin of his mother, stubbornly refused to drink milk. "I know how to fix that," said Kearns, opening a can of 7-Up and pouring a few ounces into Cyril's milk cup. After that, Cyril happily drank the strange concoction without complaint. Brian Pulsifer remembers as well how many of the young players, especially those from Boston College or Holy Cross, were devout Catholics and regularly attended early Sunday mass. They were clean cut and well behaved for the most part—despite the occasional loud breaking of wind in the middle of a movie or experimenting with alcohol for the first time living away from home—and the townsfolk looked up to them. "They were our heroes," said White. "We looked up to them for their athletic ability and as good people."

In smaller towns across the region like Truro, Liverpool, Stellarton, Springhill, Blacks Harbour, Marysville, and Grand Falls, local kids had similar access to young prospects already on the radar of major league organizations. In addition, they could attend the frequent baseball clinics that teams ran for local youth. I remember one of the first of these that I attended as a kid in Dartmouth. It was run by Dartmouth Arrows coach Art Hoch with the assistance of second baseman Bill Bergeron, All-American shortstop Johnny Yvars and pitcher Paul Susce, whose illustrious family was well-known to people in major league baseball. It may seem counterintuitive that for a couple of decades many prominent ballplayers from the eastern half of the United States interacted on a daily basis with members of the community, but this was in fact the norm. Given the derisive stereotype of the time of the Maritimes as a cultural backwater, where apparently "nothing much ever happens,"[1] the region's important place within the postwar baseball universe deserves to be remembered.

Living near the park and billeting players meant opportunities for many of us to interact closely with the players on the field. A few times I sat on the bench, and like my Frizzle cousins occasionally put up the numbers on the center field scoreboard. There were other benefits. My cousin John recalls a day as scoreboard boy when visiting outfielder "Doc" Acocella of the Dartmouth Arrows flipped him a ball at the end of the game. As we got older, there was an even more special prize: we were allowed to shag flies in the outfield with the big boys. "It was a magical time," recalled Johnny Lockhart, my boyhood friend and teammate on the "Drive-Ins" of the Apple League, as we sat together at Memorial Park watching a senior league game a couple of years ago. Johnny's association with baseball in Kentville has never waned. A fleet-footed outfielder, whose uncle Doug was a mainstay of the Springhill Fencebusters after the war, John went on to play for the Hantsport Shamrocks of the Nova Scotia Senior Baseball League in the sixties. He would not have been too out of place in a Wildcats uniform even in the import era. The Lockharts have been an enduring presence in Nova Scotia baseball for generations. John's nephews Ian and Keith were national-level ballplayers who competed at various times at the Canadian Senior championships.

Although only fourteen, I would often spend time with Armand "Babe" Sabourin, a catcher from the University of Massachusetts who roomed with my grandparents in 1958 and 1959. Another who hung around the Buckler house was Ray Stebbins, a third baseman from New Hampshire who captained the Boston College Eagles in those years. Other Wildcats, Norm Gigon, Jack McCracken and Lee Elia, from New Jersey, Pennsylvania, and Delaware, respectively, were also around. Gigon and Elia later ended up in the "Windy City"—Gigon playing for the Cubs and Elia playing for the White Sox and the Cubs. After his playing career ended, Elia, a feisty player nicknamed "Banty Rooster" by his teammates, became a controversial manager and coach for various big-league teams. He is still remembered for his profanity-laced rant in 1983, attacking Cubs fans for their lack of support.[2] McCracken, out of Gettysburg College in Pennsylvania, played in the Phillies chain, eventually making it to Double-A with Chattanooga of the Southern Association. A back injury "so bad I couldn't breathe" brought an end to his big-league hopes in 1964.

A short, hustling catcher with a winning smile, great personality, and professional approach to the game, Sabourin was a terrific individual. He had been brought to Kentville by playing coach Buzz Bowers, a veteran pitcher in the Philadelphia Phillies organization, who considered him the best young catcher in Massachusetts outside of the pro ranks. In need of a second receiver, and with a spot open on the roster after Wildcats outfielder Dick Berardino signed a bonus contract with the New York Yankees and left Kentville after a couple of weeks, Bowers asked Henry Leach, coach of the Framingham Collegians, if he would consider releasing Armand so he could come north. "OK," said Leach, "but I'm going miss him." When I spoke with Bowers in the early 1990s, the first player he wanted to talk about was Armand. "He was a great handler of pitchers and played the game the way it was supposed to be played," said Bowers. "He was always hustling and was a team leader." One example of his leadership came in his second year with the Wildcats when he confronted first baseman Ron Overcash for failing to run out a ground ball. "These fans up here know the game," he told Overcash. "They won't tolerate a lack of hustle." Overcash went on to play at Double-A Shreveport in the Kansas City organization.

Sabourin had a strong arm, speed afoot and great game-calling abilities. Always on the move, he was often only a half-step behind batters trying to beat out ground balls while he backed up throws to first base. On the day he arrived in Kentville, the first thing he wanted to do was check out the ballpark, which even today remains one of the most immaculate in the region. He asked my cousin Bev and me what positions we played, and when Bev told him second base, he grabbed his glove and said, "Let's go play catch." He had Bev play twenty feet off the bag at second, with myself at short, and delivered straight-line bullet throws one after another. After a couple dozen of these, Bev's hand was so sore that he had to quit.

I still remember how excited Armand was before his first game in a Wildcats uniform. Hal Deitz, a young left-hander from Holy Cross and ace of the staff, was on the mound. The new battery mates performed flawlessly that night. The result was a complete game, no-hit performance by Deitz, one of only six in the fifteen-year history of the league. To cap off his triumphant debut, Sabourin drove in the winning run

One. The Postwar Flourishing of Baseball in the Maritimes

Armand and Judith Sabourin at their home in Medford, Massachusetts, March 28, 1994. Sabourin was a superior defensive catcher and team leader for the Kentville Wildcats in 1958 and 1959. He boarded at the author's grandparents' home directly across from Memorial ballpark (author's collection).

with a sharp single to left, leading the Wildcats to a 2–0 victory. A few days later he hit his first home run, a high fly ball over the 315-foot marker in left field. Although the ball may not have gone more than 320 feet, it was the game-winning blow, and rather than slowly trot around the bases as was customary, he sprinted with a smile on his face that stretched from ear to ear.

After graduation, Sabourin was offered a contract by the Washington Senators but decided against turning pro. On the other hand, his battery mate McCracken couldn't wait until graduation to sign. Even as a sixteen-year-old high schooler, McCracken was considered a major league prospect, pitching a complete simulated game against the Senators' starting lineup as it got ready for its game later that day. McCracken's tryout was impressive, highlighted by a strikeout of slugger Roy Sievers, once described as having the "sweetest right-handed swing in baseball."[3] At the time, however, the Senators' parsimonious owner Clark Griffith was turning increasingly to Latin American ballplayers as a way of improving his club while cutting costs. While Griffith was ahead of the curve in giving Latin American players a chance to play major league baseball,[4] American players like McCracken often found signing with Washington less attractive than with other clubs. McCracken signed instead with the Philadelphia Phillies in the fall of 1959 while still a sophomore in college.

The Senators remained interested in Armand and wanted him to begin his professional career in the mid-minors. After serious consideration, however, he chose a career in education, where he could concentrate on coaching both baseball and football. It was probably a wise decision. Although he had major-league defensive skills and might have made a major league roster as a defensive back-up, he lacked power. Quite probably he would have struggled at the plate. After Armand's playing career was over, he became a highly revered baseball and football coach and was eventually inducted into the Massachusetts Football Hall of Fame. McCracken had a similarly accomplished and lengthy career as a baseball coach at Bel Air High School in Maryland.

I remember lengthy conversations with Armand. He would tell me about the players that he had played with and against in college, while I, having watched the Seattle Rainiers of the Pacific Coast League on Channel 13 when living in Victoria, would give him my thoughts about prospects in the Cincinnati chain. Three players with the Rainiers had played in Nova Scotia: first baseman Jim McManus with Springhill and pitchers Bob Krop and Dave Stenhouse with the Wildcats. "Who's your favourite Seattle guy?" he asked. "Vada Pinson without a doubt. What a player! He's going to be a big star," I told him. Sometime later I visited Armand in Medford, Massachusetts. "Vada Pinson," he recalled. "You were sure right about him."

Whether my assessment of Sabourin's prospects as a pro ballplayer has any merit—based as it is on a possibly clouded memory and a very limited sample—it is reminiscent of the one that Norm Gigon later provided for Joe Maddon, who managed the Cubs to their first World Series championship in 108 years in 2016. Gigon had himself played for the Cubs in 1967, his only season in the majors, before accepting a coaching offer at Lafayette University at twice his big-league salary that same year. Maddon would later play for coach Gigon at Lafayette and thought him the biggest influence on his subsequent life in baseball. Maddon's career as a player was limited to four years in the minor leagues during the 1970s, but he attributed his experience with Gigon as a reason for his exemplary big-league managing career.[5]

Although Gigon jumped at the chance to go to Lafayette, the

One. The Postwar Flourishing of Baseball in the Maritimes 21

timing was strange to say the least. After their season in Kentville, Gigon and Elia had signed Phillies contracts—only to languish in minor league purgatory for several years, most at the AAA level. Gigon spent six years at Triple-A before escaping to the Cubs at the end of the 1966 season. After a great spring training he spent the entire 1967 season in the majors, playing for Leo Durocher. In the final game of the season against the Cincinnati Reds, Gigon rapped a double to right center. As he stood at second base, the public address announcer told the crowd that it would be his last game before retiring to pursue a college coaching career. When visiting second baseman Tommy Helms heard this, he exclaimed: "You're leaving? Gig, you just got here!"[6] Elia, who also made the majors after leaving the Phillies' organization the year before, played with the Chicago White Sox in 1966 and the Cubs in 1968. He didn't fully retire as an active player until 1973, having spent twelve years at the AAA level.

One day as we sat around the table in my grandparents' kitchen, Gigon asked me, "What do you kids do around here anyway? Don't you find it boring?" I was a little bewildered by the question. Our lives were full, I thought. We ate, drank and lived baseball and chased girls when we had time! What else did we need? Looking back, I now realize how insulated we were as adolescents from the larger social issues of the day, from Cold War anticommunism to the emerging Civil Rights movement. Naïve and innocent beneath the summer sun and baseball, we were blithely unaware of the unseemliness of those years. In later years, many of us would find that small-town Kentville could not contain our dreams for the future, but the Valley town of our youth would nonetheless always retain a soft spot in our hearts.

In those days, baseball had different meanings for different people, of course. In my father's case, taking an interest in Canadian sports like baseball, hockey and Canadian football was part of his acculturation as a postwar British immigrant to Canada. A Shropshire lad and RAF veteran stationed for a time at the Greenwood Air Force base in the Annapolis Valley, he met his future bride (my mom) at a Friday night dance and, as for many wartime couples, things progressed quickly. Mom told my grandmother, "I met the man I'm going to marry last night," and they soon tied the knot. Just nine months and one day after their marriage I was born. Not a moment wasted!

As I grew up, my father became fascinated by a game often idealized as drawing the generations together. He didn't take easily to playing the game, or hockey, for that matter, remaining more comfortable with soccer and cricket. But he was always good-natured about his deficiencies. At family ball games he would invariably bunt whenever he came to bat. He used to tell me that he preferred relying on his foot-speed—and I have to admit that he did run like the wind! For a time I even accepted his excuse for not swinging away.

Once when I was about ten years old or so, Dad accompanied a group of us to frozen-over Lake Banook for a game of pond hockey. As we whizzed around passing the puck, he stood on wobbly ankles holding tightly to his stick for balance. Suddenly both feet were in the air, and he landed on his backside. Looking down at him, my friend Donny asked incredulously, "Mr. Howell, can't you skate?" Giving me a wink, he replied, "this is the way we do it in England!"

My fondest memories of that time were at the ballpark, first with Dad and later with my own teenage buddies. We often travelled between Dartmouth and Kentville, taking in games at Dartmouth's state-of-the art field, known colloquially as "Little Brooklyn," or at the Wanderers Grounds in Halifax and at Kentville's Memorial Park, where we followed our own "boys of summer." We knew this was not big-time metropolitan baseball. The H&D League would eventually send dozens of players to the big leagues, as did other circuits in the Maritimes like the Central League, the Southern New Brunswick League, the York County League, the Border League, the Cape Breton Colliery League and the Maine–New Brunswick League. From Kentville alone, a little railway hub of about 5,000 people, ten players graduated to the majors and another dozen had lengthy playing careers topping out at the AAA level. Indeed, postwar baseball in the Maritimes was as good as anywhere else in the country and probably on a par with most of the mid-level minor leagues in the United States.

A couple of decades ago when I was researching another book on baseball in the northeast, I tried to get an informed evaluation of the caliber of play in the H&D League, interviewing players and scouts familiar with baseball in the Maritimes. On one occasion my wife Sandi and I drove to the little village of Washington Corners, Maine, to talk to Clyde Sukeforth, the Dodgers' New England and Eastern Canada bird-dog, who scouted Jackie Robinson prior to Branch Rickey's inking him to a Brooklyn contract. When we arrived at the Sukeforths' lakefront home, his wife told us that the ninety-one-year-old was still in town getting a five-year extension to his driver's license. He soon arrived home, a canoe on top of his car, and jumped out looking like he could still play an inning or two. Sukeforth, who was particularly familiar with the Truro Bearcats through his friendship with general manager Clarence "Soapy" Johnson, thought that the level of play was that of the mid-minors, the equivalent of a Class B or Class A level league. (In 1962 baseball revamped its classification system. Class B Leagues were the rough equivalent of advanced A leagues of today. And Class A became AA level.) There were standout teams, of course. The 1946 Bearcats, the 1949 Dartmouth Arrows and Kentville Wildcats, the Stellarton Albions, who won three league championships in the early 1950s, the 1953 and 1958 Wildcats, the 1954 Halifax Cardinals and the 1955 Liverpool Larrupers were the class of the H&D League over its fifteen-year history. Elsewhere the 1949 Springhill Fencebusters, Fredericton Capitols and Augusta Millionaires, the 1951 Blacks Harbour Brunswicks, the 1954 Presque Isle Indians and the 1955 Edmundston Republicans could have given any of the above clubs a run for their money.

To think of the H&D League only as a collegiate summer league developing prospects for major league organizations would be a mistake, however. Teams throughout the Maritimes mixed players of different backgrounds, ages and levels of experience. Local players often contributed as much as young prospects from south of the border. Billy Harris, Vern Handrahan, Wilson Parsons, Fred Flemming, Herb McLeod, Dave Kiley, Jimmy Fox, Jackie Bowes, Johnny Graham, Carman Noiles, Mike Roberts, Billy Wade, Manny McIntyre and Johnny Harvey all played in the Maritimes before embarking on careers in Organized Baseball. Harris and Handrahan eventually made the majors. Equally talented Buddy Condy, Johnny Clark, Philip "Skit" Ferguson, Billy Carter, Roly McLenahan, Doug Ross, "Chook" Maxwell, Harry Reekie, Hum Joseph, Syd and Clyde Roy, and the Seaman brothers, Kal, Garneau and Danny, chose not to follow up on pro offers. Keep in mind that salaries were low in professional sports at the time, and for many young men with athletic talent there were often good reasons for thinking about other professional careers or furthering one's education. In addition, life in the minor leagues was grueling, often unrewarding, and always vulnerable to disabling injury.

Condy and Ferguson both had chances to play professional ball but took a longer view. Condy had his heart set on a career in medicine, and Ferguson, who received a physics degree from StFX (St. Francis Xavier University), was an aspiring engineer. Ferguson's mentor at "X," Father "Poppy" McKenna, often reminded him that baseball was "just a game, and beyond that there's more to life. Play as hard as you can when you are wearing that uniform, but when in the classroom take your education just as seriously." Skit went on to a successful professional career as an engineer and even now is an executive with the Consulting Engineers of Nova Scotia. Roly McLenahan, "Chook" Maxwell, and Art Dorrington concentrated on professional hockey careers, playing baseball only to stay in shape for the winter season. So did Willie O'Ree, who had a spring training tryout with the Milwaukee Braves in the mid-fifties.

Many other local ballplayers, like catcher "Bull" Marsh and fellow Cape Bretoner John "Brother" MacDonald, more than held their own with the old pros and imported collegians, but they had little interest in a professional baseball career. Marsh became a highly respected labor leader and president of UMWA (United Mine Workers of America) District 26 in industrial Cape Breton for more than twenty years. MacDonald was a highly respected educator and hockey and baseball coach.

Over the years, I reminisced with many of those who played in the postwar era and with a number of major league scouts who were active in searching out young talent from across North America. Along the way I also came to recognize how much people treasure memories of their sporting youth. Every Wednesday, for example, I play golf in a foursome who came of age when I did and who have intimate knowledge of baseball in the postwar era. Don MacVicar, a long-time physical educator, whose brother Jim "Lefty" MacVicar was one of the few local players on the powerhouse Stellarton Albions in the early 1950s, is well known for his butterscotch-smooth golf swing and steady play. Judge Bob Ferguson, who played on the 1959 champion Sydney Mines Ramblers, loves to talk about his days on the diamond. A big man, Bob still pounds the ball off the tee and it is easy to imagine the kind of power he must have had as a young ball player. Both MacVicar and Ferguson were recently inducted into Acadia University's Sports Hall of Fame. The third member of our group is Fred Barrett, who was a football star at Mount Allison University and the University of New Brunswick and a hockey player on various RCAF teams. Like me, Fred attended Park School in Dartmouth next to "Little Brooklyn." Today he confounds belief with the innovative use of his utility golf club.

In addition, hardly a month goes by without someone new contacting me out of the blue and wanting to talk about baseball history. Although this has been an enjoyable diversion from more formal academic pursuits that have occupied me as a professional historian, it has made me appreciate the importance of personal memory in the imagining and reimaging of the past. What follows is an expression of my gratitude to all that were part of the making of this story.

Two

Home Diamonds
Local Stars of Postwar Maritime Baseball

On 18 August 1946, eleven-year-old Burton Russell made his way into Kentville's Memorial Park to see the visiting Truro Bearcats take on the Valley League champion Wildcats. It was the opening game of the Nova Scotia playoffs and the first time Russell had witnessed a senior league game. The Bearcats, class of the H&D League that year, demolished the Wildcats. Twenty-year-old left-hander Skit Ferguson struck out eleven and held the struggling home-towners to four hits, two of them from Kentville's star shortstop Wally Barteaux. Hometown pitcher Bev Buckler eventually came in for a couple of innings to bring the game to a merciful end. Rather than leaving devastated, however, Russell became an instant Bearcats fan, intrigued by Truro's powerful lineup and more particularly a dynamic young outfielder named Johnny Clark. In a recent book, Russell wrote of his lifelong idol: "For some reason I have always been infatuated with a person's ability to make the legs move with lightning speed. This young man, whom later I was to call 'The Westville Flash,' apparently filled the bill for me.... Clark and crew quickly became my boyhood heroes."[1]

Clark, Ferguson and Joseph: "The Westville Flash," "Wonder Boy" and the "Hummer"

Truro captured the Nova Scotia crown that year and would have been odds-on favorites to win the Maritime championship, had a regional series been completed. Clark was the team's sparkplug. Although he hit only .250, his speed on the base paths and outstanding defensive play made him the most exciting player in the Maritimes. Clark's clutch playing, base-stealing ability and passion for the game impressed fans, opponents and teammates alike. Well respected among scouts and front-office personnel from Major League Baseball, he could have signed with a number of professional organizations, but his heart was always at home and he was content to play before Maritime audiences. Over the next two decades he helped develop the skills of local players and the increasing number of imports who came to the region in the late forties and fifties.

Johnny anchored the Bearcats lineup for three years before joining the Halifax Shipyards in 1949, suiting up alongside Buddy Condy, the best pure hitter—bar none—to have performed in the H&D League in its fifteen-year history. In 1950 the Condy and Clark tandem finished one-two in the H&D League batting race, hitting .358 and .350, respectively. They were teammates through the 1952 season, playing that year for Saint John in the New Brunswick League because of a dispute involving Halifax and Dartmouth over playing rights. Condy retired after that to concentrate on his studies at Dalhousie Medical School, but Clark continued to play and coach for a number of years. Throughout it all, Burton Russell remained Johnny's greatest fan, the self-acknowledged leader of the Johnny Clark fan club. (Russell's adoration of Clark had begun that sunny day in Kentville in 1946.)

Nobody outshone Ferguson that year, however. A youngster from Reserve Mines who was a student at St. Francis Xavier University (StFX), Skit gained regional notability as a member of the Dominion Hawks with a three-hit final game shutout over the New Brunswick champions, the Saint John Shamrocks, that propelled his club to the 1944 Maritime junior title. In 1945 he turned senior and the Hawks won the Cape Breton Colliery league title. By then, Ferguson's exploits were well known to Bearcats playing coach Sonny MacDonald, who strongly recommended that Truro acquire him for the initial H&D League season. General Manager Clarence "Soapy" Johnson wasn't sure what to expect from the youngster, however, and—as was his style—cautiously offered $25 a week and a job in town for an extra twenty bucks. Very quickly that arrangement went by the wayside. After a couple of outings Ferguson was hauling down $80 per week and no longer needed the extra job, and the club arranged for a doctor and dentist to look after his health. He was worth every penny! The dominant player in the Maritimes that year, Skit won eighteen games against a single loss. When not pitching, he played first base or in the outfield.

Backing up Skit on the mound was veteran Clyde Roy, a big right-hander with a blazing fastball and personality to match. During the war Clyde played for a number of teams in the Halifax Defense League, and he signed with Trois-Rivières of the Quebec Provincial

League in 1945. After a brief trial with the Double-A Memphis Chicks, Clyde headed to Truro for the 1946 season. Although he was happy to be in Nova Scotia, money was a bone of contention. Well compensated in Quebec at more than $100 a week, Clyde often complained that he deserved more than the Bearcats were paying him. Nor was he reluctant to do a little arm-twisting to add to his pay packet. Soapy Johnson—who resented the nickname since it implied that he was a little slippery in negotiating player salaries—told me the following story. One sunny Saturday, Clyde was the scheduled starter in an important game. Fans were flooding into T.A.A.C. grounds, and it looked likely that the crowd would top 2,000. When Johnson went into the clubhouse to check on things, however, Clyde was still in street clothes. All the rest of the guys were suited up. "Is there a problem, Clyde?" asked Soapy. Clyde looked up and grumbled, "Don't feel like pitching today. Not feeling well." Concerned that disaster lay ahead, Johnson motioned him outside. As they walked about, Soapy dug out a $20 bill which he flashed until saying, "It's yours if you pitch today." With a big smile Clyde pocketed the twenty bucks, saying, "You know, I'm feeling better already."

Another team leader was pepper-pot shortstop Hummit "Hum" Joseph. A streaky hitter but a good defender, Joseph was a fiery competitor and clutch performer. When he was hot, it was hard to get him out. If a rhubarb (baseball slang for a dispute or fight) happened, he was likely to be in the middle of it! Born in Springhill, Nova Scotia, a rabid baseball town that produced a generation of talented players, Hum finished high school in Truro and went on to play several years with the Bearcats, the St. John Dodgers and the highly competitive Londonderry Ironclads. Hum's career as both player and umpire spanned decades. He attended and graduated from Al Somers' umpiring school in Daytona in 1961 and became a respected ball-and-strike caller along with the rough-hewn Johnny "Fotch" Fortunato from South Boston via Lewiston, Maine. A larger-than-life figure, Fotch had a booming voice and a no-nonsense approach to officiating. Hum's three brothers were equally talented arbiters. "Bam" was a graduate of Bill McCowan's school for umpires; Kemal was a self-taught and well-respected umpire in Metro and the H&D League; and finally there was Alex, a polio victim in early childhood who nonetheless became an excellent umpire (on crutches). While living in Corner Brook, Newfoundland, in the early fifties, Alex umpired in a competitive league that included many talented American players at the Fort Pepperrell military base. The Josephs had many great stories to tell, my favorite being when Kemal threw Hum out of a game at the Wanderer's Grounds and his grandmother came out of the stands and slapped him in front of a few thousand fans.[2]

A couple of summers ago, my wife and I were sampling wines and listening to music at a Jost Wineries tasting when I spotted someone in a Red Sox hat heading to a nearby table. "You look a lot like Hum Joseph," I said. "Well, I should," he replied, "I'm his son, Danny." Thus began a long conversation about his dad's and Danny's baseball careers while we sipped on reds and listened to the band. The bass player was John Brennan, my own bass man from our group "Strawberry Jam" who plays in a number of different groups around Nova Scotia. It was a serendipitous moment when baseball and music overlapped. Later Danny invited me to give a talk about the H&D League at the Marigold Center auditorium in Truro and share fond memories of baseball in the fifties. Among the audience were Lyle Carter, former NHL goalie with the California Seals and a hard-hitting third baseman who could have played professionally had he got the chance; Glen Matheson, whose father Carl was a standout for the '46 club and a fine player in his own right; and my childhood buddy Donny Brown, who grew up with me in Kentville sixty years ago and played ball with me when we were teenagers. Donny told me a story of pitching in a recreational league in Truro. Given that his fastball hardly warranted the name, Donny relied on junk, especially a big, sweeping curveball. In one game with Hum calling balls and strikes, Donny missed the plate a couple of times, whereupon Hum shouted, "C'mon, throw them that big watermelon curve. They'll never hit that."

Also at the Marigold Center was Johnny Clark's sister-in-law, who had traveled there from Westville with her husband. I had talked to Johnny on many occasions when I was working on an earlier baseball book. At one point the conversation turned to Jack Stallings, an American boy who had played in both Truro and Stellarton and who became a coaching legend at Georgia Southern University. After a couple years in the H&D League, Jack signed a Red Sox contract and was making his way up the ladder when, like Alex Joseph, he contracted polio. After that, Jack became a Division One coach at Wake Forest and later at Georgia Southern, accumulating more than 1,100 career wins. He also coached the U.S. national team in the Intercontinental Cup, the IBF World Championship, the Pan-Am Games and the Olympics. Dr. Robert Smith, president of the International Baseball Federation, once described Stallings as the best teacher of baseball in the United States.[3]

A few years ago, Stallings was in Halifax running a coaching clinic for Baseball Nova Scotia. After it ended, I drove him to the airport and we talked baseball for almost an hour. He had the greatest respect for Johnny, remembering how the fleet-footed outfielder tracked down balls driven into the gap that others would never have gotten to. He also raved about Buddy Condy and considered him the best pure hitter he ever saw.

"And remember," said Jack, "I went to spring training with the Red Sox in 1954 when Ted Williams was there!" He considered Clark and Condy the equal of any of the imports in the early 1950s—even those who went on to the majors. "If you could have blended Condy's bat with Johnny's glove," he said, "you would have had one helluva ballplayer."

The 1946 Middleton Cardinals: Bernie Parent and the Windsor Brigade

Truro's road to the 1946 provincial championship culminated in a best-of-five playoff victory over the Middleton Cardinals. A sleepy Annapolis Valley town of about 1,000 people close to the Greenwood Air Force base, Middleton had been a prominent baseball center in the interwar years, competing against regional powerhouses such as the Yarmouth Gateways, St. Stephen Kiwanis, Marysville Royals, Liverpool Larrupers and Saint John Watermen. At both the junior and senior levels the Cardinals were among the best teams on the mainland, playing in a spacious park with a skin infield, an eight-foot outfield fence and stands that held about five hundred fans and plenty of nearby standing room when necessary. The outfield dimensions were exactly 300 feet down the right field line, 390 in left field, and a full 480 feet to straight-away center. There were not too many home runs hit either to left field or center field as a result, but in 1948 Kentville's Dick Gernert powered one well over the 390-foot sign in left field, likely measuring 450 feet.

The 1946 Cardinals assembled a mixture of players from around the Maritimes and the Detroit-Windsor sandlots. The Detroit connection had developed largely because of veteran semipro infielder Bernie Parent, a Windsor native who had played in Ontario's Nickel Belt League, the Michigan State League, and with Norfolk of the Piedmont League in the 1930s. During the war he was a star with the Victoria Air Force, hitting .477 in 1944, and was transferred to the east coast the following year. Once he arrived in Middleton, he would never leave, taking up permanent residence. So did another Windsor boy, Jimmy Dumeah, Victoria Navy's ace in 1945 and later a star pitcher in the Windsor-Detroit Baseball Federation. After a cup of coffee with the Victoria Tyees of the Class B Western International League, Dumeah married a Nova Scotian woman, traveled east to play with Middleton, and fell in love with Nova Scotia, where he lived the rest of his life. An excellent golfer, Jimmy became the club professional at the Liverpool golf club for many years.

Middleton's playing coach that year was Burt Pankratz, a burly catcher with experience in both the International League and the American Association in the late 1920s, who occasionally filled in behind the plate when regular catcher Charlie Shaulis needed a break or in the outfield when needed. Well into his forties, having worked at the Ford plant in Windsor for years, Pankratz was a smoker who would douse the embers when his cigar got down to the end and then chew the rest of it. The other imports on the club that year were three pitchers from Massachusetts, lefthander Larry Letteri and brothers Bruno and Jim Paglierani. Letteri was the best of the lot, at one point notching a no-hitter against the Liverpool Larrupers and facing only twenty-eight batters. Before the war he had traveled the Maritimes while barnstorming with the White Elephants from Cambridge, Massachusetts. After his year in Middleton, Letteri would head to the Quebec Provincial league, as had Skit Ferguson. Letteri played in the New Brunswick League after that. Letteri would continue to play throughout Eastern Canada for a number of years, ending his career after a couple of years in Quebec's Laurentide League in the early fifties.

Despite its import talent, the heart and soul of the Cardinals in 1946 were local players from the Annapolis Valley, the South Shore and elsewhere in the Maritimes. The infield lined up with Amherst native Ralph McManahan at first base and Middleton's own Carl Bruce at second—Bernie Parent would sometimes play there in Bruce's absence but otherwise would shift to left field. A junior Cardinal in the late thirties, Bruce turned senior in 1939 and led the club with a .325 average in 1946. The shortstop at the beginning of the season was New Brunswicker Manny McIntyre, who left the club in June to play for Sherbrooke of the Class C Border League, making him one of only six black players in Organized Baseball at the time. Manny left the Sherbrooke club after thirty games because of the racism he experienced when travelling across the border and returned to Middleton for the rest of the season. The third baseman for the Cards was young Haligonian Cyril Hector, still of junior age. Two other Middleton boys, six-foot, 250-pound Gerald "Fats" Ray and rangy youngster Arthur "Doc" Herman, who had been given a trial by the Brooklyn Dodgers and later had a successful stint in the Florida State League, would fill out the pitching staff. Saint John native Johnny Harvey arrived after the New Brunswick League season ended, bolstering the Cardinals for the playoff series against Truro. A flamethrower and former Chicago White Sox minor league chattel with Albany in the Eastern League in 1944, the right-hander showcased a mid–90s fastball, but his supporting stuff was mediocre. Usually dominant the first time through the lineup, he was less effective when he started to tire and went to his curveball.

Out Bustin' Fences: Springhill's Buddy Condy

Ask anyone what they know about Springhill, Nova Scotia, and you will likely get three responses: it's the birthplace of Anne Murray of "Snowbird" fame; it's the site of two disastrous mine collapses in the late 1950s that took the lives of scores of miners and brought an end to an industry that had sustained the town and shaped its identity for decades; and it's the home of the Fencebusters, a regional baseball powerhouse before and after World War II. Maritime champions in 1927, 1928, 1933 and 1945, and provincial champs in 1921, 1925 and 1936, the Fencebusters fielded a generation of great players like second-baseman Lawson Fowler—Burton Russell's choice for his all-time Nova Scotia All-Star team; the McLeod brothers, Stew, Herbie and Dingie (who once pitched to Babe Ruth); outfielder Brownie Burden; catcher Hank O'Rourke; and Len Boss, a right-handed fireballer from the 1945 squad.

Of all the town's baseball luminaries, however, none stood taller than Buddy Condy. A tremendously gifted athlete, reminiscent of Bernard Malamud's character Roy Hobbs in his novel *The Natural,* Condy grew up alongside his older brother Don watching the Fencebusters and perfecting his batting stroke by throwing up rocks and hitting them in every possible location in a nine-zone hitting area that was much wider and deeper than the regular strike zone.[4] Only fifteen when he got his chance to play senior ball in 1939, he announced himself with a grand-slam home run in his first at-bat with the Fencebusters. Soon, however, the world was at war, and Buddy had little time for baseball in the Air Force. When the war ended, Buddy entered Dalhousie University, dreaming of a medical career, but suited up with the Halifax Arrows during the summer. He continued to play through the 1952 season and returned for one last hurrah with the Halifax Cardinals in 1955. Over the years, Condy achieved the second highest career batting average in league history behind Dick Gernert of the Kentville Wildcats and just ahead of Joe Fulghum of the Stellarton Albions.

Everyone who saw Buddy play—from fellow players to coaches and major league scouts—was convinced of his big league talent. According to Bob Decker, scout and veteran minor leaguer in the Yankees organization, Condy could "run, field, and throw and could have played in the major leagues any time he wanted.... He would have been a star with any team up there." "Buddy Condy," said former New York Yankee

Zeke Bella, "was the best hitter I ever saw." Shortstop Johnny Watterson found him almost impossible to defend against. "If you played him back, you couldn't throw him out at first," he told me. "If you played him in tight, he'd kill you." Pitchers feared him. "As a left-handed pitcher, I was supposed to get left-handers out," Cleveland Indians farmhand

The author (standing) visits with general manager Clarence "Soapy" Johnson, March 19, 1994. Johnson's 1946 Truro Bearcats were the first H&D League champions. Johnson continued to oversee Bearcat operations into the early 1950s (author's collection).

Gerry Davis observed, "but Condy owned me. He was the toughest batter I ever faced." Moe Drabowsky, arguably the league's best pitcher at the time, considered Condy better than most of the major league hitters he faced during his seventeen-year big league career.

If there was a knock against Condy, it was that he was a bad-ball hitter: he would swing at anything that looked inviting. As a result, pitchers threw him outside, in the dirt, above eye level, anywhere except across the plate. "He'll never hit me," boasted Wildcats left-hander Jim Arbucho before facing him. "He'll never see a strike." Condy continued to hit the ball anyway. According to Ted Williams, one of baseball's most disciplined hitters ever, going after bad balls would turn a .300 hitter into a .200 one, but Condy's ability to command a particularly wide strike zone may well have made him an exception to the rule. When Dodger prospect Tom McMullen first faced him, he started him off with a slider that bounced three feet in front of home plate and watched it disappear over the right-field fence some 350 feet away! When asked how to pitch him, fellow Springhill native "Squirm" Noiles had the best answer. "Throw it low and behind him," he said.[5]

Tommy Linkletter: The "Mountain Boy"

Perhaps the most colorful player anywhere in the Maritimes at the time was Tommy Albert "Mountain Boy" Linkletter, a star with the Fencebusters in the thirties and with Halifax Army during the war. I never had the opportunity to meet Tommy—he died in a car crash in the mid-fifties. Since he was a relative of my wife's, however, I have heard a lot about him. Tommy grew up in the little village of Economy and was blessed with musical and athletic talent. A fine fiddler and guitar player who would perform at the drop of a hat, he was equally happy to show off his live arm. People still recall him throwing the ball up the road on Economy Mountain 300 feet or more to kids who bounced it back to him at the bottom of the hill. With the Springhill Fencebusters in the 1930s he was a leader on a first-rate pitching staff that included Edgar Cormier, Copie LeBlanc, Stew McLeod and little Purney Fuller who, according to manager Joe McCarthy of the New York Giants, had all the attributes of a major leaguer except size.

Mountain Boy's fastball was the best of all of them. Although there were no radar guns at the time, Tommy was a fireballer and was once invited to Boston for a tryout with the Braves. He was also somewhat scatter-armed pitcher: nobody knew if he would throw down the middle or over the backstop. In his trial in Boston, observers loved his velocity, but when he was asked to concentrate on getting it over the plate, he just continued to let it fly wherever it would go. My brother-in-law Joe Rector told me that one frustrated Braves coach muttered: "There is a kid with a million-dollar arm and a ten-cent head." Like Ryne Duren, the New York Yankees reliever whose explosive fast ball, lack of control and glasses as thick as a Coca Cola bottle left hitters on edge, many of those who hit against Tommy Albert did so with trepidation. Johnny Clark told me that Mountain Boy was the pitcher who scared him the most. "Guys like [Moe] Drabowsky were always around the plate," Clark said, "but Linky's rising fastball could be anywhere. No one in their right mind would dig in against him."

Halifax sportswriter Alex Nickerson considered Linkletter the most unpredictable and colorful pitcher in the province at the time and a magnet for controversy. In a game in 1946 against the Halifax Shipyards with Linky on the mound for the United Services squad, Shipyards coach Jack Carrigan was in the coaching box with a runner on third base. As Linkletter started his motion with Jimmy Gray at the plate, Carrigan yelled, "Let me see that ball!" Mountain Boy stopped his motion and threw the ball over to Carrigan, who simply moved out of the way and let the ball roll past him. The third-base runner Mick Burns strolled home. At that point, all hell broke loose, the fans screamed in protest, and both benches emptied. Umpire Bill Spinney then banished Carrigan from the game, sent Burns back to third, and ordered the game to resume. In the interim Linkletter sought out Carrigan and said, "If you ever do anything like that again, I'll kill you!"[6]

Heading for Quebec

As the 1947 season approached, fans anxiously awaited news on where the former Bearcats might land. According to newspaperman Ace Foley, "Wonder Boy" Ferguson would be the biggest catch of the year; every club in the H&D League wanted him. What most didn't know was that the exploits of Ferguson and his teammates had also attracted the attention of teams in the Quebec Provincial League. To fans' chagrin, Skit, Johnny Clark, Clyde Roy, and Billy McIntyre headed off to play in "la belle province." Middleton shortstop Manny McIntyre and Westville's Harold "Purv" MacDonald also signed with Drummondville. Slugging first baseman Joe "Pounder" Cormier from Cape Breton and Saint John native Jimmy Fox, who played for a Boston Red Sox affiliate in the Tobacco State League the year before, went to Sherbrooke, as did veteran pitcher Larry Letteri of the Middleton Cardinals.

After a mere three weeks in Drummondville, however, Clark jumped the club and headed back home accompanied by Clyde Roy. Clark's decision had nothing to do with the on-field situation. Rather, he found a French-speaking environment overwhelming. Homesick and missing his sweetheart Irene, he wanted to be back in Nova Scotia. Clark would also turn down a chance to play in the Phillies organization, knowing that he would be away from home for substantial periods of time. In an interview with Burton Russell, Johnny described his Drummondville junket. "I was my club's first batter in a then-new ball park there. Hitting-wise, I was having a good season, batting .357 in some fourteen games." A highlight came when he pounded a double down the right-field line off former Brooklyn Dodger Jean-Pierre Roy, who had knocked him down on the previous pitch. Not knowing why Clark left, club owner Camille Pinard sent him a telegram. "Johnny, you and Clyde return to Drummondville at once. The Lord knows why you left. No questions will be asked." Instead, Clyde and Johnny signed for another year with the Bearcats. Later, Clark would describe it as the "biggest mistake I ever made in my life." How far he might have gone in professional baseball we will never know, but during his twenty-year baseball career in Nova Scotia, he gained the respect of everyone in the region as well as players and scouts from south of the border.

While Johnny and Clyde returned to the Bearcats, Ferguson stayed in Drummondville and was impressed by the level of play in Quebec. At Drummondville his teammates included player-manager Joe Tuminelli, a veteran minor league pitcher and infielder who often outperformed major leaguers in winter ball in Panama. Even more notably, Montreal superstar Maurice "Rocket" Richard joined the Drummondville squad as its third baseman. In those days before "free agency" in hockey and baseball, NHLers often played semipro baseball in the summer as a way to keep in shape and earn a little side money. Norm Dussault and Doug Harvey, NHL teammates of the Rocket, were terrific ballplayers. Manny McIntyre, a natural shortstop and hockey star in his own right, was another. Behind the plate for Drummondville was Marcel St. Pierre, a veteran of the wartime Halifax Defense League who shared catching duties with fellow Quebecer Gerry Cotnoir.

Ferguson remembers Richard fondly. "We usually travelled to the other towns in the league by cab," he recalls, "and I always made a point of travelling with the 'Rocket." In one memorable game, Ferguson pitched the Cubs to an eleven-inning complete-game victory and Richard provided the game-winning blow. Afterward, someone collected bags of money for the two stars, and in a nice gesture Richard gave his to Skit, saying, "You need this more than me, kid." Richard also gave Ferguson sage advice about his education. "Don't give it up," Richard told him. "I have a grade ten education and when hockey is done, I won't have anything. I'll be done with no future." In his final appearance in Quebec Ferguson squared off against former Brooklyn Dodger and Mexican League jumping bean Jean-Pierre Roy of the St. Jean Braves, suffering a tough 4–2 loss which eliminated the Cubs from the playoffs.

The year in Drummondville was a learning experience for Skit, thanks especially to Tuminelli. Tuminelli loved the youngster's delivery, his ability to command his cut-action fastball, his sharp-breaking curveball and his ownership of the outside corner, and considered him a major league prospect. "You gotta go pro. You've got a lot of God-given talent, but you've sure got a lot of horseshit on your shoes," he said. Joe would watch Skit pitch batting practice, standing behind him and questioning him about what he was doing. "He made me think about things I never thought about," Ferguson recalls. "Why is your foot directly on the rubber? Where should it be when you are facing left- and right-handed batters? Why aren't you taking control of the inside of the plate? Show me your move to first base." Tuminelli taught him how to throw a change-up, and more importantly when to throw it and who to throw it to. He also worked for hours helping refine Skit's move to first base. By the end of the summer, Ferguson had a major league pick-off move.

Scouts and journalists from around the league came to appreciate Ferguson's talent and pitching savvy. Already surpassing former pros with AAA credentials like Ernie Balser and Pete Blumette, Skit was developing a reputation as the league's leading lefthander. According to one French-language newspaper, Ferguson "peut facilement se compare aux meilleurs, même si son style diffère totalement de ceux de Balser et de Blumette." The article went on to say that he "a merité les admiration de tous." One Friday in August, a Boston Red Sox scout took in a game in Acton Vale that pitted Skit against hard-throwing minor league veteran Jean Paul Tetreault. Although the scout had come to watch Tetreault, Ferguson stole the show, holding his opponents to three hits in a complete-game 1–0 shutout. Before long, Skit had an offer to play in the Red Sox organization and an assurance that "if you sign with us, you will be in Triple-A in two years and knocking on the door to the majors." When talking money, however, the Red Sox wanted him to play for a measly $200 per month: he was already making three times that in Drummondville. If that was not bad enough, the Red Sox also wanted him to report to Florida in January. This was a deal breaker. There was no way Skit was giving up his education and his future as an engineer to pursue a questionable chance of playing major league baseball. Having seen his share of disillusioned veteran players on their way down in Quebec, he was determined not to be one of them. When invited to return to Drummondville the next year, Ferguson agreed only if the club found him an engineering job in a textile mill. When the club refused—noting that they were a baseball club, not an employment agency—Ferguson decided to stay in Nova Scotia.

Skit returned to Halifax in 1948 and quickly demonstrated the refinements he had made in Drummondville under Tuminelli's watchful eye. His eye-popping pick-off move was so successful that Johnny Fortunato began to call balks against him even though they weren't warranted. One day, Skit and the Fotch were having lunch at Norman's restaurant and were joined by a New York Yankees scout. Ferguson's move to first quickly became the topic of conversation. "Show me it," said the scout, so Skit balled up a bunch of paper towels and proceeded to a demonstration. "That's not a balk," the scout said. After that, Fortunato was more lenient. Skit told me another pick-off story. When cocky first baseman

The 1946 Truro Bearcats were H&D League and Nova Scotia provincial champions. Back row, from left: Clarence Johnson, Billy Hepburn, Hum Joseph, Gordie Mont, Cliff Roach, Johnny Clark, John Myketyn. Front row, from left: Win Langille, Philip "Skit" Ferguson, Carl Matheson, Ab Conick, Billy MacIntyre, Angus "Sonny" MacDonald, Clyde Roy. Seated: mascot Art Dorrington (Halifax Municipal Archives, CR-67-5-990.92.01).

Don Reimer, a classy young collegian from Maine who later signed with the Yankees, arrived in town, manager Crip Polli warned him to be aware of Skit's deceptive move. Reimer blew him off, saying, "Oh yeah, I've seen the best of them." A few innings later, Skit caught a runner leaning and tried to pick him off. The ball hit Reimer flush in the stomach. "I looked over at the bench," Skit told me, "and there was Polli doubled over laughing." Nineteen forty-eight was Skit's last full year in the H&D League; a sore shoulder limited him to a single appearance with Halifax the following year.[7] How he would have fared had he chosen a pro career is the big "if," of course, but there is little doubt that he was one of the top local stars in Eastern Canada in the postwar era.

The Larrupers: Danny, Garneau, Ike and Kal Seaman

There is no better example of local players turning their backs on a professional baseball career than Nova Scotia's Seaman brothers. All four, Danny, Garneau, Ike and Kal, had demonstrated the talent to play pro ball early in their careers, but they followed their father's stern guidance, maintaining their amateur standing and playing semipro ball at home. Danny later told Burton Russell that his father "being a strong family man ... simply refused to have us separated. He always wanted the four brothers to stay together as a unit."[8] Even when all four of the boys signed with the Class C New Waterford Dodgers of the Cape Breton Colliery League in 1938, John Seaman forbade them to go, tore up their contracts, and spent three weeks haggling with the Nova Scotia Amateur Baseball Association to restore their amateur eligibility. His boys won three consecutive Maritime titles with Ike on the mound, Kal at short, and Garneau and Danny in the outfield. When Danny and Garneau accepted an invitation to spring training with the Boston Red Sox in 1940, John Seaman was dismayed. To his relief, his two boys turned down minor league contract offers and returned to Nova Scotia as playing coaches for Middleton and Liverpool, where they made considerably more money than they would have made south of the border.

When the war began, players drifted away from their town teams to play for service teams in the Halifax Defense League. Danny and Garneau ended up on opposite sides of the diamond. Garneau joined Halifax Air Force and Danny joined a Navy squad that was the equal of any club in Canada at the time and that had been Maritime champions in 1942 and 1943. Danny's teammates included Maritimers Dev and Gus Vickers, Bob "Red" Burchell, Billy Hannon, big-league pitcher

Joe Krakauskas, and outfielders Jimmy Heximer and Bobby Porter. A three-year veteran of the International League's Toronto Maple Leafs, Porter had trouble breaking into the starting outfield for the Navy squad. Heximer turned pro at war's end, playing four seasons in the minors, including a stint with Hartford of the Eastern League. Garneau's Air Force teammates were led by former Breton Colliery Leaguer Art Upper, multi-sport star Fred Thomas (perhaps Canada's best all-around athlete at the time), and Phil Marchildon, who won seventeen games for the Philadelphia Athletics in 1942. Danny went five for thirteen in three games against Marchildon in Halifax in 1943, with a double and home run. "Seaman hits the ball too hard and too often to be in Nova Scotia," Marchildon grumbled.[9] Danny stayed at home, nonetheless, becoming one the best performers in the history of the H&D League. As a thirty-nine-year-old in 1954, he added a final exclamation point to his exceptional career by slugging a game-winning, grand-slam home run against Dartmouth during the league playoffs.[10]

"Stay at Homes" and "Come from Aways": Creating a Healthy Balance

The unwillingness of Clark, Ferguson, Condy, and the Seamans to accept the blandishments of major league organizations is instructive. There is a widespread myth that anyone who had a chance would choose a pro career at the drop of the hat. This was simply not the case in the immediate postwar era. Stable employment and the opportunity to pick up an additional $100 a week playing at home often made more sense in the long run. Many young ballplayers turned down offers to turn pro as a result. This was especially true since salaries in the lower minor leagues were often far less than those in the H&D League and elsewhere in the region. Big league organizations didn't always get the players they wanted. In the summer of 1950, for example, Dodger scout Whitey Piurek, whose territory was New England and Eastern Canada, complained that getting players to sign was a difficult task since good-paying industrial jobs diverted them from signing on to play ball for far less money. Piurek spent the summer holding tryout camps in places like Meriden, Connecticut; Taunton and Fitchburg, Massachusetts; Woonsocket, Rhode Island; and Concord, New Hampshire, and in Saint John, Moncton, Fredericton, Halifax and Kentville in the Maritimes. He was only able to sign six players that year despite being impressed by the potential of a number of young Maritimers. Other organizations, Piurek lamented, were experiencing the same challenges.[11]

Gerry Davis, another Windsor, Ontario, product, who came to Nova Scotia at the end of the decade, provides a different look at the circumstances affecting young ballplayers as they pondered their future lives. Davis arrived in Nova Scotia in 1950, having heard good things about the H&D League from Bernie Parent, Jim Dumeah and old Cape Breton Colliery League player "Nap" Ross of the Windsor Ryancretes. When Middleton dropped out of the H&D League, Dumeah returned to Windsor briefly to manage the powerful Ryancretes, whose roster included a number of players with a Nova Scotian connection. Gerry Davis was one of them. While with the Ryancretes, Davis came to the attention of the Chicago White Sox, who signed him to play with their Wisconsin Rapids club. A contract dispute ended that arrangement, however, and Davis followed the advice of Ross and joined Liverpool for the last half of the 1950 season. The following year Gerry had another opportunity in Organized Baseball in the Class B Colonial League, but the league fell victim to baseball's retrenchment and folded early in the season. He returned to the Larrupers for a second year.

I had the chance to talk at length with Gerry at the H&D League reunion in 1989 and carried on a correspondence with him for some time after that. He loved his time in Liverpool. Davis was impressed by the quality of play in the league but even more by the working conditions. Playing in the H&D League was far more congenial than life in baseball's minor leagues. In the Border and the Colonial leagues he played seven days a week, practiced daily, and took home less than $100 weekly. In Liverpool he played and practiced five days a week, made considerably more money, and boarded with a local family for next to nothing. "It was like I was reborn and had gone to Heaven." Over two seasons in Liverpool, Davis averaged around three earned runs per game, good enough to land a new contract with the Cleveland Indians, who assigned him to Class C Fort Smith, Arkansas, for the 1952 season. In 1953 he joined St. Hyacinthe in the Quebec Provincial League, but after only one game with them "my dad called me ... to tell me the house my soon-to-be wife and I had purchased before I left for spring training couldn't be mortgaged because of my baseball career. So, I walked out the door." It was the end of his baseball career and the beginning of life as a successful insurance broker.[12]

Irving "Peaches" Ruven: An Enigma

Small-town baseball in the late forties involved a delicate balancing of local stars and imports from south of the border. Despite the increasing numbers of Americans on club rosters, locals had a role to play. In Halifax, for example, the Shipyards, the Arrows, and the United Services clubs were stocked with veterans of the wartime Halifax Defense League, many of them Maritimers. Among the starriest was Jimmy Gray, a flashy third baseman and .300 hitter with the Shipyards who had played with Halifax Air Force during the war. A broken ankle sliding into second base brought his career in both hockey and baseball to an end. The Shipyards were a powerhouse at the time. In the outfield, Leo Woods was in the middle of a ten-year career in senior baseball, sparkling defensively and putting up consistent numbers at the plate. Fans remember the booming voice of his father, who accompanied every base hit or running catch with "That's my boy." In his five-year H&D league career, Woods usually ranked in the top ten in batting. Behind the plate for the Ships was Donald "Chic" Charlton, one of the classiest receivers in the H&D League. Charlton handled a pitching staff led by Manitoba native Mike Genthon and Paul Oleynik from Windsor, Ontario, and shared catching duties with one of the most enigmatic figures in Maritime baseball at the time, Irving "Peaches" Ruven.

Ruven was an itinerant professional who made a living on the fringes of baseball in the "Dirty Thirties," playing for various independent Quebec Provincial League teams. His choice of a baseball life is intriguing and stands in contrast to many postwar ballplayers who had more expansive employment opportunities. During his teens and early twenties Ruven played with Les Royaux, Montreal Senior League champions, Tupper Lake of the New York Vermont League, and the Canadian National Railway and YMCA teams located in Montreal. He was a youthful prodigy of two former major league catching greats, Tom Daly and Wally Schang, both of whom instructed him in the intricacies of handling a pitching staff and tutored him on in-game baseball strategy. In 1936 Ruven took his talents to London, England, as playing coach of the Hackney Wick team, and he remained there until war broke out. He returned to Nova Scotia as starting catcher for the powerful Halifax Navy club, Maritime champions in 1942 and 1943, and played in the H&D League until 1948, including a short stint with the 1946 provincial champion Truro Bearcats.

Before the 1947 season got underway, the Whitney Pier club in the Cape Breton Colliery League offered thirty-six-year-old Ruven a contract as playing coach. While critics considered the salary offer exorbitant, Ruven told fans, "I come high, gentlemen, but the price in no way exceeds my value. If there's anything I know, it's baseball. I've had a steady diet since I was fourteen and my main diet was served by no less a figure than Tom Daly."[13] A Saint John native and baseball legend in the Maritimes, Daly had played eight years in the major leagues for the White Sox, Cubs and Cleveland Indians and thirteen more years of minor league ball, including two years with the Montreal Royals in the early thirties. As for the offer from Whitney Pier, a bitter coal strike threw the Cape Breton baseball scene into disarray in the spring of 1947. Many of the best players on the Island left to find roster spots with teams on the mainland. Ruven ended up staying with the Halifax Arrows, where he hit over .300 that season, helping Halifax to another Maritime championship, his third in five years.

Despite his lengthy baseball pedigree Ruven had a somewhat unsavory reputation. His career was reminiscent of those traveling circus and carnival performers who eked out a living through sheer force of personality and the talent to perform. Many who knew him recall an edgy character who always seemed to have a scam of one sort or another going on, replacing new baseballs with older, roughed up ones and selling them or running poker games where he was not above "bending the rules." On the diamond he used his accumulated knowledge to steal an advantage whenever he could. I have always wondered, however, whether these assumptions about his character reflected contemporary stereotypes of people of Jewish heritage, given the widespread anti–Semitism of the time. This remains an open question. What was never in doubt, however, was his knowledge of the game. "Peaches was smart," remembers Ferguson, his part-time battery mate with the 1946 Bearcats. Although Ruven was only in Truro for a brief time—filling in when Win Langille was injured—he quickly picked up on how much energy the youngster wasted snapping off his curveball. Ruven encouraged him to let the ball spin off his fingers a bit more. "After that I wasn't as tired at the end of the game as I had been before," said Ferguson.

By the end of the forties, the number of players from south of the border increased dramatically but local players still stood out. Dartmouth's curve-baller Neil "Ozark" Staples won nineteen games in 1947 and another dozen in 1948, vaulting him into H&D League's top pitching quartet that included fellow Nova Scotian Ferguson and import pitching sensations Art Raynor and Jack Halpin. Over his lengthy career Staples won 42 games, more than any H&D League player of the forties and fifties. Eventually, however, the flood of American collegians and minor league vets would turn the Maritimes into the "NCAA North." Among the best of the college boys were future major leaguers Dick Gernert and Art Ceccarelli in Kentville, Hal Smith and Mike Roarke in Blacks Harbour, George Alusik in Saint John, "Turk" Farrell in Springhill, and Emmanuel "Sonny" Senerchia in Middleton.

Although the import experiment ended in Cape Breton after 1950,

Maritime baseball's geographical footprint continued to grow as fast as its reputation. Rivalries involving hometown stars, young American collegians, and established minor league veterans attracted large crowds, and new ballparks were constructed with lighting for night games. In turn, major league scouts crisscrossed the region to keep tabs on the young prospects they might send north. Former big-leaguers "Stuffy" McInnis in Stellarton, Bill Cronin in Springhill, "Crip" Polli in Halifax, Emerson Dickman in Kentville, and Ray Fisher in Blacks Harbour and Truro were enlisted to manage them. As Maritime baseball began attracting increasing attention, moreover, competitive summer leagues south of the border were collapsing. This meant an expanding talent pool was available to local clubs. It is not surprising that a barrage of barnstorming clubs from south of the border—including those with major league stars on their rosters—arrived to challenge teams that blended talented home-town players with big-league prospects from the United States.

Three

The Barnstorming Era
American Baseball's Northward Glance, 1948–50

On August 2, 1948, an overflow crowd of over 4,000 fans squeezed into the Wanderer's Grounds in Halifax to watch a select squad of young players from the Halifax and District Baseball League take the field against the touring Brooklyn Junior Dodgers. Chosen to represent Flatbush in the "Brooklyn-Against-the-World" classic, an annual event co-sponsored by the *Brooklyn Eagle* newspaper and the major league Dodgers, the baby Brooklynites had split two games against juniors from Washington, D.C., and triumphed over Toronto and Montreal before boarding the Ocean Limited for a twenty-three-hour train ride from Montreal to Halifax. Led by their sparkling right-hander Billy Loes, Gotham's best schoolboy pitcher of the postwar period, the baby Dodgers' roster also included future major leaguers Don McMahon and Joe Pignatano and players like Pete Gentile who would go on to lengthy minor league careers. A slugging outfielder who had won the Lou Gehrig award as MVP in the Hearst Classic that year, Gentile signed an $18,000 bonus contract with the Yankees soon after returning from Halifax.[1] He received an invite to spring training with the Yankees in 1949 along with another junior-age player, Clark Wojtowicz, who had a sensational year with the Springhill Fencebusters in 1948.[2]

Loes was the most sought after, however. Only a couple of weeks away from signing a $22,000 bonus contract with the big-league Dodgers, he had dazzled scouts for a few years while pitching for Bryant High School. Dodgers GM Branch Rickey was determined to sign him to the Dodgers organization. The Dodgers began the Canadian swing with a 4–2 victory over the Toronto Junior All-Stars and beat the Montreal Juniors handily, 15–9. In Halifax they lost their only game by a 5–3 count, with Loes and Harry Owens sharing the mound duties.³ Saint John native Joe Breen's towering home run, and the combined efforts of four Halifax pitchers who held Brooklyn to three hits, were enough to send the crowd home happy. After the loss, the Dodgers returned to New York via Providence, Rhode Island, where they finished off their tour with a 2–0 victory led by Loes' fifteen-strikeout performance.

The Brooklyn-Against-the-World series was one of two classic postwar showcases of young baseball talent. The other was the Hearst Sandlot Classic, which originated in 1945 and pitted an all–New York squad against a team representing major urban centers across the United States.⁴ Locked in a battle for circulation with William Randolph Hearst's *New York World*, the *Brooklyn Eagle* newspaper responded with a series of its own that highlighted an "international" component. Marketing it as Brooklyn-Against-the-World was both brilliant and ironic, implying that Brooklyn was the international capital of baseball and that the *Eagle* was more worldly than the *World*. It was also a way for

An all-star team drawn from the three Halifax H&D clubs, the Shipyards, Capitals and Dartmouth Arrows. Many of the players seen here helped Halifax defeat Billy Loes and the touring Brooklyn Junior Dodgers in the 1948 Brooklyn versus the World Classic series. Back row, from left: Tom Dulmage, Jack Halpin, Bob Fitzgerald, Nurse McKenzie, Joe Breen, Duke Morgan, Ted Narleski, Buddy Condy. Front row, from left: John Duarte, Doc Acocella, Herb Rossmann, Don Reimer, Philip "Skit" Ferguson, Jimmy Gray (Halifax Municipal Archives, CR-67-5-992.20.01).

the Dodgers to extend what was already the most far-flung scouting network in all of baseball. Two members of the 1946 World All Stars would have connections to baseball in Eastern Canada. Roger Bréard was a mainstay of baseball in Quebec, while Hawaiian pitching sensation Hank Tominaga would play for the Blacks Harbour Brunswicks and Kentville Wildcats in the early 1950s.

Shepherding the club into Halifax were Brooklyn's director of scouting, Mickey McConnell, and former Dodgers pitcher Ownie Carroll, who managed the team on the field. While watching their recruits perform, McConnell and Carroll also kept tabs on players that the Dodgers had sent to Nova Scotia earlier in the year. Drawn from both the Halifax Junior and H&D League, the locals had a number of players of interest. Second baseman Herbie Rossman was already well known, having grown up on Long Island and having played with the *Brooklyn Eagle* All-Stars in the 1947 classic. At shortstop was seventeen-year-old Ted Narleski, son of a former major leaguer and brother of pitcher Ray Narleski, a mainstay on the mound for the Cleveland Indians in the mid–'50s. Others on McConnell's watch list were slugging first baseman Don Reimer of Bowdoin

Blacklisted Mexican Leaguer Bucky Tanner (left) towers over the 1947 Middleton Cardinals pitching staff, including, from his left, Gerald "Fats" Ray, Cy Burnam, Jim Dumeah, and Maurice DeLoof. DeLoof was a Red Sox scout dispatched to Middleton to follow Tanner and players from the Detroit-Windsor area (author's collection).

College, speedy African American outfielder Milton "Bomber" Neal, and two seventeen-year-old pitchers, Charlie Greene and Albert Pare. Of the six Nova Scotians on the club, only Puddy Reardon and Albert Pinaud were technically of junior age. Home run hero Joe Breen, outfielder "Twit" Clarke, and third baseman Cyril Hector had already turned twenty, and veteran catcher Harold Duke Morgan was older still. Breen already had had a successful stint in the Quebec Provincial League in 1945, and Morgan, who was already on the Dodgers' radar, spent 1947 in the Class D Eastern Shore League.

The Brooklyn press was quick to praise the "crack" Halifax team but made it clear that the higher age limit "gave the Nova Scotian players a jump on the Brooklyn boys in both experience and general physique." The difference was particularly noticeable in the field, where the Haligonians played solid defense. The Dodgers, on the other hand, performed sloppily. Three Brooklyn errors and a couple of bad decisions not noticeable in the box score plagued the New Yorkers.[5] McConnell told a Halifax columnist that he had watched the defeat of the Dodgers with mixed feelings "since several of the players who put the lash on the Brooklyns were themselves members of the Brooklyn organization and had been sent by him to the H&D League." He was particularly impressed with Rossman, who went two for three with a stolen base, and Breen, who along with his home run made two fine running catches in center field.[6]

Off to the Valley: Scouting Talent in Kentville and Middleton

After leaving Halifax, McConnell and Carroll travelled to Kentville to scout Valley talent, taking in a double-header between the Wildcats and the Halifax Shipyards. Topping the prospect list were Dick Gernert, a power-hitting first-sacker out of Temple University and still in his junior year, outfielder Jack Kaiser from St. John's University, and pitchers Tom McMullen, Jim Arbucho, and Art Raynor. Raynor had starred in the 1947 Brooklyn-Against-the-World series, one of two New York starting pitchers, the other being Eddie Ford, who would later go by the nickname "Whitey." Ironically, Gernert and Kaiser were kept in check by Shipyards pitchers. The Dodgers also had interest in players from the nearby Middleton Cardinals, including seventeen-year-old infielder Emmanuel "Sonny" Senerchia and Mexican League veteran William "Bucky" Tanner, who had been blacklisted by major league baseball for jumping his contract with the Dodgers a couple of years before. As an eighteen-year-old, Tanner had made it to Triple-A in the Dodgers organization. Eventually the Dodgers signed McMullen and Raynor, but lost Gernert and Kaiser to the Boston Red Sox.

Although my baseball loyalties were strongly linked to the Wildcats, I also had some fondness for the Middleton Cardinals since I had been born in the sleepy little Valley town. Later I became intrigued with "Sonny" Senerchia who, like me, blended baseball with a passion for music. A wonderful musician who performed at Carnegie Hall as a ten-year-old and later shared the stage with the likes of Jack Benny and Ella Fitzgerald, Senerchia completed his college degree at Monmouth State College in the spring of 1952. In his one season in Nova Scotia, the youngster was overmatched and found H&D League pitching too tough to handle. He would not be invited back the following year and played instead in the Class D Ohio league. Still hoping to return to Nova Scotia, he attended a New England tryout camp in 1950 run by Braves scout Jeff Jones, who was putting the Truro Bearcats team together. Once again, Senerchia failed to make the cut. After his graduation from Monmouth, where he played in the infield and took turns on the mound, he eventually signed with the Pittsburgh Pirates. He played the first half of the 1952 season in the Class B Carolina League before being called up to the big leagues. In 100 at-bats for the Pirates, he hit an anemic .220 but collected five doubles and three home runs, and started twenty-six games at third base.[7]

Despite his stint in the majors, Senerchia remains something of a forgotten figure in Nova Scotia baseball lore, overshadowed by his more successful Middleton teammates Johnny Wingo, Gerald "Fat" Ray, Carl Bruce, Manny McIntyre, Herbie McLeod and Mexican Leaguer "Bucky" Tanner. Tanner was a free spirit, occasionally appearing at the park in a wide-brimmed sombrero. A hard-throwing, six-foot-eight, two-hundred-pound right-hander from Rattlesnake, Florida, Tanner signed with the Dodgers as a seventeen-year-old whiz kid. A front-page story in *The Sporting News* described him taking the Dodgers spring training camp by storm in 1944. "Long, loose and loquacious" was the verdict, audacious as well, but that would have destroyed the alliteration.[8] In his first season of pro ball, the teenager chalked up two no-hitters, already showing more velocity than fireballing Kirby Higbe of the big league Dodgers. In one of those encounters, Bucky walked the first eight batters, but Newport News manager Jake Pitler told him not to quit since Brooklyn scouts in the stands wanted to see how long he could smoke the ball. Tanner finished the no-hit game with thirteen walks and lost 6–0. After Tanner appeared for the International League Montreal Royals in a game early in 1946, Jorge Pasquel offered him more than twice his salary to jump his contract with the Dodgers and play in Pasquel's upstart Mexican League.[9]

Tanner told Ted Cumming, who was living in Middleton at the time, that Pasquel showed up at his hotel room and counted out twenty $100 bills and threw them on his bed. It was the most money Tanner had ever seen in one place. Already married with four kids, the twenty-year-old quickly agreed to play in Mexico and was assigned first to Veracruz and later to Torreon. Although he pitched admirably, even besting Max Lanier in a pitcher's duel that broke Lanier's six-game unbeaten streak, Tanner chose not to return after the 1946 season. In 1947 he turned up with the Middleton Cardinals of the H&D League, accompanied by catcher Matt Batts, who didn't stay and later that year made the Boston Red Sox roster. With Tanner already in tow, the Cardinals also sent an offer to Lanier, but his asking price of $10,000 would have been too rich even for big league clubs.[10] Tanner returned to the Valley town in 1948 and was no doubt interested in the visit of the Junior Dodgers that year. Reinstated by MLB in 1949, he would gain notoriety with an eleven-inning no-hitter for Fort Lauderdale of the Florida International League against the Miami Marlins in 1950. The first televised no-hit game in baseball history, it was Tanner's third.[11]

The baby Dodgers were by no means the only touring squad to visit the Maritimes in the late 1940s. As the H&D League and the New Brunswick League played at an increasingly high level, touring teams from the New York area and New England made the Maritimes a priority. Clubs from New England had already turned the Maritimes into something of a baseball burned-over-district prior to the war. Both the Red Sox and Braves had played in-season exhibition games in New Brunswick and Nova Scotia in the 1930s. In addition to big-league clubs, the Boston Royal Giants, led by Negro League stars Burlin White and Bill Jackman, barnstormed by bus through New Brunswick and Nova Scotia each year in the style of the Bingo Long Traveling All-Stars. Other tourist clubs included the Georgia Chain Gang, the Philadelphia Colored Giants, the Chappie Johnson All-Stars, the African Zulu Giants, the Detroit Clowns, the Boston Hoboes, New York Equitable Life, the Brooklyn Bushwicks, the New York Black Yankees, and the bewhiskered House of David squad. Many of these teams had former major leaguers in their lineups, while the black clubs had players denied a chance to play professionally in organized ball. Often, touring clubs would find the talent in the H&D League to be far more than expected. The 1951 Georgia Chain Gang, led by ex–major leaguers Ray Martin, Sam Gentile and Charley Osgoode, for example, were seriously outclassed, losing to Stellarton 6–0, Truro 10–1, and the Halifax Capitals 6–4.

The Birdie Tebbetts Traveling All-Stars

In addition to the visit of the Junior Dodgers, a second major event of the 1948 season occurred when the Birdie Tebbetts Traveling All-Stars undertook a tour of New England and New Brunswick at the end of the major league season. Although Tebbetts had planned to visit Nova Scotia, the uncertain weather in late October led to the cancellation of the last part of the schedule. Tebbetts knew the Maritimes well. A native of Vermont and a self-proclaimed "baseball nomad," he was a veteran major league catcher and four-time all-star whose career spanned fourteen big league seasons.[12] Tebbetts brought with him a lineup that drew heavily on his baseball connections to Boston, New York, and his native Vermont.

The All-Stars were a star-studded crew. Earl Torgeson of the Braves was at first base. The middle infield included New York Yankees second baseman George "Snuffy" Stirnweiss, a former American League all-star in 1946, and Red Sox shortstop Vern Stephens, who hit twenty-nine home runs and joined teammate Tebbetts on the 1948 American League all-star team. Slick-fielding Eddie Pellagrini, who had tried unsuccessfully to break into the old Cape Breton Colliery League before the war, was the third baseman, replacing Red Sox infielder Johnny Pesky, who had to withdraw from the team due to the death of his father. In the outfield were two Red Sox prospects, Walt "Moose" Dropo, who hit .359 for Birmingham in 1948, and Jimmy Piersall, an eighteen-year-old phenom who spent the season playing for Scranton of the Eastern League. The other outfielders were Tony Lupien, like Tebbetts a native of Vermont, and Carl Scheib of the Philadelphia Athletics, who shared duties as outfielder and on the mound. New York Giants catcher Gus Niarhous and pitcher-outfielder Johnny "Red" Barrett were the backups.

Part of the Red Sox "youth movement" in 1952, Piersall was a five-tool player. He could run, could field, had a strong arm, and could hit both for average and with power, which explains his subsequent seventeen-year career in the majors. At the same time Piersall struggled with a bipolar disorder made worse by the pressure of making it to the major leagues. His struggles, recounted in his autobiography *Fear Strikes Out*, were made into a movie starring Tony Perkins as Piersall and Karl Malden as a demanding and domineering father. A review in the March 13, 1957, edition of *The Sporting News* by columnist Fred Lieb described the film as "packed with drama, pathos, suspense and tension, the same tension that sent Piersall into a sanitarium [sic] in 1951."[13] Although the film's baseball scenes displayed Perkins' awkwardness rather than Piersall's physical talent, the film highlighted many social trends evident in the postwar era. One of these was a changing conception of fatherhood that witnessed the replacement of the stern and demanding patriarch by the mild-mannered dad venerated in the TV series *Father Knows Best*. The film also testified to a growing postwar faith in psychiatry as a profession and to the ability of psychiatrists to provide surrogate parenthood for those suffering from neuroses and more serious mental disorders.

The All-Stars opened their Maritime swing on October 21 with a 5–1 victory over the Saint John St. Peters, league champions in the New Brunswick city league. To the delight of the overflow crowd, Saint John opened the scoring in the first inning. Lead-off hitter Aukie Titus singled, Dave Kiley then executed a perfect sacrifice, and a ground out moved Titus to third. Then, as visitors' starter Ray Scarborough peered in for the sign for the next pitch, Titus took off for home and beat the tag. Tebbetts protested but to no avail. For five innings it was anyone's match. Saint John starter Johnny Harvey, a one-time Chicago farmhand who had been on the White Sox 40-man roster in 1944, limited the All-Stars to a single hit entering the fifth. In the fifth, a Tony Lupien double and singles by Tebbetts and Pellagrini knotted the score and Harvey was done for the day. Art Wilson replaced the tiring Harvey in the sixth but gave up four runs over the next three innings. Cecil Brownell, a dependable workhorse for many years with the Saint Stephen-Kiwanis club, finished the game with a clean inning.

On the following day, the All-Stars travelled to Grand Falls for two games against the local Cataracts. On the mound for the Tebbetts club was Frank Shea, who had broken into the majors in spectacular fashion the year before, winning fourteen games for the New York Yankees. New Hampshire native Bob Savage of the Philadelphia Athletics finished up for the All-Stars, saving a 4–2 victory for the touring squad. "Muck" Carroll, the Grand Falls starter, went four innings and gave up four hits and two runs, striking out two and walking none. The locals garnered ten hits off Shea and Savage, while the All-Stars managed eleven off four Cataract pitchers. In iron-man fashion, Carroll was on the mound again the following day, this time lasting six innings and giving up four runs on seven hits in a 6–1 loss to the All-Stars. Joe Coleman went the distance for the major leaguers, giving up a run and four hits, including a triple to Bill Mulherin. A 400-foot three-run homer by shortstop Vern Stephens in the seventh inning iced the victory for the touring club.

The visit of the All-Stars attested to the close baseball connections between New England and the Maritimes after the war. Although bad weather interfered in 1949, the Tebbetts club returned to the Maritimes in 1950 and 1951. Supplementing a returning core of players from 1948 were household names Phil Rizzuto, Al Rosen, Sal Maglie, Whitey Ford, Johnny Pesky, Jim Hegan, Vic Wertz, Mike Garcia and Bobby Thomson. Such an array of big-league talent may seem surprising today, but player salaries remained artificially low at that time and touring meant a few extra dollars. Even star players like Thomson, whose "shot heard around the world" off Dodgers pitcher Ralph Branca clinched the 1951 National League pennant for the New York Giants, were attracted to barnstorming. Unfortunately, fan support began to dwindle as televised baseball and other forms of summer entertainment diverted people from the ballparks. After the 1951 tour, a disillusioned Tebbetts gave up the ghost. "We had the best team I've ever assembled," said Tebbetts. "Bobby Thomson and Sal Maglie were the hottest attractions in baseball.... In other years, fans would have packed the ballparks, but not this year. The fans already had seen them in their own living-room."[14]

The Waning Fortunes of the Vermont-Northern League: A Boon to Maritime Baseball

In addition to the tours of the Brooklyn juniors and the Tebbetts All-Stars, the 1948 season was a pivotal year for baseball in the Maritimes. For years, stretching back to the 1930s, the Vermont-New York Northern League was considered the strongest summer league outside of Organized Baseball, bringing together collegiate stars, top-flight prospects, and older pros. At the end of the 1947 season, however, the East Coast Athletic Conference (ECAC) declared the Northern League professional. This decision was at once a blow to Vermont and a boon to baseball north of the border. When four players from Michigan State lost their college eligibility by playing in Vermont, many collegians looked to the Maritimes as a safer place to play for pay during the summer months.

In 1948 the Northern League played before dwindling crowds, and many of its fans expressed displeasure that the H&D League had escaped similar sanction. On June 19, 1949, the *Burlington Daily News* reported that "the ogre-like ECAC ... has turned its frown on the Nova Scotia League" and hoped that it might soon be blacklisted. "Perhaps this may mean that with all the concentration on ... leagues which were getting away with murder the Northern League may be left alone this summer. Let's see how they like being ECACized."[15] In fact, summer leagues in the Maritimes escaped sanction for another decade. Unable to survive the NCAA sanction, the Northern League suspended operations in 1951 and shut down for good in 1952. As a result, the H&D

League could claim its status as the finest summer league on the east coast of North America.

The struggles of the Northern League were a mixed blessing for teams in the Maritimes. On the one hand, a new pool of college prospects provided a temptation for local clubs to add to their complement of imports. On the other hand, the influx of talent from south of the border meant diminished opportunities for local players. As a result, the balancing of locals and "come-from-aways" was difficult to maintain. During the 1947 season, for example, the Kentville Wildcats assembled a healthy balance of Canadian and American players. Two home-town boys, pitcher Bev Buckler and track star Gordon Troke, were joined by well-known veterans of baseball from Cape Breton: catcher Bull Marsh, infielder-outfielders Leo Fahey and Eddie Gillis, and first baseman Joe Cormier. The imports were led by infielders Johnny Watterson and Soc Bobotas and outfielders Hal Burby and Emile Krupa, all from the University of New Hampshire and all of whom had played in the Northern League on occasion. Teenage sensations John "Bruce" Blount from the University of Rhode Island and high-school prodigy Art "Chic" Ceccarelli from New Haven, Connecticut, rounded out the pitching staff. Beginning the following year, however, the Wildcats replaced a number of competent Maritime players with college prospects from south of the border, many of them having been sent north on the recommendation of the Dodgers.

Hank Swasey's 1948 Wildcats joined the H&D League for the season—led by Jack Kaiser, Dick Gernert and Bobotas at the plate. New Yorkers Dom Novak, Art Raynor, Tom McMullen and New Hampshire boy Gerry Girard sparkled on the mound. Paul O'Neil, a cigar-smoking veteran in the Reds and Dodgers organizations, handled the pitchers capably. Despite a successful season in the H&D League, the Wildcats opted to join the Central League the following year and dominated their opponents. While the on-field results were outstanding, the switch to the Central League had its liabilities. In a league where pitching performances were sub-par, leading to high batting averages and blow-out games, crowds at Memorial Park were disappointing and the club lost money. In addition, travel arrangements were less than ideal, including a number of trips across the Bay of Fundy. New Hampshire's *Portsmouth Herald*, which followed the exploits of the boys from UNH closely, reported that Coach Hank Swasey may be "the only seafaring manager in baseball, as his team crosses the Bay of Fundy twice weekly in a one-masted schooner."[16] Undertaken to save money, sea travel was not without risk. According to the *Kentville Advertiser*, Swasey had a number of close calls. "En route to Amherst last week, Hank just missed having his brains bashed out by scant inches when a forward hatch was lifted by the heavy wind and blown directly over the spot where he was sitting." There were other problems. When the tide was against them, players would get home "just when the average farmer is making ready to milk the cows." This perhaps explains both Swasey's decision not to return the next year and the club's eagerness to return to the H&D League fold.[17]

Dodger Dandies: Brooklyn's Maritime Connections

Sent to the Wildcats by the Dodgers, Ceccarelli had a solid season, winning eleven of thirteen decisions and recording a no-hitter against the Windsor Maple Leafs. The seventeen-year-old had a quality fastball but, like most hard-throwing youngsters, experienced control and command issues. Just a kid, and away from home for the first time, he was mocked by some of his older teammates about his naivety. Bev Buckler remembered a night in Truro when Ceccarelli was late getting his gear together and couldn't find his way back to the hotel, only a few blocks away. He took quite a ribbing from his older teammates.

Happy with Ceccarelli's year in Nova Scotia, the Dodgers signed him to a minor league contract. As a twenty-year-old in 1950, he was at Elmira of the Eastern League but experienced arm problems that would plague him throughout his fifteen-year professional career. Unhappy that the Dodgers kept him relatively inactive for the second half of the 1950 season even though his arm felt fine, he decided to keep his arm problems to himself. "I wouldn't admit to any discomfort, since major league organizations would often write you off if you did." Although he lost a little velocity and often played through pain, Ceccarelli persevered and went on to play five years in the majors with the Athletics, Orioles and Cubs.

When I caught up with him at his home in Connecticut after his retirement from the game, Art was by no means averse to talking about his days in Nova Scotia and his later career. At the same time he emphasized that his baseball exploits represented a mere half-inning in the longer game of life. "I was so young, and this was just a small and fleeting time in my life, and hardly the most important," he observed. "My life as a father and educator are the things that are the most important to me." When Art revealed that his son had been recently diagnosed with a brain tumor, it emphasized to me that any baseball life requires a deeper understanding beyond statistics, contractual relationships, or on-field performance. It also helped me understand why so many players chose not to follow a professional baseball career. For most young players, a competitive career wouldn't outlast their twenties. For others, it was a prelude to lifelong careers as high school or college coaches. Most imagined a future as medical doctors, lawyers, engineers, insurance agents, priests and ministers, businessmen, journalists or a variety of other occupational opportunities that emerged in the postwar industrial economy.

United States National Amateur Baseball Champions: New York Equitable Life

The healthy complement of New York area players on Nova Scotian diamonds, and the particular interest of the Dodgers in their development, set the stage for the third major series involving touring teams from the United States. In 1949 the New York Equitable Life team, National Amateur Baseball champions in 1948 and 1949, played a three-game set in Halifax against the Capitals and Shipyards of the H&D League. In his memoir, veteran sportswriter Ace Foley of the *Halifax Herald* remembered "the greatest game ever played in my life on a Nova Scotia diamond. It went into extra innings, the home team won ... and it had everything including a triple play.... There were no homeruns but only because the outfielders were leaping high in the air and grabbing the liners as they headed for the bleachers."[18] The Equitable Life squad dominated play against amateur, military and college teams in New York and had a club which included former major leaguers Al "Dutch" Mele and Vince Ventura and veteran minor leaguers. The club was competitive with the Class A teams and had its share of wins against teams at Double-A.

According to first baseman Fred Price, a former New York Giants prospect whose career was sidetracked by a serious wartime injury, his club expected to face teams that played at the level of a Class C team in Organized Baseball. Instead, they found the caliber of play in Nova Scotia "as good as anything being played in the Class A leagues in the United States."[19] After splitting the first two games of the series against the Capitals and Shipyards, Equitable Life played the rubber match against a team drawn from the two Halifax clubs. Like the game before, the deciding game went into extra innings, with the visitors pushing across a run in the 10th to win 5–4. Tom Casey, an All-American pitcher from NYU who signed to play in the Red Sox organization the following year, went the distance for the Americans, scattering nine hits and striking out five.

Halifax residents were delighted with the tightly contested series and large crowds that exceeded 12,000 paid spectators. Across the harbor in Dartmouth, there was annoyance and resentment, however. Conflicts between the rival owners of the Halifax teams and the Arrows denied Dartmouth an opportunity to participate in the series and receive a share of the substantial gate receipts that would have followed. To make matters worse, the Arrows had the best record of the three metro teams.

Dartmouth gained its revenge at the end of the season. In the first round of the playoffs, the Arrows went undefeated, outscoring the Shipyards 35 runs to 22. Decker's Texas League teammate "Smokey Jim" Heller was the pitching star. Dartmouth then faced the Halifax Capitals, who were hopeful that local stars Buddy Condy and Johnny Clark and dominant lefthander Jack Halpin would lead them to victory. Dartmouth's lineup included future big-leaguer Zeke Bella, slugging catcher Stu O'Brien and gritty right-hander Heller. The teams swapped victories in the first two games, but Dartmouth's pitching did not allow a single run after that. Heller was again the star of the series, spinning two five-hit shutouts. Although Heller had a good fastball and average control, his greatest asset was deception. According to Johnny Watterson, he delivered the ball "out of his pocket almost," making it hard to pick up the spin. "It was on you in an instant."

Having copped the H&D League championship, the Arrows prepared for an even tougher challenge against the Central League champion Kentville Wildcats. The mainland championship between the Arrows and Wildcats would become the highlight of the 1949 baseball season in Nova Scotia. Generally considered the class of the entire region, the two clubs were as evenly matched as one could imagine. All of the first four games of the series were decided by a single run, and the following two knotted the series at three games each. In the seventh game in the Valley town, a ninth-inning Wildcats comeback evened the score. A rain delay and eventual darkness created confusion and a dispute arose over where the eighth game should be played. Facing the loss of some of their prized collegians, the Wildcats refused to play the deciding match that the NSABA mandated be played in Halifax. With Kentville's forfeit, the Arrows were chosen to take on the Cape Breton Colliery League champion Sydney Mines Ramblers for the provincial championship. In an anti-climactic final, the Arrows won the five-game series in four games.

Across the provincial line in New Brunswick, the hard-hitting Fredericton Capitols squared off against the Moncton Legionnaires in the provincial championship series. Sporting a solid core of homebrews and a sprinkling of imports, Fredericton dominated the seven-game series, winning in five games. Earlier in the year they had overpowered their rivals in the province and across the border, knocking off the strongest squads in Maine; had a Maritime championship been played, they would have given the H&D League champions a run for their money. Homebrews Rollie McLenahan, Buster Mills, Manny McIntyre and Charlie Pyle led the club at the plate with solid support from import center-fielder Art "Whitey" Weinstock and moundsmen Lefty Letteri, Bob Watts and Bob Bagwell. A 21-year-old pitcher in his third season with the Capitols, Bagwell was a native of Watertown, Massachusetts, and often made his way to Fenway to watch the Red Sox. "I was a big Ted Williams fan," Bagwell said, "and I used to go to college at Northeastern, and sometimes I'd sit in the bleachers. Baseball is a big part of my life."[20] His love for baseball also rubbed off on his son Jeff, a fifteen-year veteran of the Houston Astros who was recently inducted into Baseball's Hall of Fame.

Bob Bagwell first came to Fredericton in 1947 from Northeastern University when the swing toward imported players was in its initial stages. At the time, most teams had a solid core of local players and would occasionally bring in collegians from Maine, New Hampshire, and Massachusetts to fill gaps in their rosters. Each year saw more imports on league rosters. As the 1949 season opened, the *Daily Gleaner* predicted a "Big Season for Maritime Baseball" with lots of imports and twenty-six different senior teams across New Brunswick and Nova Scotia.[21] The import parade had begun a couple of years before, but by the late forties, fans increasingly demanded the high quality of play that the flow of talent from south of the border promised. It was not just the bigger towns in the region like St. John, Fredericton, Moncton and Grand Falls that went the import route. This was also true of towns close to the border with Maine. In the small railroad hub of McAdam, which played a schedule with teams on both sides of the border, thirteen players on its 1949 squad came from the United States, most from Maine and Massachusetts. Furthermore, in the sardine-canning industry town of Blacks Harbour, the local Brunswicks would become one of the province's most competitive clubs of the day, sporting a roster that included future major league catcher Mike Roarke and former New York Giant Johnny Gee. Before 1950, New Brunswick teams nonetheless drew heavily on a pool of local talent that included the likes of Joe Breen, Johnny Harvey, Doug Ross, Aukie Titus, Rollie McLenahan, Hum Joseph, Dave Kiley, Don Johnson, Curt Moore, Moon Mullen, Pius Gaudet, Alonzo Gaudet, Billy Harris, Jackie Bowes, Jimmy Fox, Sonny MacDonald and Fred Flemming. Although the reliance on imports would grow in the years to come, baseball at the end of the 1940s in the Maritimes still rested on a foundation of good local players.

As the decade drew to a close, baseball flourished throughout the region. In addition to a solid core of local performers who honed their skills in the highly competitive Halifax Defense League, top-level college prospects brought a growing sophistication of play. The contraction of minor league and independent league baseball south of the border, evident in the troubles of the Northern League, the Blackstone Valley League in Maryland, and the Albemarle League in the Carolinas, also meant a surplus of talent for teams in the Maritimes to exploit. By 1950, Maritime baseball was on the verge of a "golden age." The H&D League was reputed to be the fastest summer league anywhere on the eastern seaboard, a destination for college players and prospects from as far south as the Carolinas and westward to the Great Lakes.

Four

Tipping the Balance

*The American Influence
and the Marginalization of Local Players*

As the 1950 baseball season approached, Kentville Wildcats infielder Johnny Watterson had a decision to make. Having finished his student years at the University of New Hampshire, the slick-fielding shortstop had to decide whether to accept a minor league contract with the Brooklyn Dodgers or concentrate on a coaching career. A Pacific war veteran, Watterson had starred in military ball in the Philippines and Okinawa, playing alongside and against a number of major leaguers. Although barely out of his teens, he became convinced of his ability to compete against well-known stars with much more experience. An at-bat against eventual Hall of Famer Early Wynn stood out in his mind. Rather than coming with his usual delivery, Wynn, who had the reputation as a head-hunter, dropped down and threw a submarine-style heater that almost grazed Watterson's head, sending him sprawling to the ground. Incensed, Watterson dusted himself off and readied himself for Wynn's next offering. "There was no reason for him to drop down like that," Watterson recalled, "so I wanted to make it clear to him that I wasn't intimidated. On the next pitch I hit the ball as hard as I had ever done on a straight line into left field." When his military hitch was up, he returned home to take advantage of the educational opportunities offered up by the GI Bill. He played summer ball for the Keene Blue Jays of the Vermont Northern League and in Kentville from 1947 through 1949.

In considering his future, Watterson sought out Dodgers scout Jim Ferrante for a frank assessment of his baseball prospects. Ferrante pulled no punches. In Watterson's case he was a Class A- or AA-level player, not a major league prospect. His drawbacks were twofold: size and age. Standing only five foot five and weighing 145 pounds, Watterson was a line-drive hitter with no power, and despite hitting .335 for the Keene Bluejays of the Northern League in 1946, he was only a .260 hitter over his three years in Nova Scotia. Furthermore, like many players whose careers were delayed by the war and who then chose to get their college education, Watterson was approaching age twenty-five in 1950, too old to be considered a prospect. With this in mind he contemplated a coaching career, hoping that the Wildcats might be interested. Johnny told me that he had absolutely loved his years in Kentville and was considering moving his wife and family north to settle permanently in Nova Scotia. He was also aware that Hank Swaysey would not be returning to the Wildcats for the 1950 season and that there was a possible opening for him in Kentville as playing coach. The Dodgers had different plans, however, and wanted Emerson Dickman, former Boston Red Sox pitcher and baseball coach at Princeton, to take over the Wildcats. The Dodgers were interested in a number of players on the Princeton roster at the time, among them bespectacled Dave Sisler, who would later go on to a major league career with the Red Sox; Ray Chirurgi, the ace of the Princeton staff with a 9–2 won-lost record; and Harry Brightman, who would later sign with the Cardinals organization. Chirurgi and Brightman each won ten games for the Wildcats in 1950. Mearle Strachan, a former AAA pitcher, served as an assistant coach to Dickman and contributed another five wins.

With the Wildcats out of the picture, Watterson decided to shop his services to other clubs in the province. He requested and received his release from the Wildcats and signed with the Stellarton Albions as playing coach. In a letter dated April 1, 1950, Kentville club president Dr. J.P. McGrath told Johnny that "we certainly would not have let you go if it had not been that you wanted to coach, and the Brooklyn Dodgers wanted to send a coach of their *own* selection." McGrath also confided that the Dodgers had not expressed an interest in retaining Paul O'Neill, a veteran catcher with a number of years' experience in the Dodgers organization, or second baseman Tom Jones of Villanova, "so if you wish to contact either one of these there will be no difficulty in obtaining their release, but as far as [Chris] Tonery, [Gerry] Girard and [Jack] Curran are concerned, Brooklyn has earmarked them for this year again, and we, consequently, cannot release them."[1]

At the Helm: "Stuffy" McInnis and John Watterson in Stellarton

Watterson had big shoes to fill in Stellarton. In 1948 and '49, the Albions field manager was "Stuffy" McInnis, member of the famed

$100,000 infield of the Philadelphia Athletics during the 1920s and baseball coach at Springfield College and later Harvard. McInnis, who had family ties to Nova Scotia, brought a dozen prospects from New England to flesh out a squad of mostly local players. Except for young shortstop Joe Lamonica, who hit .368 in 1949 and signed a Red Sox contract, and Waterville, Maine, native John Hafeneker, a three-year Central League veteran who signed with the Yankees, local players proved to be the heart and soul of the team. To McInnis' surprise, the locals often outperformed his prized imports. According to homebrew pitcher John "Twit" Clarke, McInnis couldn't get over the fact that most of the locals worked all day in the mines before playing in the evening. "They come home, wash the coal dust off, then head to the diamond to play, and they play well," said McInnis. The old major leaguer was particularly impressed by outfielder Harry Reekie and felt that if he could convince him to go south he had a reasonable shot of making it to the majors.[2]

During his two seasons in Stellarton, McInnis kept an eye on opposing team players, serving as an informal scout for the Boston Red Sox. Dick Gernert and Jack Kaiser of the Wildcats, Paul Aylward of the Westville Miners, Truro Bearcats catcher Bob Atwood, Springhill's Joe Lamonica and Hal Buckwalter of the Amherst Ramblers especially impressed him, and he recommended them to the Bosox organization. The Red Sox invited Kaiser and Gernert to Fenway for tryouts, and after watching them power the ball over the Green Monster, he signed them to pro contracts. Aylward, who had grown up in Boston near Fenway, was a tall, lean righthander who according to *The Sporting News* could "fog the ball past hitters" and elicited comparisons to Dizzy Dean.[3] Buckwalter, like Gernert, had played baseball and basketball for Temple University and had a major league bat. According to Pinky Higgins, just because players were in Class C or D, they were not necessarily Class C- or D-level players. Many young ballplayers could hit .300 in every league they played in, and Higgins considered Buckwalter one of those.[4] The problem was finding a position for him. He was a below-average defender wherever he played. When the Red Sox went to spring training in 1952, Gernert made the big league roster and the twenty-year-old Buckwalter was sent to Triple-A Louisville, where he ended up hitting a respectable .276, splitting his time between first base and third base. Kaiser and Aylward were farmed to Albany of the Eastern League, and Atwood and Lamonica were farmed to the California League.

In the coal-mining town of Springhill, former Boston Red Sox catcher Bill Cronin started the 1949 season managing the Fencebusters, but his abrasive personality and fondness for drink alienated many of his players. Dick Maloney, out of Springfield College, replaced him, and Providence College coach Billy Wise advised a number of his players to play in Nova Scotia, among them Walt Modleszewski, Len Smith, Jim Sullivan and team-captain Art "Whitey" Weinstock, who had been the Boston Braves' bullpen catcher while still in college. A proud and closely knit community with a history of labor solidarity, Springhill adored the Fencebusters and baseball augmented a sense of civic pride and collective sensibility that had grown out of its coal mining history. Even today Fencebuster fans remember the exploits of Brownie Burden, Lawson Fowler, Len Boss, "Dingie" McLeod and others from the years before and after the war. Canadian historian Ian McKay recalls that while interviewing miners who struggled against absentee ownership, unsafe conditions underground and life-threatening cave-ins, more often than not the conversation would turn to the Fencebusters and their proud history.

Rather than relying on the homebrews who had played so well for McInnis, Stellarton's Watterson concentrated almost exclusively on imported players, a formula that had worked for the Wildcats the year before. He brought in veterans like Bill Brooks, his former Keene Blue Jays teammate in the Vermont Northern League, and Jim Arbucho, another Northern League teammate of Robin Roberts, Jack Kaiser and Buzz Bowers on the 1947 Montpelier club. Arbucho had played for Kentville in 1948 and in the Giants minor league system in 1949 and would split the 1950 season between the Albions and Trenton of the Class B Interstate League. The rest of Watterson's recruits were drawn from front-rank colleges in the northeast. His infield included Jack Kurty of Penn State behind the plate; Dick Oviatt, a .300 hitter for the Als in 1949, at first; and third baseman Huck Keany, a football star later inducted into the UNH Football Hall of Fame. Watterson played short. Stellarton native Reekie anchored the outfield and led the club in hitting. John Kuharetz, a star right-handed pitcher in his sophomore year at NYU; Ray Slivocka of Bayonne, New Jersey; and Don Wiederecht from Fordham joined holdover local boy Syd Roy on the pitching staff. Kuharetz and Roy were workhorses, racking up thirteen wins and more than 200 innings between them. Slivocka later settled permanently in Nova Scotia. Weiderecht's teammate at Fordham, Tom Casagrande, had planned to join him in Nova Scotia but at the last minute decided to stay in Massachusetts where he put up a 10–2 record in the Blackstone Industrial League. Casagrande eventually made the majors with the Phillies in 1955 but didn't make an on-field appearance.

Shunted Aside: Local Players and the Import Model

As the import trend continued, being shunted aside was a fate shared by a number of local players who made key contributions to the Albions over the years. John "Brother" MacDonald, Harry Reekie and Syd Roy all fell victim to the "good old Southern boys" strategy adopted by the Stellarton management. Although it was natural that American coaches would draw upon players that they knew from their experiences south of the border, it meant that roster spots were few and far between for local players. In addition, the baseball season in the south was longer, and collegians and minor league vets were already in mid-season form when they arrived in the Maritimes. A columnist for the New Glasgow *Evening News* suggested on May 22, 1951, for example, that Reekie, Roy and MacDonald should "crank up their training so they can hold their own against the imports, or they might be riding the bench. The American boys will all be in shape."

Reekie and Roy had no trouble making the squad, however, and made important contributions to Stellarton's pennant-winning season. MacDonald was consigned to the bench for the most part. His limited use had nothing to do with conditioning or his ability. Rather, Stellarton's new playing coach Bill Brooks, the Als' starting catcher in 1950, had brought Leroy Sires, a .400 hitter at Duke that year and a veteran of the Albemarle League, to be his starting catcher and moved himself to first base. MacDonald told me that Brooks came to him at the beginning of the season, saying, "Now 'Brother' Macdonald, you know that I'd like to play and play at first base. You wouldn't mind if I played, and we kept you in reserve in case I got hurt would you?" "What could I say?" Brother recalled. "I just had to grit my teeth and accept it." A couple of years later, Reekie also found himself on the outside looking in. Before the season started, he wrote an open letter to the media complaining that the Albions had not even approached him with an invitation to try out. Reekie decided to move to Ontario looking for work and played for a time in Ontario's Inter-County League. Before that, he numbered among the best local players in the region, hitting .300 while playing in the Central League for a couple of years and about .270 in his time in the H&D League.

The pushing aside of local players in favor of imports was already a contentious issue as the new decade opened. In June 1949 the Truro Bearcats of the Central League had ceased operations, citing "phony amateurism" and inflated salaries ranging from $70 to $150 per week. Low gate receipts and long road trips had led to significant losses in a town that only three years before had won the H&D League championship with a team made up entirely of local players such as Skit Ferguson and Johnny Clark. The 1946 Bearcats had a lineup drawn of players from across the province, including Ferguson, Clark, pitcher Clyde Roy, catcher Win Langille, hulking first baseman Carl Matheson, infielders Hum Joseph and Billy McIntyre, and speedy outfielder Cliff Roach. An editorial in the *Truro News* complained that "importing baseball players like kings of old hired armies" was destroying community baseball and led to the withdrawal of the Bearcats from the league. No longer was it a question of what town had the best athletes but which community could raise the most money. Some small towns like Springhill survived only because "the Fencebusters have become more or less a tradition with the miners ... somewhat like the Dodgers to the people of Brooklyn. The whole town is interested in the team."

Concerns about the direction that baseball was taking were by no means limited to Truro. The 1950 edition of the *Maritime Baseball Pictorial Yearbook* complained of "overpaid College players from south of the border, who straggle in when the season is almost half spent and, more important, return home again before even league playoffs have been completed." The early departure of college players who headed home for fall football practice at the end of August was a particular annoyance, since the teams that went on to play in provincial and Maritime championship competition were not the same as the ones that played day to day throughout the summer. For some observers, like the *Truro News* columnist quoted above, the answer was a return to amateur play and restrictions on the number of imports; for others, a solution lay in formal affiliation with Organized Baseball and an end to college players.

The 1950 season gave some solace to those who argued for maintaining a healthy balance between local and imported players. In the H&D League that year, five of the top ten hitters were local players. The two best players in the league, hands down, were Springhill native Buddy Condy and Johnny Clark, the "Westville Flash." Condy led the league with a .358 average over 260 at-bats, followed by Clark at .350. Stu O'Brien, who had played a couple of years in the Quebec Provincial League, was next. A native of Manchester, New Hampshire, O'Brien was outstanding both at the plate and behind it for the Dartmouth Arrows, handling a solid pitching staff that included local boys Neil Staples, Terry Iceton and Howie Martin. O'Brien returned to the Arrows for the 1951 season and continued his torrid hitting before suffering a career-threatening injury to his throwing hand. "So badly splintered was the Dartmouth catcher's little finger, after he had blocked a foul tip Wednesday night," wrote columnist Alex Nickerson,

New Hampshire native "Stu" O'Brien, who played summer ball in Vermont, Quebec and Nova Scotia, goes after a pop-up at Dartmouth's "Little Brooklyn" ballpark (Halifax Municipal Archives, CR67-5-989.01.141).

"it was feared for a time that it would be necessary to amputate the top joint."[5]

The only other two players to exceed the .300 plateau in 1950 were Liverpool native Mac Bowers and eventual major leaguer Zeke Bella. Dartmouth outfielder Joey Lay, well known in the Maritimes as well as in Ontario's Border League and the Quebec Provincial League, had broken that barrier as well but fell short of the required number of plate appearances to be ranked in the batting race. Cape Breton native "Red" Burchell, a mainstay at first base for the Shipyards, and outfielder Leo Woods of the Shipyards at .286 rounded out the top ten. On the mound, local boy John "Twit" Clarke of the Halifax Shipyards put up a marvelous 1.66 ERA—the best in the league that year—to go along with a 5–3 won-lost record. Other locals who turned in good years included Howie Martin, Warren Iceton, Neal Staples, Syd Roy, Hilton Boss, Norm Fitzgerald and Jackie Rudderhamm.

Despite the exceptional performances of many native Nova Scotians, the trend was definitely moving in the direction of imported players. "It was unfortunate," Johnny Clark observed. "Gradually the average player in the league would be an import rather than a local. We may not have been stars, but neither were many of those who came in and took our jobs." Ironically, as local players found it difficult to find spots on Maritime rosters, some of the better players were signing pro contracts and leaving the region. Moncton Cubs pitcher Billy Harris signed with the Dodgers and would go on to a couple of cups of coffee with the major league club; Wilson Parsons of Halifax signed with the Yankees and quickly established himself as a top pitching prospect in their minor league system; and Jackie Bowes of Saint John signed with the Cleveland Indians and moved quickly up the chain before arm trouble brought an end to his hopes.

Ironically, despite folding for a time in 1949, the Truro Bearcats entered the 1950 season with a team made up almost exclusively of imported collegians and ex-minor leaguers. Clary Johnson, general manager of the Bearcats from 1946 to 1955, realized the need to follow the lead of other clubs by paying more for imported talent. To offset increased player salaries, he employed a strategy of supplementing revenues with 50–50 draws, bingos, benefit dinners and even wrestling matches. On the recruitment side, Johnson developed close ties with both the St. Louis Cardinals and the Boston (later Milwaukee) Braves through their regional scouts, Harry Greenaway and Lucius "Jeff" Jones. Before the 1950 season, Jones and Greenaway held tryout camps throughout New England, arranging a series of exhibition games and winnowing the number of hopefuls from about three dozen to a dozen or so. At times there was a regular airlift of players to and from New England. Johnson remembers Truro having the equivalent of three teams, one going, one there, and one coming!

A Different Approach: Cape Breton and the Return to Local Players

As the 1940s came to an end and the new decade opened, teams in Nova Scotia and New Brunswick had turned increasingly to American-born collegians and veteran pros who had been pushed aside as the number of teams and leagues within Organized Baseball shrank year by year. One exception to the import trend was in Cape Breton, where most teams stopped importing players after 1950. This was ironic in a way, since the old Colliery League in the 1930s was the only Maritime league before or since to affiliate itself with Organized Baseball's minor league system. In 1936 local teams began to recruit former major leaguers like Fred Maguire, Billy Hunnefield and Del Bisonnette and young players Lenny Merullo and Ed Turchin who went on to play in the big leagues. The league operated independently that season, before joining Organized Baseball as a Class D outfit for two years and as a Class C organization in 1939. There had been expectations of a further reclassification to Class B status in 1940, but the war ended that hope.[6]

After the war, the Colliery League moved cautiously into the import market. In 1947 it announced its intention to add players from around the region and the United States, but a coal miners strike beginning in May of that year intervened and a limit of one import per team was adopted. The following year, the league raised the import limit to four per team. Among the initial arrivals from south of the border were infielder Johnny Carroll, a student at Duke; Gerry Gervais and Al Zaijor from Detroit; pitchers Bud Niles and Art Chartier; and outfielders Dick Murphy and Johnny Boston from Tufts University. Import restrictions were lifted in 1949 and 1950, leading to a new crop of American players. Third baseman Al Ware, a Detroit native, led the league in hitting in 1949 with a .399 average, while catchers Tom Cassell and Doug Cossey, second baseman Bill Bergeron, and pitchers Ritchie Colombo and Tom McCarthy had solid seasons. All would go on to play in the minor leagues. In 1954, Ware started at third base for Charleston of the AAA International League. Bergeron played four seasons in the Phillies chain before returning to the H&D League in 1954. McCarthy was a Yankees prospect who shocked the organization in 1956 when he jumped to the Knoxville club in the Sally League and later starred in independent ball.

Even in the years when the imports arrived, local players continued to play a significant role in the Colliery League. Cape Breton had supplied teams throughout the region with a number of quality players over the years.[7] Eddie Gillis, who teamed up with Lenny Merullo as Glace Bay's double play combo in 1936, would later play a few seasons with Kentville of the H&D League. Gillis sometimes mused about young American players who often asked him "where in the States are you from?" Charley Pyle ended up in Fredericton in 1949, as the Capitols captured the Provincial championship. John "Brother" MacDonald, as good a first baseman as anyone in the region, played in Halifax in the forties and with the Provincial champion Stellarton Albions in the fifties and finished third in the 1949 Cape Breton Colliery League batting race, ahead of another long-time island star, Oscar Seale. Another Cape Breton native, "Red" Burchell was a mainstay at first base for the Halifax Shipyards for a number of years and finished in the top ten in the 1950 H&D League batting race with a respectable .295 average.

After 1950, baseball in Cape Breton relied almost exclusively on home-grown talent, but the trend elsewhere was in the other direction. Players from south of the border dominated the rosters of H&D League clubs, and this was increasingly true for others, from Westville and Springhill in Nova Scotia to Moncton, Fredericton, Saint John, Grand Falls, Blacks Harbour, and Edmundston, New Brunswick. The Maine–New Brunswick League entered the import era in 1950 with teams in Presque Isle, Fort Fairfield, and Houlton, Maine, as well as in Edmundston and later in Grand Falls. In New Brunswick the import era eventually ended after the 1955 season with the collapse of the Maine–New Brunswick league—although it would resume sporadically as an amateur circuit after that. Meanwhile in Nova Scotia, the H&D League relied upon imported talent until its collapse after the 1959 season.

In many ways the 1950 season was important in moving Maritime baseball in new directions, hastening the movement toward import-dominated rosters, reducing the opportunities for local players—many of whom had shown their ability to outperform those recruited from south of the border—and turning over the responsibility for roster construction to those with experience in the United States. Playing coaches like Johnny Watterson, Bob Decker, and Danny Seaman, scouts from major league organizations, and coaches from Division One baseball programs were happy to oblige, since their players could play against high-quality opponents and avoid NCAA sanction while doing so. For major league organizations, the region offered a chance to assess their players' abilities alongside the best collegiate talent from New England to the Carolinas and beyond. NCAA college powerhouses, including College World Series champions of the early fifties—Holy Cross, the University of Michigan and Wake Forest—would in turn encourage their players to head to Nova Scotia. In the process, summer ball in the Maritimes was transformed into what might be called "NCAA North."

Five

Bill Brooks, Art Hoch and the Carolinian Connection

Of all the Americans coming north in 1950, none would have a greater impact on the history of the H&D League than Bill Brooks. Brought to Stellarton by Johnny Watterson after the two played together for the Keene Blue Jays of the Vermont Northern League, Brooks was a North Carolina native and Wake Forest University graduate with a number of years of experience in minor league and semipro baseball. A rangy, six-foot-three-inch catcher, Brooks played three postwar years in the New York Giants chain. His first season in Stellarton was more solid than spectacular, but his veteran presence in the clubhouse and steadying influence on the field made an impression on the club executives. When Watterson was recalled to military service and unable to return for the 1951 season, team executives Bob Munroe and Clary Semple asked Brooks to assemble the roster and serve as playing coach.

Turning over the coaching reins to Brooks inaugurated a close connection between baseball in Nova Scotia and the Carolinas that lasted until the H&D League ceased operations at the end of the fifties. Brooks was well known throughout the South and well positioned to access a deep pool of Southern talent that included collegians angling for a career in professional baseball and a number of old pros from the upper levels of the minor leagues. As the H&D League expanded its footprint beyond New England, New York, and Pennsylvania, moreover, opportunities to play summer ball elsewhere were closing down, making the Maritimes increasingly attractive. Minor league and small-town baseball was contracting all across North America, and attendance nosedived. Between 1950 and 1951, minor league attendance fell from 34,735,967 to 27,625,527 and the number of functioning professional leagues dropped from 58 to 50. The same trend was at work with respect to independent semipro baseball leagues. Like the Vermont Northern

League—which chose not to operate in 1951 because of ECAC restrictions—the Albemarle League also gave up the ghost, leaving a clear field for clubs in the Maritimes to fill their rosters with high-level collegiate prospects. For the most part, Southern players were drawn from Wake Forest, Duke, North Carolina State and the University of North Carolina. Led by its Carolinian brigade, the Albions dominated the H&D League in the early fifties, winning three successive league titles from 1951 through 1953.

Stellarton's dominance was not just a function of player excellence and the pool of talent that the Albions could draw upon. It was connected as well to the fortunes of the coal mining industry. Part of a complex of coal mining communities that included nearby New Glasgow, Westville, and Pictou, and River Hebert, Joggins and Springhill to the west, Stellarton had been known for much of the 19th century as Albion Mines. Providing coal for iron and steel production in Trenton, Londonderry, and Sydney, the town prospered in the early 20th century, encouraged by the artificial demand of two world wars. In 1951, when the Albions won their first H&D League championship, its population stood at 5,575, its highest ever, then and now.

Stellarton's success on the ball diamond, however, disguised the weaknesses of the regional economy and the coal mining challenges that grew increasingly severe year by year. By 1955 the Albion Mines were essentially tapped out, and despite continuing production at the mines in Westville and Springhill, tragic accidents loomed. In Springhill, mine cave-ins in 1956 and 1958 shattered lives and eroded the town's economic health. Not surprisingly, the crisis of the coalfields affected the ability of these coal towns to sustain import-based semipro baseball in the way they did when Bill Brooks and his Carolinian contingent first arrived in Stellarton.

Some years ago, well after Bill Brooks' playing career was over, I had the pleasure of spending a couple of days with Bill and his wife in Wilmington, North Carolina. A tall and imposing figure, Brooks cast a giant-size influence over the athletic programs at UNC Wilmington, where he would serve as baseball and basketball coach and athletic director for almost forty years. The baseball stadium there still carries his name, testifying to the importance of his work in building the school's baseball program. He directed the baseball Seahawks to two national JUCO baseball championships in 1961 and 1963, was NAIA coach of the year in 1975, and was inducted into the National Junior College Baseball Coaches Hall of Fame in 1990. His career at UNC Wilmington began in 1951, the same year that he signed on as player coach in Stellarton.

Five. Bill Brooks, Art Hoch and the Carolinian Connection

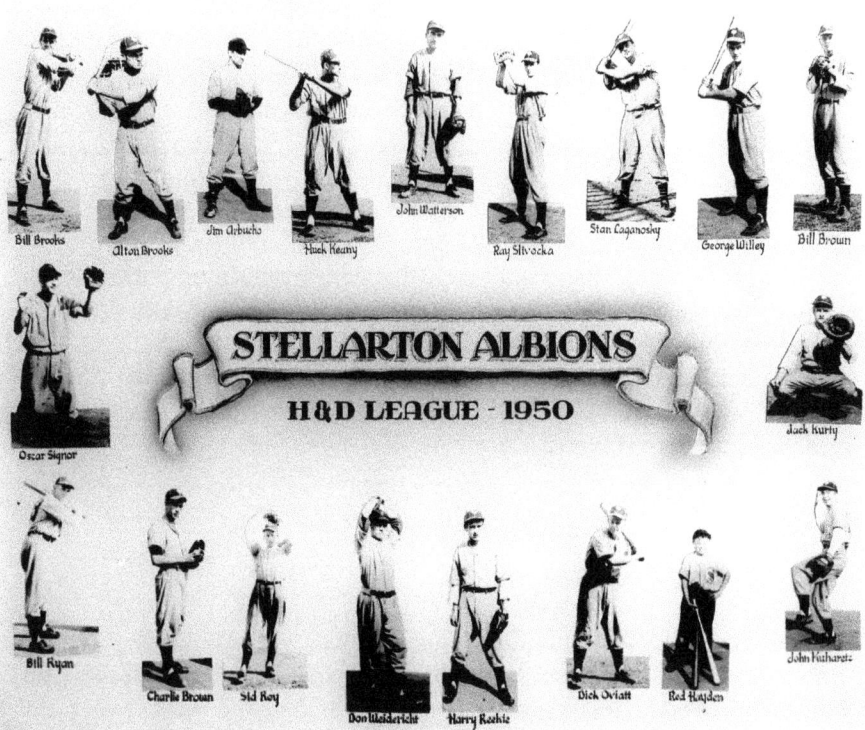

The 1950 Stellarton Albions led by coach Johnny Watterson and playing coach Bill Brooks, who brought a number of players north from the Carolinas in the 1950s, transforming the H&D League in the process (Halifax Municipal Archives, CR-67-5-2012.01.189).

Along with being introduced to the delights of Southern barbecue, I had the chance to play golf on that visit to Wilmington with Bill and his brother "Toomey," who also played in Stellarton. The final member of our foursome was "Doc" Murphey, the Albions' third baseman, who took over from Huck Keany in 1952 as Brooks relied increasingly upon players and good friends from the south. It was a beautiful spring day with lots of sunshine, and the azaleas and rhododendrons were in full bloom, making the occasional bad tee shot or missed putts easy to forget.

A lively raconteur and humorist, Murphey regaled us with stories that kept us in stitches that day. At the time of his arrival in Stellarton, he recalled, the local Catholic priest doubled as the team's official scorekeeper. Unaware of the spelling of Doc's last name and assuming him to be of Irish heritage, the priest sought him out. A couple of

Sundays had passed, and the priest expressed surprise and disappointment in not having seen the young Carolinian in church. When Murphey replied that it was probably because he was a Baptist, the vibe changed instantly. After that, if there was a questionable scoring play either defensively or offensively, he recalled, "I would never get the benefit of the doubt. It would always be an error." Another memory was of a car trip home from a game in Liverpool when they accidently hit a racoon crossing the highway. Stopping the car and finding the animal in serious distress, they reluctantly decided it should be put out of its misery. Murphey took a bat and swung three times at the poor creature, but every time it would move its head strategically at the last moment. He passed the bat along to the other players, who were equally ineffective. "It was our worst hitting performance of the summer," he laughed. "Struck out three times in a row by a racoon!"

The Wake Forest Deamon Deacons as Stellarton Albions

Stellarton's 1951 club was almost a replica of the Wake Forest Deamon Deacons. Runner-up to the University of Texas in the NCAA College World Series in 1949 after a remarkable 27–2 record that year, the Deacons were one of the elite squads in collegiate baseball in the United States at the time. As CWS finalists in 1949 and 1950, the Deacons were given the honor of representing the United States at the 1951 Pan Am Games in Buenos Aires. The twelve-man squad captured the silver medal behind the Cuban national team, which won gold. Almost all of the players on that Wake Forest team as well as those after that would turn up in the Maritimes at one point or another.

Among the dozen or so Wake Forest players with the Albions in 1951 were a number of standouts. Shortstop Gair Allie, already on the radar of the Pittsburgh Pirates; infielder-outfielder Art Hoch, who completed his degree in 1949 before playing a season in the minors; and hard-hitting outfielder Joe Fulghum from Wilson, North Carolina, were the leaders on offense. Second baseman Kent "Baby" Rogers, who spurned pro offers from the Cardinals and Yankees in favor of an athletic scholarship at Wake Forest, was in the first of his four years with the Albions. Hailing from a working class family from the mining districts around Bluefield, West Virginia, Rogers was more than comfortable in the hardscrabble Pictou County community. "I played four years in Nova Scotia and loved every minute," he told me. "It was the best four summers of my life." The other infield regular that year was

Five. Bill Brooks, Art Hoch and the Carolinian Connection

holdover Walter "Huck" Keany, one of Watterson's teammates at UNH. Stellarton's outfield contingent had Fulghum in right, Hoch in left and starry homebrew Harry Reekie in center. Wake Forest's Johnny Alford served as fourth outfielder and utility player. With no spare room on Stellarton's fifteen-man roster, another member of the Pan-Am squad, infielder Bob Coluni, signed with the Kentville Wildcats.

Art Hoch was a particularly valuable contributor that year since he could play all over the outfield and infield. Although his natural position was shortstop, Hoch graciously gave way to Allie, a bona fide major league prospect as Hoch himself had been at a similar age. While a teenager Hoch played alongside a number of wartime big leaguers at Ft. Lee and was regarded as a "can't miss" prospect by the New York Yankees. Rather than sign a Yankees contract when the war ended, however, Hoch took advantage of the G.I. Bill, which allowed him to play ball and complete a college degree in physical education. The Edenton *Daily Advance* raved about him, even suggesting that he was the best college shortstop in the nation. "[T]he scintillating Edenton shortstop, is continuing to prove that he is by far the best defensive shortstop in the Albemarle League," said one column. "Hoch is fast and rangy and covers a lot of territory. In addition, he possesses probably the finest infield arm in the circuit."[1]

As for the pitching staff that year, homebrew Syd Roy was a leader on the mound with an 8–2 record, heading a starting rotation that included Wake Forest boys Vern "Preacher" Mustain, Ray Moring, and Don Woodlief and UNC star Joel Pazdan. Maine native Andy McAuliffe and John Kuharetz rounded out the relief brigade. Before coming north, Brooks had intended to bring along Billy Joe Davidson, a highly sought-after pitcher from North Carolina and Allie's college roommate, who had played summer ball earlier in the Blackstone Industrial League. Brooks was a friend of the young left-hander's father, Troy Davidson, and had a commitment that Billy Joe would join the Albions, but he signed a $120,000 bonus contract with the Cleveland Indians. Described at the time as "the best Indians prospect since Bob Feller," Davidson would never make the majors. A freak injury playing basketball ended his career in 1955, and he was never heard from after that.[2]

In 1950, while playing for Coach Watterson, Bill Brooks had been the Albions' regular catcher, the position he had played in the New York Giants organization. When putting the 1951 team together, however, Watterson decided to shift Brooks to first base in order to open a spot for catcher Leroy Sires, a former Southern Conference all-star at Duke. A naval veteran who played summer ball in the Albemarle League during his college years, Sires was highly regarded. According to the Elizabeth City *Daily Advance*, he was the best position player in the 1949 Albemarle League. When big league clubs seemed reluctant to sign him, local observers continued to scratch their heads. The apparent knock against him was a throwing arm that fell below major league standards.[3] It was also likely that because he was twenty-four, big league teams thought him too old to take a chance on. A vicious line-drive hitter, he put up a .282 average for the Albions, almost identical to Brooks. With Sires behind the plate and Brooks at first base, one of the better players in Nova Scotia at the time, first baseman John "Brother" MacDonald, remained stapled to the bench that summer.

The Albions were the class of the H&D League in 1951, winning 45 of 61 games and finishing twelve games ahead of the second-place Halifax Capitals. Nineteen-year-old shortstop Gair Allie had an excellent season, leading the league in home runs with nineteen, hitting over .300 and demonstrating great range and a bullet-like arm at shortstop. When a friend of mine, Ken Clare, who assisted me for a while with interviews, caught up with him at his sports bar in San Antonio, Allie joked about fielding sharp grounders, holding the ball momentarily and yelling, "Run, you bastard, run!" before gunning the ball to first for the out. Pittsburgh's general manager, Branch Rickey, already an admirer, quietly endorsed Brooks' decision to take Allie north to Nova Scotia, hoping that he might escape the attention of other major league organizations.

After Allie's summer in Stellarton, the Pirates signed him to a $30,000 bonus contract. Although he hit a meagre .216 in his first pro season, Allie remained a top prospect. In 1953 the Pirates held spring training in Cuba, clearly in need of infield help. Allie turned out to be one of the best players in camp, hitting around .300 and impressing manager Fred Haney with his play at shortstop. As the Pirates were about to break camp, Allie went two for four with a home run in a 4–2 victory over the Philadelphia Phillies. Haney decided to add him to the twenty-five-man roster and penciled him in as his opening day shortstop. Unfortunately, on the very last day of spring training, Allie broke his ankle sliding into home and sat out most of the season. According to *The Sporting News*, it was Haney's worst day of the spring since he was "secretly grooming the 19-year-old ... as his No. 1 utility infielder and had high hopes for him."[4] In 1954 Allie started at short for the Pirates and played an important part in the team's youth movement.

Although Allie had a tremendous year in Stellarton in 1951, outfielder Joe Fulghum had an even better one, winning the league batting title with a .417 batting average. He was considered a major league prospect at Wake Forest, and his professional baseball aspirations ended

Five. Bill Brooks, Art Hoch and the Carolinian Connection 75

The 1952 Stellarton Albions were the class of the league that year. Front row, from left: Ed Morris, "Doc" Murphey, Tunney Brooks, Sonny Way, Joe Willard, Joe Pazdan, Kent Rogers. Back row, from left: Harry Reekie, Syd Roy, Don Woodlief, Bill Werber, Bill Brooks, Joe Fulghum, Vern Mustain, Rudy Williams. Halifax Municipal Archives. CR67-5-2001.111.01

when he suffered a severe arm injury. He was also a somewhat lumbering, slow-footed runner, moving, according to one observer, at "the pace of a snail."[5] When I first met Joe at the H&D League reunion in 1990, he impressed me with his polite and soft-spoken manner, and his fond recollections of summers in Nova Scotia. He was also one of the few players that I interviewed over the years who was willing to speak of the racism that existed in the years when intercollegiate baseball south of the Mason-Dixon line was still a lily-white affair. I came away from those conversations with even more respect for him as a person. A year or so ago, Fulghum passed away just two weeks shy of his 95th birthday.

Art Hoch, the Truro Bearcats and UNC Tarheels

The success of Stellarton's Carolinian strategy in 1951 led to even closer connections to the South Atlantic states in subsequent years. After playing alongside Brooks that year, Art Hoch received an offer from Soapy Johnson to help assemble and coach the 1952 Truro

Bearcats. Now twenty-eight years old and no longer the New York Yankees prospect that he once was, Hoch was intrigued. He had already set his mind on a future in coaching. Worried that an acceptance of Johnson's offer might be seen as disloyal to Bill Brooks, his response was to demand what he thought was an exorbitant salary well over $100 a week. Johnson surprisingly agreed, and Hoch began a seven-year stint as a playing coach in the H&D League.

Hoch loved coaching. In the many conversations I had with him both in Nova Scotia and at his North Carolina home in Raleigh, he emphasized how proud he was to have helped so many players realize their potential. Like other notable developers of young talent—coaches Eddie Gillis and Bob Decker come to mind—he stressed fundamentals, hitting the cut-off man, throwing to the right base, backing up the play, bunting when the game required it, and knowing the tendencies of your opponents. He also had a cantankerous streak and was a master at needling his opponents. "He was something of a mouthpiece," Kentville native Brian Pulsifer recalls, "the kind of guy that opposing players and fans loved to hate." Always assertive and never one to keep his opinions to himself, he kept up a running battle with Truro newspaperman Harry Flemming, who was equally opiniated. After a column critical of Hoch, the Carolinian responded in less than gentlemanly fashion, referring to Flemming as a "snaggle-toothed prick."

In my own dealings with Hoch, he was ever genial but he would make his feelings about the game clear. Now and then we would talk about Bill James and the then-new sabermetrics that has since spawned all sorts of new measurements of on-field performance, but Hoch remained old school. "Colin," he once said to me, "you sure know statistics, but I know the game on the field, and as a coach I needed to emphasize preparation, baseball fundamentals, and to be something of a psychologist as well." Art was convinced that the responsibilities of teaching younger players and managing his lineup on a daily basis took a toll on his own performance on the field. "I was a better ballplayer than the statistics suggest," he once mused. Putting together the lineup, managing his pitching rotation, making strategic in-game decisions and keeping his players motivated and satisfied was not only distracting but also left little time to focus on his own game-readiness. Although he would undoubtedly balk at having his career reduced to statistics, Art had a solid but unspectacular H&D League career, hitting .260 during his eight years in the league while playing all over the diamond.

Hoch's career as a coach in the H&D League drew heavily on his connections at UNC and elsewhere throughout the south. He also publicized baseball in the Maritimes. On May 29, 1952, for example, the

High Point Enterprise reported that Hoch "will take three of the Tar Heels' brightest diamond prospects to play with him in Nova Scotia this summer. Hoch will manage a team in the fast north-country semipro league and will have Billy Lore of Smithfield, outfielder Connie Gravitte of Roxboro and shortstop Fred Dale of Hickory on the team."[6] Other UNC notables, pitchers Joe Morgan, Dennis Parrish, Don Marbry and Joel Pazdan; second baseman Harry Lloyd; catchers John Motsinger and Walter Frye; and veteran outfielder Fred Stowe, also accompanied Hoch to Truro. From Wake Forest came shortstop Jack Stallings, college roommate of golfer Arnie Palmer, who led the Bearcats in hitting that season; second baseman Dickie Harris (son of Bucky Harris, the manager of the Washington Senators); and right-hander Bill Walsh, a youngster just at the beginning of his college and eventual four-year career in pro ball. Throughout the years, Hoch played on his connections to the Old South. The Halifax *Herald* reported that in Truro a hot recording of the Confederate marching song blared from the speakers before every home game.[7] I vividly remember a Confederate flag being unfurled on top of the Bearcats dugout in Kentville as well. At the time, nobody seemed to reflect upon the darker connotations attached to these Confederate items.

Blue Devils from Duke: Billy Werber, Al Spangler and Dave Sime

In 1952 the quality of baseball in the Maritimes reached its highest level since the war. Almost the entire Duke Blue Devils roster surged north into New Brunswick and Nova Scotia that year, led by catchers Jack Tarr and Johnny Carroll; pitchers Joe Lewis, Dave Traynor, Bob "Dizzy" Davis, Lew Klein and Tom Blackburn; first baseman Stu Erickson; infielders Tom Powers, Ralph Kehoe, Bill Bergeron, Dick Brewer and Bob LeClercq; and talented outfielders Footer Johnson and Johnny Gibbons. George Carver also had a short visit that year before playing with the Albions in 1953. Although Carver subsequently chose against a professional career, he gained notoriety while in the service for leading the 1955 Lake Charles Air Force Base to the championship of the World Wide Air Force tournament. Carver won three games in the double-elimination series, including a 3–2 victory over Hickham AFB in the championship game.

Of the many Blue Devils coming north, outfielders Billy Werber, Al Spangler, and Dave Sime were the most notable. The son of a former New York Yankee and Red Sox infielder and one-time teammate of

Babe Ruth, Werber was a blue-chip major league prospect. According to Yankees scout Paul Krichell, he was a better all-round player than Duke teammate Dick Groat, who at one point planned to come north if he didn't sign a major league contract. "Werber runs faster than Groat, hits the ball farther, has a good arm and is just as aggressive," said Krichell. "There is something about him that suggests he should be an outfielder."[8] At Duke, Werber was a first-team Coaches All-American at first base and demonstrated power potential that had major league scouts drooling. In Stellarton he would play mostly in the infield, either at first or second base.

During Werber's two summers in Stellarton, scouts from all sixteen teams regularly checked on his performance. *The Sporting News* reported that, while in Nova Scotia, he was "scorning fancy offers from big league clubs and will enter his father's insurance business, a $50,000 decision."[9] Werber continued to show flashes of power but was only a .250 hitter in the H&D League. After the 1953 season in Nova Scotia, he was called to military service and played the next two years for a U.S. Marine club that won the Pacific championship. This only added to the interest of big league scouts. Werber eventually accepted an invitation to spring training with the Cincinnati Reds in 1956, but since the Reds had no need for a first baseman—all-everything Ted Kluszewski had clubbed 47 homeruns the year before—he agreed to shift to the outfield.

Despite attending spring training with the Reds, Werber was still not committed to a baseball future. Columnist Shirley Povich of *The Sporting News* wrote of his anomalous situation. "Major League Baseball's rarest rookie is now cavorting in the uniform of the Cincinnati Reds," said Povich, "yet strictly speaking, he's not getting a tryout, he's putting major league ball on trial." Given his acceptance for postgraduate work at the Wharton School of the University of Pennsylvania, and since his father was "one of the most successful writers of insurance in the United States," Werber had more leverage than most players.[10] He told the Reds that he wouldn't be a bench player and would play a year in the minors, but if he wasn't a starter at the major league level the following year, he would give up his baseball completely. Although Major League organizations at the time were unaccustomed to this kind of perceived impertinence, general manager Gabe Paul was all right with Werber's stance. Had he not restricted his commitment to a single season, however, the Reds would likely have signed him as a "bonus baby."[11] Werber was another example of those who placed a longer-term livelihood ahead of a few years in a professional sport.

Werber showed well that spring, hitting over .300, mostly with the

"B" squad, and impressing the Reds with his strong outfield play.[12] Knowing that he would quit rather than ride the bench, the club had to make a choice as to who would start in left field. Would it be Werber, who had shown good power and solid defensive abilities, or twenty-year-old phenom Frank Robinson? Ultimately the Reds chose Robinson. Who could blame them? Not only was Robinson named the National League Rookie of the Year but also he played twenty years in the majors and later was inducted into the Hall of Fame. True to his word, Werber retired from baseball after a successful season with Nashville of the Southern Association. Notably as well, there was a third outfield prospect in the mix for the left field job that year, a young eighteen-year-old named Curt Flood, who, despite being optioned to the Class B Carolina league that season, went on to an auspicious fifteen-year big league career and was instrumental in securing free agency for MLB players.[13]

In the spring of 1998 I had the good fortune of meeting Robinson, who was the special guest at the Diamonds in the Desert spring training baseball conference organized by my good friend Bill Kerwin. The banquet that year was held on the fifth deck of the new Bank One Ball Park in Phoenix before its official opening. At one point I asked Robinson if he remembered that spring and if he recalled Werber. "Oh yes," he replied, "It was him or me. I have to say I'm glad it was me." At another point during the conference, my wife made her way to the top row of the stadium, sitting all alone in Bob Uecker fashion, wondering how she was going to make it back down the steep steps.

Al Spangler, a teammate of Werber's at Duke, played with Halifax in 1952 and 1953. He was a Richie Ashburn–type player. "Deacon" Jones described him as one of those "pain in the ass guys" that could beat you in so many different ways. Spangler showed good outfield range and hit .270. Contemplating a return to Halifax in 1954, he instead signed a Milwaukee Braves contract and joined the major league Braves in June without seeing any action. Spangler's contract allowed him to stay at the big league level if he wanted, but he accepted assignment to Evansville of the III League. He would eventually play thirteen years with Milwaukee, Houston, California, and the Chicago Cubs. Spangler's liability was a lack of power in a day when power took precedence over speed and getting on base. According to SABR biographer David Skelton, it was ironic "that Spangler's 13-year career eclipsed any of those players who were ushered ahead of him, while also sad to note that Al's Ashburn-like talents were not both appreciated and utilized in a manner that might have brought untold success to team and player."[14]

Dave Sime was the most skilled of all the Blue Devils at the time and certainly the most interesting. In 1954 he shared time between

Halifax of the H&D League and the Edmundston Republicans of the New Brunswick League. Later chosen Duke's most outstanding athlete of the 20th century, he initially had aspirations of playing professional baseball while following a career in medicine. His idol was Dr. Bobby Brown, of the New York Yankees, who was able to balance both careers at once.[15] Sime was a track star and pro-level basketball and football player as well. He clocked a world record 9.3 seconds in the 100-yard dash four times and won a silver medal at the 1960 Olympics, finishing second to Germany's Armin Hary in the 100 meter. His speed was an obvious asset, as he roamed the pasture in center field with grace and tracked down fly balls that other outfielders couldn't even imagine getting to. According to Ace Parker, his coach at Duke, he was "the only man who can go after a line drive and catch up with it."

Sime was another world-class athlete with larger horizons than professional baseball, and he made it clear that if he chose to play, it would be on his own terms. He had no interest in playing in the minors or sitting on the bench. "He wanted to realize a lifetime ambition to become a doctor," *The Sporting News* reported, "and the diamond game would interfere with these plans." In 1959 the Detroit Lions selected him in the NFL draft, but he had even less intention of playing pro football than baseball. By then he was in medical school and well on his way to becoming a highly regarded and nationally known ophthalmologist. His numerous celebrity patients would later include Richard Nixon, Marilyn Monroe, Bob Griese, and Mickey Mantle. Observing Mantle's often dysfunctional life, Sime concluded that it confirmed the wisdom of avoiding the life of a professional athlete.

The Southern pipeline to Nova Scotia continued until the H&D League ceased operations at the end of the 1950s. By my tally, thirty players from Wake Forest followed Brooks, Hoch and Fulghum to Nova Scotia. I have also identified twenty-six more from Duke and two dozen from University of North Carolina and North Carolina State. The Atlantic Coast Conference at the time also supplied a number of players such as Connie Hemphill and Russ Duffy from the University of Maryland, Paul Susce from Georgia, Ty Cline and Hal Stowe from Clemson, and Bucky Luck and Vance Long from the University of Richmond. Little Rollins College, runner-up in the 1954 College World Series, supplied a number of others, including Art Brophy, Doug Baxendale, Bill Cary and Al Fantuzzi. Rollins lost 4–1 in the championship game to the University of Missouri that season. It is likely that more than a hundred players from elite college programs in the south travelled north, as the Maritimes found itself transformed into NCAA North. (See Appendix 4.)

Paradox: A Poverty of Riches

The great paradox of these years was that the surplus of talent on the field could not disguise weaknesses on the balance sheet accompanying rising player costs and shrinking gate revenues. These financial challenges were harbingers of what was to come. Eventually the growth of television and automobile ownership provided a range of leisure alternatives that drew fans away from the ballpark and undermined the financial stability of community baseball. Increased mobility allowed people to spend vacation time camping, staying in cottages, and touring the region to take in its natural beauty. Of course, the new consumerism of the fifties was hardly unique to the region. That these influences came somewhat later to the Maritimes than to other parts of North America may explain to some extent the ability of the H&D League to continue operating until the end of the fifties as others fell by the wayside. With the collapse of summer leagues south of the border, the Maritimes were in the enviable position of attracting, year by year, players who had reached the finals of the College World Series, beginning in 1952 with Holy Cross, then Michigan in 1953, Rollins College in 1954 and Wake Forest in 1955. On the field, at least, the level of play was the best it had ever been.

Six

"NCAA North"
CWS Champions, Bonus Babies and All-Americans

In the early 1950s, baseball in the Maritimes was transformed by an influx of players from the Carolinas and other Southern states. While the Southern strategy changed the complexion of baseball throughout the region, it by no means diluted the close historical connection between the Maritimes and the "Boston States." Collegians from all over New England as well as New York and Pennsylvania were drawn north as the reputations of the H&D League and the Maine–New Brunswick League strengthened year by year. Boston College, the University of Massachusetts, Holy Cross College, St. John's, Fordham, NYU, Penn State and Temple were only a few of the elite college programs that fashioned working relationships with clubs throughout the region. In addition, big league organizations played a leading role in recommending and placing players of interest with clubs managed by coaches of their choice. More than three dozen players who spent summers in the Maritimes were eventually chosen as All-Americans by the American Baseball Coaches Association (ABCA). Others signed five- and six-figure bonus contracts with major league clubs that sent them directly to the big leagues as a result of a curious "bonus baby" regulation inaugurated in 1953.[1]

By the mid-fifties, the Maritimes had been transformed into "NCAA North," and scouts from major league organizations crisscrossed the region keeping tabs on young prospects. The fact that three College World Series champions, Holy Cross (1952), the University of Michigan (1953), and Wake Forest (1955), sought out the H&D League and New Brunswick League as summer training grounds for their players only enhanced the reputation for high-quality play. According to Holy Cross shortstop Don Prohovich, "the H&D League was the place to play for collegians interested in a professional baseball career."

In addition, veteran players attracted by salaries higher than those of minor leagues clubs often flitted back and forth between the Maritimes and clubs within Organized Baseball. Their experience and the guidance of playing coaches, including Jack Kaiser in Liverpool, "Buzz" Bowers and Eddie Lyons in Kentville, former big leaguer Stan Benjamin in Stellarton, Ray Fisher and George Owen in Truro, and Artie Hoch and Bob Decker in Dartmouth and Halifax, was important to the development of younger players destined for futures in professional ball.

The 1952 Holy Cross Crusaders

Long recognized as a northeastern baseball and basketball power, 1952 College World Series champion Holy Cross had connections to Maritime baseball that went back before World War II. Their legendary coach Jack Barry knew the Maritimes well, having played professional baseball in Cape Breton before embarking on an eleven-year major league career. A second baseman with the Philadelphia Athletics in the 1920s, Barry played alongside first baseman Stuffy McInnis, who had family roots in Cape Breton and spent two summers at the helm of the Stellarton Albions. Two other Crusaders—fifteen-year big leaguer Fred Maguire, who played in the interwar Cape Breton Colliery League, and long-time Brooklyn Dodger "Doc" Gautreau, whose mother hailed from New Brunswick—were deeply involved in the Nova Scotian baseball scene as well. In New Brunswick, former major leaguer Bill Lefebvre, a Holy Cross grad whose mother was an Acadian from Nova Scotia, served as a player and scout for various major league clubs interested in the development of young college prospects.

One of the 1952 Crusaders, second baseman Paul "Breezer" Brissette, came north before enrolling at Holy Cross and later shared his fond memories of Nova Scotia with me. "I had two or three stints in Nova Scotia," he recalled. "After my year in Springhill where I did ok but not great by any means, I enrolled at Holy Cross. After that I played summer ball ... in the Blackstone Industrial League. In 1952, however, the Blackstone League was in trouble and a lot of guys didn't know whether to stay or not so I decided to go Nova Scotia and play for Danny Seaman in Liverpool. I roomed with centerfielder Art Moossmann in John Seaman's house, above his clothing store and we shared a bed. Here I was at 165 pounds and Moossmann probably at 225, but we were both from blue collar families and used to sharing a bed. Joe [Morgan] was planning to go to Nova Scotia as well but he signed with the Braves and went into their system."

Brissette's memories of Nova Scotia went beyond baseball since, among other things, he met and married local girl Estelle Cooke. He also attended summer courses at Saint Mary's University, commuting from Liverpool to Halifax and staying with Tommy Sweet, whose Spring Garden Road restaurant was a gathering place for ballplayers throughout the fifties. Brissette felt at home at Saint Mary's, a small Catholic school with a solid commitment to student athletics, similar in many ways to Holy Cross. After a couple of solid seasons in the White Sox organization Brissette returned to Nova Scotia for a third time in 1957, harboring thoughts of taking up permanent residence. Brissette was hitting over .300 for Colorado Springs that year when the White Sox, happy with Nellie Fox at second base, decided to shift him to third base. Rather than make a position change that required more power than he could deliver, Brissette quit pro ball and played the rest of the year with the Dartmouth Arrows.

While Brissette's Holy Cross teammates Art Moossmann, Gene Schiller, and pitcher Ron Cote spent their initial seasons in Liverpool, his other teammates Ron Perry, Don Prohovich, and Jim Kelly landed in Kentville. Perry was the pitching star of the 1952 CWS champions along with All-American James O'Neill, who ended up going to Saint John. Perry came to Kentville on the recommendation of Wildcats coach Bill Kearns and Braves scout Jeff Jones. Jones told Perry that the H&D League was as good a league as any on the east coast of North America. The fact that Kearns was bringing Prohovich, who had played alongside Perry on both the basketball court and the diamond, made up Perry's mind. Also accompanying Kearns was future major league pitcher Dave Stenhouse, who, like Prohovich, played for Edmundston in 1952, and catcher Steve Korcheck from George Washington University. Perry and Stenhouse were the workhorses of the 1953 Wildcats staff, logging over 250 innings and winning 20 games against 10 losses, and they became great friends in the process. Stenhouse and Korcheck would later play together with the Washington Senators in the early sixties.

Over the summer, Perry billeted with the Pulsifer family, who welcomed a player—sometimes two—into their home every year. Most of the Wildcats stayed in the west end of town on Park or Main Street or the little avenues that ran off of them. On numerous occasions Stenhouse and Bunker would hang at the Pulsifer house; Kearns was just around the corner on Park Street, staying the summer with the White family. Brian Pulsifer remembers the anticipation that preceded the arrival of the new crop of imports each season. "We wouldn't leave the house until our guys would arrive," he recalled. The year that Perry came to board with them, "young Cyril White was out on the street

Ron Perry, longtime athletic director at Holy Cross University, in his 1953 Kentville Wildcats uniform, after the Holy Cross Crusaders captured the 1952 College World Series (courtesy Brian Pulsifer, author's collection).

yelling 'we got the coach, we got the coach.'" Many who opened their homes, including the Buchanans, Bucklers, Hales, and Cochranes, came to think of their billets as part of the family. "They were like older brothers to us, and we often kept in touch with them for years after that, exchanging Christmas cards and occasional letters." When they returned home, they often left their collections of comic books and other mementos behind. Pulsifer remembers the year that outfielder Tom McBrien left him a Rawlings glove, which was almost impossible to get locally at the time. Cyril White would now and then be gifted a pair of oversized, worn-down cleats that he had to lace up around his ankles.

Some years ago I had the chance to talk at length with Perry about his time in Kentville. He was the athletic director at Holy Cross at the time and was well remembered as a great all-around athlete and All-American on the basketball court. In a poll of the greatest Crusader athletes of the 20th century, Perry placed fourth, trailing NBA Hall of Famers Bob Cousy and Tom Heinsohn. We spent the entire morning talking about his career. "I loved Nova Scotia," he said. "In fact, I liked it so much that after my year with the Wildcats in 1953, I came back again the next year on my summer vacation and pitched a couple of weeks before the July player deadline." Perry signed a pro contract later that year and spent a number of years in the White Sox system before retiring at the end of spring training in 1958.[2]

1953 CWS Champions: Ray Fisher's Michigan Wolverines

Like Holy Cross, the University of Michigan Wolverines maintained a connection to the Maritimes over a number of years. A farm boy from Vermont and a hundred-game winner in the majors, Michigan coach Ray Fisher was well known for what SABR biographer Chip Hart called his "unjust banishment" from baseball after a contract dispute with the Cincinnati Reds in 1921. Although a major league outcast, Fisher was head baseball coach at Michigan for almost forty years, winning fourteen Big Ten titles along the way. He was also a leading figure in the development of the game in the northeastern borderlands. Before coming to the Maritimes he managed the Twin City Trojans of the Vermont Northern League. When the NCAA designated the Vermont Northern an "outlaw" league and banned four Michigan players from future varsity competition, Fisher moved north to Blacks Harbour in 1951, winning the Southern New Brunswick League championship that year behind the stellar play of youngster Charley Lau and former New York Giant Johnny Gee. Fisher spent three years in Blacks Harbour before moving to Truro of the H&D League in 1954.[3]

Gee played both basketball and baseball for Michigan and led the Wolverines' run to the Big Ten baseball championship in 1936. Like

Fisher, Gee had a running battle with major league baseball because of a contract dispute with the New York Giants. Refusing to re-sign with the 1947 New York Giants for a salary that he could almost match teaching school and playing semipro ball, Gee decided to pitch where and when he wanted and was blacklisted as a result.[4] An imposing figure on the mound, standing six-foot-nine and looking like an earlier-era Randy Johnson, he still had major league talent. In the 1951 playoffs he was virtually unhittable, making two starts, both of them shutouts. Gee's battery-mate Lau was a Michigan high schooler coveted by Fisher as a future Wolverine. Only seventeen at the time, Lau hit .291, third best on the club. To Fisher's disappointment, Lau signed with the Detroit Tigers and went on to a lengthy career in the majors as a player and batting coach. His influential book *The Art of Hitting* found a special disciple in future Hall of Famer George Brett. "Little did I realize at the time what [his system] was going to do and how it was going to change my life," said Brett. "I've never looked back."

When Fisher returned to Blacks Harbour in 1953, it was with an NCAA championship under his belt, and he brought a solid core of Wolverine regulars with him. All-American shortstop Bruce Haynam, a veteran of two seasons in the Maritimes, led the brigade, and pitchers Jack Ritter, Marv Wisniewski, Jack Corbett and outfielder Bob Gordynec were returnees as well. Newcomers on the squad were Rich Leach, Howie Tommelin, Robert Pollard, Paul Lepley and third baseman Don Eaddy, who would go on to a lengthy pro career and a cup of coffee with the Chicago Cubs. A third team All-American in 1953, Lepley signed with the Tigers after his summer in New Brunswick, as did Ritter, who went straight to AAA Toledo of the International League as a twenty-year-old. Two-year New Brunswick League veteran Richard Leach also signed with the Tigers. His son Rick Leach, Jr., was selected in the first round of the major league draft in 1979 and had a ten-year career in the majors with the Tigers and Toronto Blue Jays.

When Blacks Harbour decided not to operate in 1954, Fisher took his players to Truro in the H&D League. With Lepley, Ritter, Leach and Eaddy lost to the pros, the Bearcats roster was an amalgam of Wolverines and other recruits brought to Nova Scotia by Jeff Jones and Clary Johnson. Two Michigan first-team All-Americans, Ken Tippery and Bruce Haynam, gave the Bearcats a slick double-play combination, and Howie Tommelin completed the left side of the infield. Johnny Gee and Dick Peterjohn led the Michigan contingent on the mound. High on Fisher's wish list for general manager Soapy Campbell that year were twin brothers Ron and Don Eason from Northeastern, who played for him in Blacks Harbour, and infielder Grover "Deacon" Jones from

Ithaca College and the Grand Falls Cataracts. Johnson obliged, traveling to Boston to sign the Eason twins, who were virtually inseparable and would only sign together. As for signing Jones, Johnson did Fisher one better; in addition to "the Deacon" he recruited the heart of Ithaca's pitching staff: Walter Judd, Don Kern and Bob Thwaites. Johnson also brought Gene Lary from the University of Alabama, a member of a well-known baseball family. Gene's father was a former major leaguer, as were brothers Frank and Al. Frank made his debut with the Detroit Tigers later that same season.

Another notable Bearcat signing was Norwalk, Maine, native Bill Thurston, who so impressed Fisher in Truro that he recruited him for the Wolverines, where he led the Big 10 Conference with a .470 batting average in 1955. Later that year Thurston was named the outstanding pitcher in the New Brunswick-Maine League with the 1955 Edmundston Republicans. Some years ago I visited Thurston and his assistant Dave Jauss at Amherst College in Springfield, Massachusetts. Thurston spoke of growing up on a dairy farm and playing for a semipro club in Farmington. He considered his two years in the Maritimes as highlights of his youth, but turning pro in 1956 was a dream come true. After a few years in the minors, however, Thurston came to the realization that he was a borderline prospect and that a major league career was unlikely. "It was a tough thing when I realized that my dream was at an end," he recalled, "but I wouldn't trade my coaching career here at Amherst where I've had the chance to help a lot of kids move into pro ball." Thurston's most notable protégé at Amherst was pitcher John Cerutti, who spent a few years with the Blue Jays. Dave Jauss later coached in New Brunswick before becoming a member of the Boston Red Sox coaching staff.

Fisher's 1954 Bearcats had a disappointing season, ending up out of the playoffs. Eason led the pitching staff with a 9–3 record, but the rest of the staff was mediocre at best. Johnny Gee was finally beginning to show his age, and youngster Lary was surprisingly ineffective, given his later success with the Cleveland Indians at the Triple-A level. Deacon Jones, a .300 hitter everywhere he played during his twenty-year career, hit less than .250, and All-American Bruce Haynam was even worse. When I talked to the Deacon about his mediocre season, he laughed heartily. Not only was it his worst season ever, but two years later he led all of minor league baseball, hitting over .400. The best player on the Truro club that year was not one of the classy imports but local boy Stan Maxwell, who was in his rookie season. Maxwell led the club in hitting, excelled in the outfield and impressed major league scouts with his all-around athletic talent.

Another CWS Champion: The 1955 Wake Forest Deacons

At the beginning of the decade, Wake Forest graduates Bill Brooks, Art Hoch and Joe Fulghum helped establish a Carolinian connection to the H&D League that eventually supplied over a hundred players to teams throughout the Maritimes. College World Series runner-up in 1949 and United States representative at the 1951 Pan-Am Games, the Deacons were one of the most powerful college teams anywhere in the United States during the fifties, capping it off with a College World Series championship in 1955. Jack McGinley was outstanding that year, posting an 8–2 record in Atlantic Coast Conference play, racking up two more wins in playoff qualifiers and another three in Omaha despite a sore arm that he treated with "Atomic Balm" liniment.[5] A pitching duel against Colgate's Larry Bossidy, attended by a raft of major league scouts and Baltimore Orioles manager Paul Richards, was particularly notable. McGinley posted a four-hit shutout, Bossidy a two-hitter. Future H&D Leaguer Luther McKeel knocked in the winning run in the Deacons 1–0 victory.

McGinley played the next four years in the H&D League, and Bossidy starred in New Brunswick in 1955. Neither would sign pro contracts: McGinley because of a gimpy arm and Bossidy because of his parents' insistence that he follow a business career. Every time a scout would appear on the Bossidy doorstep, his mother would lock the door. For the Deacons, John Stokoe and Bill Walsh also made significant contributions to the playoff run. Stokoe racked up a 2–0 complete-game shutout over Oklahoma State, and Walsh sparkled as a spot starter and reliever. Right after the Omaha tournament they travelled north to play for Art Hoch's Dartmouth Arrows. Catcher Lyn Holt, who hit .352 on the road to Omaha and earned a spot on the 1955 American Baseball Coaches First Team All-American squad, accompanied them.

All-Americans and Bonus Babies

Holt was not the only All-American to play summer ball that year in the Maritimes. Two other dream-squad selections, infielders Bud Getchell from Springfield College and Wolverine third baseman Don Eaddy, played in New Brunswick. Sixteen first-team All-Americans played summer ball in the Maritimes between 1952 and 1959. When the ABCA added second- and third-team selections beginning in 1955, the number of All-Americans increased significantly. Among those honored were Tom Gastall, Ron Weidenhammer, Connie Gravitte, Phil Tarpey and Art Brophy (1955); Don Prohovich, Carmen Santoli and Neil Stinneford (1956); Ken Tippery, Marsh McLean, Tom Clarkson, Dave Sime and Jim Raugh (1957); Bob Wedin, Frank Saia, Hal Deitz, Tom Morgan, Marsh McLean, Rex McMillan (1958); Moe Morhardt (1959); and Gene Malinowski and Ty Cline (1960). More than forty All-Americans played in the Maritimes in the fifties, a clear indication of the level of talent arrayed across the diamonds of the region.

Another indication of the H&D League's reputation as an incubator of young talent was the signing of "bonus babies" who ended up going directly to the big leagues without a stop in the minors because of a curious and ill-considered regulation instituted by Major League Baseball in 1953. Trying to stop wealthier clubs from stockpiling college talent, the "bonus rule" required any team that signed a player to a bonus exceeding $4,000 to keep the player on its twenty-five-man big league roster for two full seasons.[6] Three players who played in the H&D League in 1954—Tom Carroll of the Halifax Cardinals and the Liverpool Larruper battery of Tom Gastall and Art "Red" Swanson—thus found themselves on major league rosters for both the 1955 and 1956 seasons. Larruper pitcher "Wild Bill" Oster preceded them, but an arm injury while he was negotiating the size of his bonus interfered with his progress. Oster went directly to the Philadelphia A's in 1954 and appeared in eight games but was not required to remain with the big league club. Al Spangler, who was planning to join Carroll in Halifax, signed below the $4,000 limit with the Braves but had a contract that allowed him to stay on the big league roster if he wished. Ron Jackson was another player destined for Halifax but signed as a bonus baby. Jackson already had a train ticket to Halifax when the Chicago White Sox offered a tryout and large signing bonus that may have been as high as $40,000.[7] Moe Drabowsky and Ralph Lumenti were signed to bonus contracts with the Chicago Cubs and Washington Senators, respectively, after that.

From Halifax to Gotham: Tommy Carroll

In February 1955 the New York Yankees held a Manhattan press conference to announce the dual signings of thirty-six-year-old shortstop Phil Rizzuto and eighteen-year-old bonus baby Tom Carroll, Rizzuto's heir apparent. It was what veteran New York reporters and *The Sporting News* referred to as a "two cheesecake" event, reflecting its special significance. Apparently there were four levels of Yankees press events, the routine one with no embellishments, a slightly more important one with sandwiches, a third with sandwiches and a cheesecake from a well-known restaurant around the corner, and this one, which included a couple of the tasty desserts. Carroll signed a bonus contract reportedly worth $40,000 although in an interview for the SABR oral history project in 1991 he remembered receiving $50,000 over three years. "This is a ballplayer," said Krichell of Carroll, "he's got a great arm, he runs well, has terrific hands for ground balls and hits the long ball."[8]

The year before Carroll's signing, Krichell insisted that Carroll play for Bob Decker in Halifax and introduced the two during a workout at Yankee Stadium that spring. "I liked Decker," said Carroll in a recent interview, "and I was flattered that the Yankees were interested in me and I went up there ... and had a good summer."[9] Carroll's teammates in Halifax included future major leaguers Zeke Bella and Yale pitching sensation Bob Davis; outfielder Bill Cline, who played six years after that in the Yankees chain; and local boys Billy Carter, Johnny Clark and Don Boudreau. Decker also relied on a couple of veteran pitchers: "Smokey Jim" Heller and Braves farmhand Gerry Levinson, who had played with Decker in 1949 and was eager to return to the Maritimes. "I was already thinking of another career when Decker called to offer me a job," Levinson told me during an H&D League reunion, "and didn't hesitate for a moment." Six-year pro Amby Foote, the father of Montreal Expos catcher Barry Foote; Phil Tarpey, a hard-throwing right-hander who later signed with the Cubs: and nineteen-year-old George Player, who split the season between Halifax and Quebec City of the Provincial League, rounded out the roster.

Carroll had a solid year in Halifax, hitting .281 with seven home runs in a little over 200 at-bats before joining the Yankees. Manager Casey Stengel recognized Carroll's potential and often spoke highly of him, but as with most bonus babies, compliments didn't translate into playing time. In fact, it wasn't until the middle of the 1955 season that Carroll made an appearance in the lineup, and then only as a pinch runner. He would not make a plate appearance until the final two games of the season, starting both games of a double header and going one for three in each.

In 1956, his second year with the Yankees, Carroll had a good spring training, hitting close to .400 and starting a number of games in a row at third base. According to *The Sporting News*, "he comported himself with credit both in the field and at bat.... Few Yankees can outrun him." Stengel raved about Carroll and spoke of the emerging kid infield of the future: Marv Throneberry at first, Bobby Richardson at second, Tony Kubek at short and Carroll at third. "They are better than

The 1954 Halifax Cardinals. Three players, Zeke Bella (front row, second from left), Tom Carroll (second row, fourth from left) and Bob Davis (third row, third from left), signed Yankees contracts and went on to the majors. Other players on the team included Smokey Jim Heller (third row, at left) and Billy Carter (third row, second from right) (Halifax Municipal Archives, CR67-5.989.01.10).

some major league infields already," said Stengel. "Carroll can't miss. Watch him during a workout. When he bats, he won't just walk off after his turn. He will run to first and then pretend he is in a game and continue around the bases. He watches intently and is as good a hustler as you will find in any camp.... The kid has great power now. Watch him in another year."[10] Unfortunately for Carroll these were just testimonials. He finished his two years in New York with less than thirty at-bats, hitting .359 in regular season play and slightly better than that in spring training. Carroll was an obvious victim of the bonus rule; here was a youngster with immense talent who spent two years stapled to the bench while other Yankees prospects Bobby Richardson and Tony Kubek honed their craft playing every day in the minors.

Liverpool's Bonus Kids: Tom Gastall and Arthur "Red Swanson"

Tom Gastall signed a bonus deal with the Baltimore Orioles in 1955 after three seasons in Liverpool. Although an average hitter, he was already a superior defensive receiver with a strong arm and good game-calling abilities, and he was considered the Orioles catcher of the future. Unfortunately, when he arrived in Baltimore, he found himself third on the club's depth chart. Hal Smith, a veteran of the New Brunswick League, was a solid major league starter, and backup Gus Triandos had prodigious power and could also play first base. Like most bonus rookies, Gastall fought for playing time. Quite often his impatience irritated manager Paul Richards, who resented that the bonus rule limited his roster flexibility. He made his position clear to a reporter from *The Sporting News.* "I know that there has been talk about Triandos and Smith being used in deals this winter, but you can forget that," Richards said. "Both figure in my future plans, and I won't dispose of either."[11] Over two seasons, Gastall came to the plate fewer than a hundred times and appeared in just fifty-two games. He played well in spring training, however, and if one combines his performances, he grades out as a .230 hitter and a more-than-adequate defender.

All of this became irrelevant at 6:21 p.m. on September 20, 1956, when the control tower in Baltimore received an ominous radio message from Gastall as he piloted a small plane across Chesapeake Bay. "75 Hotel I'm going into the water," Gastall declared. Nobody at the airfield saw the plane go down, but an emergency search discovered an oil slick and some seat cushions. It would be five days before his body was recovered. Gastall had been careful to keep his flying from manager Paul Richards, who would have grounded him if he'd been aware of it. Flying would have exacerbated an already strained relationship. Teammate Gus Triandos, who had driven him home after the game that day and was one of a handful of players who knew of his hobby, had unsuccessfully tried to dissuade him. "I knew he was going up anyway," said Triandos. "He kept talking about what a great day it was flying and how he could hardly wait to get up there."[12]

When funeral services were held at St. Patrick's Church in Fall River, Massachusetts, throngs of people stood outside of the church. Among the mourners were Triandos, Jack Dunn, Joe Cusick and Frank McGowan representing the Orioles, and Cape Breton Colliery League veteran Lenny Merullo, who had followed Gastall closely during his four summers in Canada. Richards did not attend, but he made the following comment to columnist Bob Addie of *The Sporting News.* "He was a funny kid. He always had to prove something to himself—which is perhaps the reason he took up flying. He'd get mad at me because he thought I didn't use him enough. I never saw such restless energy in any kid. There could be a thing, I guess as too much hustle. If there is, then Tommy Gastall had it."[13]

Gastall's battery mate in Liverpool, Red Swanson, was the third bonus boy from the H&D League to play major league ball that year. Swanson arrived in Nova Scotia in 1954 as an inexperienced seventeen-year-old and low man on the Liverpool pitching chart. His record with the Larrupers was unremarkable, two wins in six decisions and more hits given up than innings pitched. The Pirates were nonetheless intrigued. They liked his poise, his ability to throw strikes and his bloodlines—his father was head baseball coach at Louisiana State—and offered him a $20,000 bonus. Swanson appeared in one game as the 1955 season wore down, and 1956 was not much better. Swanson's manager, Bobby Bragan, a vehement critic of the bonus rule, was annoyed when three bonus pitchers—Swanson, Lauren Pepper and Paul Martin—took up roster spots in 1957. "I don't like my situation with three bonus pitchers," Bragan told *The Sporting News*. "All they're doing is beating someone out of a job who could help me on this club. Lauren Pepper's time is up in June and he will be sent out.... Art Swanson has the pitches and seems to have guts out there ...[but] I know one thing. I'll not use them unless I absolutely have to, or one of them comes along very fast."[14]

Although there was every indication that Swanson would be sent packing, he looked good in spring training and Bragan seemed more willing to use him in 1957. After a number of solid relief appearances, Bragan finally gave him a start. Making the most of the opportunity, the young redhead scattered four hits in an 8–1 complete-game victory over the St. Louis Cardinals. Swanson hadn't surrendered a hit through four innings when official scorer Paul Veech gave Alvin Dark a scratch infield single on an obvious error to first baseman Dee Fondy. The Pirate bench was incensed. Then in the seventh, Stan Musial hit a line shot that popped out of right-fielder Paul Smith's glove. It was declared a hit as well. These were the only two "hits" that Swanson had surrendered as the ninth inning began. Bragan told his players that if Swanson escaped without another hit that they should rush to the mound and carry him off holding their fingers up as a zero to indicate a no-hitter. That marvelous performance cancelled a ticket to the minors. He finished the season with a 3–3 record and a respectable 3.72 ERA, yet it was his last in the big leagues.[15]

Bearcat Bonus Boys: Moe Drabowsky and Ralph Lumenti

While most bonus kids like Swanson had to fight to make their mark, "Moe" Drabowsky was an instant regular. A hard-throwing right-hander out of Trinity College, Drabowsky arrived in Truro in 1955 with a number of his college teammates. Although he won seventeen games at Trinity that year, he found the H&D league far more challenging, posting a 6–8 record with 103 strikeouts and 61 walks in 121 innings. Drabowsky's initial season made it clear that he needed to work on commanding his pitches. The stuff was there; it just needed to be refined. With Truro in 1956 he racked up one dominant performance after another, holding opposing batters to a .163 batting average and winning six of eight decisions. Major league scouts followed him closely, especially the old Cub Lenny Merullo, who every year crisscrossed the region signing young prospects. On Merullo's recommendation, the Cubs signed Moe to a $60,000 bonus and he left Truro for the big leagues in late July.[16]

It wouldn't take long for Drabowsky to make his mark. After a brief appearance on August 7, in which he struck out Henry Aaron, and a sparkling exhibition start in the annual White Sox vs. Cubs game, Drabowsky made his first major league start on August 18. The Cubs won 8–1, and Drabowsky impressed with his poise and command of the strike zone. Drabowsky finished the year with a 2–4 record, pitched three complete games and held opposing batters to just 37 hits over 51 innings, the beginning of a seventeen-year big league career.

On a visit to British Columbia in the late 1980s, I talked to Moe about his Nova Scotia days. He was a pitching coach with the Vancouver Mounties at the time but still remembered his H&D League experiences as though they were yesterday. His most vivid memory was of the semi-final championship game of the 1955 season when Art Hoch drove a Drabowsky fastball into the left-center-field bleachers at Halifax Wanderers Grounds for a walkoff victory. "I'll never forget it, an amazing day in a great league!" Drabowsky exclaimed. When Art visited Chicago the next season, Drabowsky introduced him to all the guys in the clubhouse. "I told them this is the last guy to hit a home run against me before I came to the majors."

Hoch had equally fond memories of his walk-off homer. Drabowsky had been the starter the day before and had been brought in to finish off the final game by getting Hoch out. "I was thinking that Moe was likely tired after pitching the previous day," Hoch recalled, "and also that he was a strike thrower who liked to get ahead of you, so I made up my mind that if I saw a fastball I was going to take advantage of it." North Carolina State catcher Bob Kennell, who came to Halifax to play for Hoch, said jokingly that Hoch "would never let anyone forget [the homer]" and never missed a chance to remind people of it. "He was a fierce competitor," said Kennell, "but truly a good man."

When Drabowsky left Truro for Chicago in July 1956, future bonus baby Ralph Lumenti was in his initial season in the H&D League. A lanky six-foot-three, 185-pound lefty from Milford Massachusetts, Lumenti signed a $35,000 bonus contract with the Washington Senators in September 1957.[17] Every major league club was bidding for his services at the time. One who followed him closely was Bill Lefebvre, a former major league pitcher and first baseman, who was scouting for the Senators and still playing occasionally in the Maine–New Brunswick League. "I watched him first in Presque Isle ... then I followed him in the Nova Scotia League with the Truro and Liverpool clubs," said Lefebvre. "Every time I watched him I was more impressed."[18]

Lumenti's best asset was what his Topps baseball card described as a "supersonic" fastball. "I could throw the shit out of the ball," Lumenti told me. "But it took a lot out of me in the process." When Senators manager Cookie Lavagetto first saw him, he thought his fastball "far better that any we now have on the club" including that of hard-throwing Camilo Pascual. Watching him smoke the ball in bullpen sessions, Lavagetto was itching to start Lumenti, even though the youngster was enrolled at the University of Massachusetts for the fall term and commuting to Washington only on the weekends. His debut came on Saturday, September 7, against the Yankees, a scoreless-inning relief appearance, giving up a hit and generating eight swinging strikes. All thought his fastball top tier, as good as anyone's in the league. Prophetically, Yankees broadcaster Phil Rizzuto declared, "He's got it if he can control it."[19] The following weekend Lumenti threw a three-hitter over seven innings against Kansas City.

As his second season with Washington began, the youngster admitted that he was "scared to death" about what was coming, aware that he had to improve his change-up.[20] Relying on his high-nineties fastball, he had a great spring and won a starting job. The only cause for concern was that he walked as many batters as he whiffed. In the longer term, a lack of command would be his undoing. After four starts and a 1–2 won-lost record, he was banished to the bullpen. In June the Senators sent him to Chattanooga. He would continue in the Senators organization until his retirement in 1962 without reaching his potential. I asked him if he was bitter about not achieving a solid major league career. "Not at all," he replied. "The Senators gave me my chance and I blew it. I just couldn't get the ball over the plate." His good memories were of the H&D League. "I think the best pitching I've ever done was in Nova Scotia," he told a reporter for *The Sporting News*. "In the playoffs there in 1956 I was hot for a week. Twice I came in with the bases loaded and nobody out and struck out the side. I pitched 35 innings and walked only one." Lumenti was the last of the classic bonus babies to go directly from the H&D League to major league baseball.

Major league baseball finally rescinded the controversial bonus baby regulation in 1957. Unfortunately for many caught up in the experiment, including those with experience in the H&D League, sitting on the bench at the major league level interfered with their development. In the future there would be many H&D Leaguers signing lucrative bonuses, but they would be allowed to develop their skills in a traditional manner as they proceeded through the minor leagues. By that time, the league was a four-team operation made up almost exclusively of young prospects sent to Nova Scotia by major league organizations.

Seven

Playing in "Color Bar Limbo"
Black Players in the Maritimes, 1946–60

The history of sports and race in the 20th century has frequently been romanticized as a journey from segregation to inclusion and a gradual triumph over various forms of intolerance. Despite the optimistic note sounded by Jackie Robinson's breaking of baseball's color bar in 1946, however, widespread discriminatory practices involving housing and employment, residential schooling for First Nations peoples, the legacy of Japanese internment, and the segregation of restaurants, movie houses, and golf clubs—and of recreational clubs like the Halifax Waegwoltic Club that excluded Jews—continued to be the norm in postwar Canada. In November 1946, shortly after Robinson finished his season with the Montreal Royals, businesswoman Viola Desmond attended a movie at the Roseland Theatre in New Glasgow. After purchasing a balcony-only ticket, she took a seat in the "whites-only" lower area and was arrested, fined twenty dollars and kept in jail overnight. Although the Desmond case has since become recognized as a landmark event in race relations in Canada, it was hardly an isolated incident at the time.[1] A year later a West Indian student engineer, who was employed with the Nova Scotia Department of Highways and was on a work assignment, was denied service in a local restaurant on what the black newspaper *The Clarion* called a "flimsy pretext." According to Carrie Best, New Glasgow was "fast becoming a town that the Bilbos and Huey Long can be proud of."[2] Not long after that *The Clarion* reported a cross burning in the wee hours of the morning at the house of Chinese restaurant proprietor Joe Mong. The perpetrators wore white hoods while gathered around the burning seven-foot cross.

The Clarion was an important voice for postwar black Nova Scotians. Associated with the Second Baptist Church in New Glasgow, it championed education and Christian character-building and emphasized the careers of successful black men and women in various walks of life including sports. Carrie Best's son "Cal," who subsequently became Canadian High Commissioner to Trinidad and Tobago and served on the three-person panel that released an influential report on the future of Canadian sports in the wake of the Ben Johnson doping scandal, was the *Clarion*'s associate editor at the time. His column "Here and There Around Sports" emphasized the important contributions of black athletes to the struggle for social justice.[3] Although his emphasis was on male athletes, Cal also encouraged black women to get involved with sports. Noting the establishment of a black women's softball team in Saint John, for example, he thought the local Truro Women's Royals, organized by Bill Dorrington, should prepare for competition throughout the region. Right-fielder Phyllis Reddick particularly impressed him. "She plays the position like a veteran and she is not afraid to take a good healthy cut at the ball."[4] He also encouraged involvement in track and field as a way of improving basic athletic prowess among girls and women.[5]

Although many of Cal's columns involved American athletes like Robinson, Joe Louis, Roy Campanella, Satchel Paige, and Larry Doby, he extolled Canadian multi-sport athletes such as Cape Breton's Oscar Seale, boxers Percy Paris and Crossley Irvine, hockey and baseball players and cousins Doug and Art Dorrington, and footballer Willie Strode in equal measure. He had special praise for Windsor, Ontario, native Freddie Thomas, who broke the Eastern League color line in baseball in 1948. Tremendously gifted, Thomas was a star basketball player both at Assumption College and with the Harlem Globetrotters and had a brief gridiron stint with the Toronto Argonauts in 1949. Thomas played semi-pro baseball in the Maritimes, Quebec and Ontario throughout the forties and fifties.[6]

Although the Maritimes produced several exceptional black athletes prior to the Second World War, the number of blacks playing alongside whites on baseball diamonds and hockey rinks increased dramatically after that. The postwar era, of course, witnessed what historian Jules Tygiel dubbed "baseball's great experiment,"[7] the breaking of the unofficial color barrier excluding black players from major league baseball's "Organized Baseball" system. By then, black players figured prominently, competing on all-black clubs in towns scattered throughout the Maritimes and displaying their talents on integrated teams. During the war, players such as Alvin Paris, Charles and Morton Berry, Bob Mentis, Oscar Seale, Gordon Maxwell and Charlie Pyle were household names in regional baseball circles. So were various members of the McIntyre, O'Ree, Dorrington, States, Borden, Downey, Skinner and Clyke families.

Pyle and Seale played for Canadian Army teams overseas and starred on local diamonds after the war in the Cape Breton Colliery League and on the mainland. Pyle played two seasons with the Central League's Truro Bearcats and helped the Fredericton Capitols to the New Brunswick championship in 1949. Seale, meanwhile, was runner up to Al Ware and John "Brother" MacDonald for the 1949 Colliery League batting title. A few years later Ware was the starting third baseman for the White Sox's Charleston affiliate in the Triple-A American Association. Around the same time Seale attracted the attention of legendary softball hall of famer Eddie Feigner who invited him to travel as a member of his four-man squad "the King and his Court."[8]

Manny McIntyre: A Pathbreaker in Baseball and Hockey

One of the early pioneers in black sports at the time was Vincent "Manny" McIntyre, a history-maker in both baseball and hockey. The first black Canadian to play professional baseball when he signed with the Sherbrooke Canadians of the Class C Border League in 1946, he also gained fame as a member of the first all-black line in pro hockey alongside brothers Herb and Ossie Carnegie. With Timmins in the Northern Ontario League and later the Sherbrooke Saints, the "Black Aces," as they were known, were outstanding. Despite their ability none of them got a real shot at the National Hockey League. Rather, like a whole generation of black stars, they found themselves consigned to "color bar limbo." The gradual weakening—but not the real eradication—of the color bar in both hockey and baseball meant that many black players had to content themselves with playing at a minor league or semipro level, despite knowing that they had the talent to play at a higher level. "We never worried about playing in the NHL because we knew we were good enough to play there," said Manny in an interview with Ian MacDonald of the Fredericton *Daily Gleaner*.[9]

In 1947 Manny and Ossie decided to take their hockey talent to Europe as stars of hotelier Charles Ritz's Paris Racing Club team and in doing so gained the kind of recognition that had been denied them in Canada. Referred to as "les Noirs," the duo played before immense crowds that at times exceeded those in the National Hockey League. The Paris squad played against all-star teams from Sweden, Switzerland, Czechoslovakia and Great Britain on their way to a sensational 54–4–2 record. Ted Cumming, who had watched McIntyre play baseball and hockey in Middleton right after the war, and who also took his hockey skills overseas, remembers playing for the British national team against the Racing Club before 22,000 enthusiastic Parisians. Cumming was a member of the Brighton Tigers of the English National League at the time and an early champion of hockey's internationalization. In the early seventies, Cumming teamed up with promoter Gary Davidson in the creation of the World Hockey Association, with the intention of eventually expanding professional hockey to cities in Britain and on the continent.

The son of a lumberyard and sawmill worker on the Saint John River, McIntyre grew up in Devon, New Brunswick, played ball for Fredericton High School and led Devon to the New Brunswick junior baseball championship in 1938. After a year of senior baseball with the Truro Bearcats, Manny spent much of his time playing wartime baseball in Halifax, first for Halifax Army and then for the powerful Shipyards club. In 1945 he moved to Trois-Rivières of the Quebec Provincial League, suiting up alongside fellow Maritimers Joe Breen, Clyde Roy and Joe Cormier, and played occasionally for the Shawinigan Falls Cataracts. By then Manny had garnered attention from both the New York Black Yankees and the Cuban Giants, who saw him as a future recruit. "The coloured baseball star from North Carleton Ward made a flying visit ... en route to New York City to sign with the New York Cuban Stars in the Negro National League," the Fredericton *Gleaner* reported in August 1945. It was at the tail end of the season, however, and McIntyre would only play in a single game. "I joined the Cubans for a game in Yankee Stadium," McIntyre recalled in an interview for the *New Brunswick Reader* in 1995. "It was something. That was where I first saw Jackie." In June 1946 Manny signed a contract with Sherbrooke of the Class C Border League, making him one of only six black players in professional baseball at the time, and a Canadian at that. When Minny Minoso signed a major league contract with the Cleveland Indians prior to the 1948 season, the Cubans came calling once again, but Manny had already committed to play for Drummondville of the Quebec Provincial League and turned the offer down.[10]

Manny's earlier experience playing cross-border baseball in the Border League for a couple of years earlier may have influenced his decision to stay in Quebec. He had not enjoyed his experience in semi-pro ball. Many of his teammates in the Border League were Southerners, and Manny was often ignored by them when they were traveling across the border to play. He lasted with the Sherbrooke team for thirty games, but after another lonely night in Ogdensburg, New York, he informed manager George "Pappy" Smith that he was quitting. It wasn't because of poor performance. Manny was hitting over

Manny McIntyre from Devon, New Brunswick, was the first Black player from Canada to play professional baseball after the war, signing with Sherbrooke of the Border League in 1946. Offered contracts by Negro League clubs, McIntyre preferred playing in Canada (courtesy Canadian Baseball Hall of Fame and McIntyre family),

.300 when he made the decision, although a sore arm had resulted in a number of throwing errors from his shortstop position. Smith tried to dissuade McIntyre, since McIntyre and Sherbrooke-native Norm Dussault were his two best players, but to no avail. Instead, Manny chose to return to Nova Scotia and suited up with the Middleton Cardinals of the H&D League along with fellow New Brunswick native and NHLer Roly McLenahan. Manny finished the season with a .263 batting average. The following year, Manny signed with the Drummondville Cubs and remained there for another year before leading the Fredericton Capitols to the New Brunswick championship in 1949. Manny closed out his baseball career in 1951, playing with Waterloo of the Ontario Intercounty League.

Art Dorrington: Another Two-Sport Star

As Manny's career wound down in the late 1940s and early '50s, Art Dorrington's pro career was just beginning. Dorrington was a pathbreaker and, like Manny, played both hockey and baseball at the professional level. Growing up in Truro—a town that has produced an impressive array of hockey and baseball players over the years—Art was always hanging out around the rink and the TAAC ball field as a kid. In his early teens he worked out with the senior Bearcats and in 1946 served as the team's bat and ball boy. Two years later he played his first season with the Bearcats and later suited up with the Saint John club in the Southern New Brunswick League, playing alongside Manny McIntyre. Ontario native Fred Thomas was a teammate in 1950 when Art finished near the top of the Southern New Brunswick league with a .295 average.

Later that same year, Art made hockey history as the first black player to sign an NHL hockey contract with the New York Rangers organization. Assigned to Atlantic City in the Eastern League, he was an immediate sensation: a prolific scorer and speedster who led the club to the league championship in his first year. Like other black players in the forties and fifties, however, Dorrington would never get a chance to play in the NHL. Instead, he played six seasons in the Eastern League with Washington, Johnstown and Philadelphia and one season in the International Hockey league. His best year was 1954–55, when he tallied 33 goals and 35 assists in 49 games with the Washington Lions. Dorrington's experience mirrored that of Manny's in baseball's Border League; he remembered not being allowed to socialize with his white teammates and having to eat and billet with black families. His hockey life consisted of going to and from the rink. A broken femur after just eleven games with the Philadelphia Ramblers in 1957 ended his hockey career.

Baseball continued to be a part of Art's life. When the EHL season came to a close in 1951, Boston Braves scout Jeff Jones offered him a chance to play professional ball. He was assigned to Wellsville of the Pony League, where he showed real power, hitting three home runs in 43 at-bats. Unfortunately, Art contracted pneumonia and called it quits after just fourteen games. "I realized then," he told me, "that playing two sports at the professional level was just too demanding." After his retirement from hockey, however, Dorrington returned to the diamond with the Hap Farley All-Stars in Atlantic City. His manager was Negro League legend Pop Lloyd, who would eventually be inducted into the Baseball Hall of Fame in Cooperstown. The All-Stars were sponsored by New Jersey state senator "Hap" Farley, a former baseball and basketball player at Georgetown University and political boss in Atlantic City who had succeeded Enoch "Nucky" Johnson as the most powerful man in the city. Both Johnson and Farley organized baseball teams as a way to promote their own interests and public visibility, but with Johnson's conviction for tax evasion, the Johnson All-Stars took on the Hap Farley moniker. Many will recognize Johnson as a central character in the popular HBO series *Boardwalk Empire*.[11]

Stan "Chook" Maxwell: H&D League Star

Another Truro native, Stan "Chook" Maxwell, would follow in Dorrington's footsteps. Not only was he one of the finest black hockey players anywhere in the fifties and sixties, but he also was one of a handful of local black players to play regularly in the Halifax & District League. Only infielder Billy Carter, who played for both Dartmouth and Halifax over six seasons, would play as long in the import-dominated H&D League as Maxwell. Other talented black players like Bobby "Cook" Mentis and Frank "Danky" Dorrington would have brief cameo appearances in the league; Chook's older brother Warren Maxwell and Johnny Mentis from Truro—as good a ballplayer from the Maritimes as anyone—migrated to Central Canada in search of steady work or would likely have played in the League as well. Mentis would establish himself as one of the top players in the history of the Quebec Provincial League in the 1950s and '60s and starred in hockey at the junior and senior level. Warren ended up working in the mines in Sudbury and was a dominant pitcher for Garson in the Nickel Belt League.

Chook began his competitive baseball career as a seventeen-year-old with the powerful Londonderry Ironclads, playing alongside local luminaries Herbie McLeod, Hum Joseph, Carl Matheson and Len Boss. Although in a lower-ranked circuit, the Ironclads would have held their own in any league across the Maritimes. After two solid years with the Ironclads, Chook returned to Truro in 1954 to play for Ray Fisher and his starry crop of collegians. The other black player on the roster that year was Grover "Deacon" Jones out of White Plains, New York, and Ithaca College. A star in American Legion ball who won the Silver Bat for highest batting average in minor league baseball by hitting .409 for Duluth of the Northern League in 1956, Jones was a second baseman and catcher with the Bearcats. I still remember being at a game when Jones was behind the plate; my dad and I had driven to Truro to catch a game against the visiting Wildcats. As the game went on, we heard singing coming from the field; finally my dad pointed at Deacon and said, "he's the one singing." An early edition of *The Sporting News Baseball Register* listed singing as a one of Jones' hobbies, which was not surprising since his father was a minister and Deacon grew up as a regular in the church choir.

It was Deacon's bat and not his voice, however, that led him to a major league stint with the Chicago White Sox in the early 1960s. Signed as a second baseman, Jones went to spring training in 1956 with the big league club, but he injured his shoulder badly sliding into second base after smashing a double off Sandy Koufax. A later injury to his other shoulder relegated him to first-base duties. While Deacon was a major league hitter with power—and would have been a great DH today—two lame arms limited his major league opportunities.

Major league scouts were intrigued by the potential of Truro's two nineteen-year-old black players. At one point during the 1954 season, Braves scout Jeff Jones sat at the Maxwells' kitchen table, hoping to sign Chook to a pro baseball contract. Jones told the family that if Chook signed his bonus contract, he would be in the major leagues the following year. (As we have seen, signing a bonus of more than $4,000 meant going directly to the majors for two years, and this was the context for that comment.) There was one catch, however, and it was a deal breaker. Chook had to agree to play winter ball in the Caribbean. Unwilling to forego his professional hockey dreams, Chook refused. He later turned down an offer to play in the Pittsburgh Pirates organization for the same reason. Instead, Chook headed to Trois-Rivières for his final year of junior hockey and then signed a $3,000 contract to play for Punch Imlach's Quebec Aces.

Willie O'Ree: The Jackie Robinson of Hockey

In the spring of 1956, Willie O'Ree joined two hundred prospects at the Milwaukee Braves spring camp in Waycross, Georgia. A fine baseball player, he met Jackie Robinson a few years before while touring New York with a teenage all-star squad from Fredericton. A middle infielder with Fredericton and Marysville of the New Brunswick Baseball League, O'Ree caught the eye of Milwaukee scout Jeff Jones, who offered him the spring training tryout. O'Ree's experience in Georgia helped Willie decide on a hockey career rather than baseball career.

O'Ree found Georgia to be a hostile environment. He was treated with suspicion and undisguised hatred by segregation-minded Southerners and was refused service at lunch counters. He remembers vividly being followed around a local drugstore by a glowering owner when just looking to pick up a couple of postcards to send home. At camp, moreover, he was often ostracized by his white teammates. Although he hated every moment of his tryout, he played well enough to make it to the last day of camp before receiving a bus ticket home and an invitation to return the following year. "There was no way I was going back," he told me. For one thing, it was clear that major league organizations still had unofficial quotas on the number of black players that each had in their system each year. For another, like Art Dorrington and Chook Maxwell, Willie had the option of a professional hockey career.

Convinced that his future lay in hockey rather than in pro ball, O'Ree happily boarded a Greyhound bus for the trip back home. As the bus rolled north, Willie felt the weight of intolerance lessen with each mile. In addition, as the sweltering humidity of the deep south gave way to the crisp freshness of impending spring, he anxiously awaited getting back to New Brunswick. When leaving Waycross, he was forced to sit in the back of the bus, of course, but he recalls moving forward whenever the bus crossed a state line. "By the time I crossed the border into Canada," he told me one night when the two of us were being inducted as player and builder into the Black Hockey and Sports Hall of Fame, "I was sitting right up by the driver." His next bus trip took him to Quebec that fall and the beginning of his professional hockey career with Punch Imlach's Quebec Aces.[12]

Johnny Mentis: A Legend in the Quebec Provincial League

Although he would not make it to the NHL or to baseball's major leagues, Johnny Mentis was another of those who experienced the "color bar limbo" of the 1950s and '60s. Born in Truro in 1938, Johnny grew up in a sporting family. His father Robert was a track, hockey and baseball star in the thirties and may have been the best black hockey player of his generation. Everyone knew that Robert had NHL talent. Indeed, there is a widely told story involving Bob and Hockey Hall of Famer Gordie Drillon, a Moncton boy who won the NHL scoring championship with the Toronto Maple Leafs in 1938. At the end of that season, King Clancy approached Drillon, wanting to know if there were any other guys down in the Maritimes who might make a similar mark in the NHL. "There is a guy down there named Bob Mentis who is so good I couldn't even carry his skates," said Drillon. When Clancy expressed interest, Drillon added that "there is only one problem.

Mentis is black." End of conversation, end of a familiar story line in the age of the color bar![13]

A generation later, Robert's sons Johnny and "Cook" displayed similar talents. As teenagers they joined Chook Maxwell and Clobie Collins, another black player, playing baseball and hockey for the Truro Sheiks, Brookfield Elks and the junior Bearcats. Clobie would pursue his hockey career to Newfoundland along with Frank "Danky" Dorrington, who became a hockey legend in Cornerbrook. The Mentis boys were fine all-round athletes. Johnny was a graceful skater and hockey playmaker and a terrific baseball player whose competitive baseball career stretched over fifteen years in a number of semipro leagues in Quebec. Although Johnny never played in the H&D League, fifteen-year-old Cook played a couple of games with the Bearcats with two hits in three plate appearances. Younger brother Berton would later suit up with the Vaughan Furriers on the way to the Maritime junior baseball championship in 1961.

The 1950s were not a congenial time for blacks in Nova Scotia, of course, and Johnny—like his father and others—faced racial taunting and other forms of discrimination. It is worth remembering that even ten years after the Viola Desmond incident, the most popular restaurant in Truro still refused to serve blacks. In addition, young black men could serve as caddies at the Truro Golf Club, but their parents were barred from playing. Racism was hardly confined to Truro. Johnny remembers playing for the Truro Eagles on their way to the provincial juvenile hockey finals in 1956 and a controversial game in Berwick. Along with racial slurs, the crowd serenaded the young teenager with a derisive rendition of "Old Black Joe." When Truro ended up winning the game, the crowd erupted in anger and the police had to be called to escort Johnny out of the building.

In September 1956 Johnny and Cook were invited to the Boston Bruins camp of the Quebec Aces. Johnny was later cut and sent to the Chicoutimi Sagueneens. In Chicoutimi he roomed with Jacques Allard, who was also a star on both the ice and ball diamond. Allard would become well-known throughout the Maritimes when he led the Windsor Maple Leafs to the Maritime title and Allan Cup semi-finals in 1963. Johnny stayed in Quebec. In 1966 when playing with Victoriaville, Johnny was invited to play against the Russians in Montreal on a team that included Doug Harvey, Gump Worsely and Red Berenson. Although the Canadians lost 3–2 before 15,000 fans at the Forum, Johnny gained recognition as the first black hockey player anywhere to play against the Russians. At about the same time, he was hired as a guard at the new federal penitentiary in Cowansville, Quebec, and may well have been the first black prison guard in Canada. He worked at the prison for more than 30 years, following his father's advice of getting a good secure job rather than thinking about a career in a professional sport.

After their early stint as hockey roommates in Chicoutimi in 1956, Johnny and Jacques decided to play off-season baseball with Kenogami of the Saugenay League. This marked the beginning of Johnny's illustrious career in baseball that stretched over fourteen seasons. He and Allard held down the corner outfielder spots for two seasons. Johnny won the league batting title with a .398 batting average his first year and finished second the following year at .331. At one point the touring Indianapolis Clowns arrived in Kenogami. When Johnny led his team to victory, he was invited to tour with them, but he would not give up his new job in the corrections system. He also turned down an offer to play in the Phillies organization, having no interest in playing professional baseball in the south. He joined Waterloo in the Quebec Provincial League in 1959 and hit over .400 before moving to Granby. He would also suit up with Sherbrooke, Trois-Rivières and Quebec City before retiring from baseball after the 1970 season. Johnny's .340 career batting average was unmatched in the history of the Provincial League. His average dipped below .300 only once, with Granby in 1967 he hit .283, but a running battle with his coach left him in a less than positive frame of mind and affected his performance.[14]

In addition to Mentis and Chook Maxwell and others native to the Maritimes, there were a handful of black players numbered among the imports of the postwar era. Third baseman Don Eaddy, a member of the University of Michigan NCAA champions, played for Ray Fisher's Blacks Harbour team in 1953 and would have likely come to Truro the following year but signed with the Chicago Cubs. Eaddy made a brief fifteen-game appearance with the Cubs in 1959. The other eventual big leaguer was Dave Ricketts, a catcher and third baseman who had a productive six-year major league career mostly with the St. Louis Cardinals.

A number of other African Americans from south of the border played at least a full season during the H&D League's fifteen-year history. All of them would have brief careers in the minors. Milton "Bomber" Neal played for the Dartmouth Arrows in 1948 and against the Dodgers when the junior all-stars visited Halifax. A speedster on the basepaths, he played three years in the Baltimore system. Kentville outfielder Al Griggs was signed by Branch Rickey of the Pirates and went directly to the Eastern League in 1954. He put up almost identical numbers to those for his year with the Wildcats. Returning from a two-year military hitch, he got an invite to spring training with the

Pirates in 1957 and picked up three hits in four at-bats. And finally, Clarence "Sonny" Thomas spent the 1958 season with the Dartmouth Arrows and played a year in the Florida State League. Bob Dawson, a member of the first all-black line in intercollegiate hockey and an excellent ballplayer as well, was a good friend of Sonny's. The Dawson family stayed in close contact with Thomas over the years.

When the import era ended, a number of black players who had not gotten the chance to play in the H&D League would become fixtures in Maritime baseball. Black teams like the Truro Sheiks—which occasionally included white players like Johnny Graham—and similar clubs elsewhere fielded highly competitive squads. One of these was the Vaughan Furriers club in Halifax, which drew players from around the province on their way to the Maritime junior baseball championship. Their exploits are highlighted in Frank Mitchell's book, *The Boys of '62: Transcending the Racial Divide*. I often play golf with Frank as we swap "falsehoods" about our old playing days while overlooking our strikeouts at the plate or errors on defense. One of a handful of white players on the Furriers club, Frank provides a number of short biographies of the team's starry players, among them Berton Mentis, Denny Clyke, and Luke Maxwell. Mitchell's book helps flesh out in greater detail the history of baseball in the era of "color bar limbo."[15]

Eight

Borderlands Baseball
New Brunswick and Maine

Although most observers would consider the H&D League the most competitive summer league in the postwar northeast, it would be unwise to ignore New Brunswick baseball, given the province's central location and its historic connections throughout the northeastern borderlands. As early as the 1880s the province had an enthusiastic baseball following, especially in Saint John, Fredericton, Moncton and St. Stephen, and Canadian teams forged links across the border with Bangor, Augusta, Portland and as far south as Boston. By 1888 Halifax and Saint John were importing professional players from New England, many of whom had or would play in the National League. Other New Brunswick towns along the American border—Edmundston, Grand Falls, McAdam, St. Stephen and Woodstock—also had a rich history of playing against community and college teams in Maine and against barnstorming teams from New Hampshire and Massachusetts. In the years before World War I, most teams in the Maritimes operated as semipro independent clubs, filling their rosters with players from Organized Baseball and northeastern colleges. Besides baseball in New Brunswick and Maine, the 1912 Nova Scotia Professional League had teams in Halifax, Westville and Stellarton anchored by players like Saint John native Tom Daly, who went on to a twenty-year professional career. Daly was behind the plate for the Albions that year, hitting close to .400.

Baseball on the Border: The Early Years

By 1910 a New Brunswick-Maine League was already operating as a six-team circuit, with teams in Saint John, Fredericton, St. Stephen, Woodstock, and Calais, Maine. Occasionally these teams played exhibition matches with Houlton, Bangor and Portland. Maritimers Shorty Dee of Halifax and Art McGovern of Saint John were leaders on the St. Stephen club. Former Boston Red Sox catcher Pat Donahue was a mainstay with Saint John along with battery mates Andy Harrington, Casey Hageman and George Winter, and Houlton native and center-fielder Happy Iott served as playing coach with Calais. All would play at some point in the major leagues.

In August 1912, a crowd of 8,000 turned up to watch the New Brunswick-Maine League champion Saint John Marathons host Houlton. A three-game series that year against the New England League champion Lowell club went down to the wire with Lowell winning the deciding game in extra innings and attracted enthusiastic crowds as well. Lowell also played exhibition matches in Calais and St. Stephen. The success of these exhibitions quickly attracted promoters such as Frank Leonard of the Lynn Baseball Club and Montrealer Joe Page, sports agent for the Canadian Pacific Railway, who envisaged a network of Maritime baseball centers linked by rail and connected to the New England baseball scene.[1] The result was an affiliation with Organized Baseball. In 1913 the Saint John Marathons, Fredericton Pets, St. Croix Downeasters and Bangor Maroons played in a Class D New Brunswick-Maine League. These teams also maintained inter-provincial connections with teams in Nova Scotia and Prince Edward Island on an exhibition level. Further south, Portland and Lewiston fielded teams in the New England League before World War I.[2]

Although the war and subsequent depression undermined the growing connection to Organized Baseball in the borderlands, touring teams from the Boston area were regular visitors, as they had been earlier. Some players like Danny MacFayden from Somerville, Massachusetts, who had family connections in the Maritimes, ended up playing summer ball in the region. MacFayden played part of the summer in Nova Scotia in 1924 and 1925. He went directly to the Boston Red Sox the following year and ended up spending seventeen years in the big leagues. Now and then, clubs in the Maritimes lured star players from touring aggregations. Nova Scotia had a professional league in the mid-twenties stocked with players like third baseman Jersey Joe Stripp and pitcher Phil Page, both of whom would eventually go on to major league careers. Saint John entered a team in the Greater Boston Twilight League in 1925. That same season the Boston Red Sox visited Saint John and knocked off the locals by a 7–5 score. After that, Maine and the Maritimes continued to fall under the metropolitan influence of Boston. In 1934 the Boston Braves came to St. Stephen to play the Maritime champions, handily defeating the Kiwanis squad by an 11–3 score, and then travelled to Nova Scotia the following season to take on the Yarmouth Gateways. Both the Braves and Red Sox played against teams in Maine in the mid-thirties. In-season games between major league clubs and clubs from small towns of a couple thousand people would be unheard of today.

Along the way, a number of players from New Brunswick and Maine would end up in the big leagues. Among the more notable were Saint John natives Bill "Tip" O'Neil, an outfielder with the World Series champion White Sox in 1906; catcher Tom Daly, who played eight seasons at the major league level; first baseman John "Chewing Gum" O'Brien, a six-year veteran of the National League; and Maine natives "Colby Jack" Coombs and catcher Bill "Rough" Carrigan from Lewiston and Holy Cross College. Many New Englanders came to New Brunswick from further south. Bob Ganley from Lowell, who played five years with Washington and Pittsburgh, and Pennsylvanian Casey Hageman, who came to Saint John after a contract dispute in 1912 left him suspended from pro ball for more than a year, were particularly notable. Hageman had played for the Red Sox the year before and returned to the big leagues with St. Louis in 1914. Eight-year veteran of the major leagues George Winter was the Marathons' player coach and along with Hageman and Andy Harrington gave Saint John a one-two-three big-league punch on the mound. Between the wars, big Del Bissonette from Winthrop, Maine, and center-fielder Charley Small of Auburn suited up in the Cape Breton Colliery League as their professional careers wound down. Small played a few seasons in the Can-Am and Border leagues after the war and had a short stint in the H&D League as an umpire. In addition, Plaster Rock, New Brunswick, native Vince Shields made a brief appearance with the St. Louis Cardinals, and Augusta native Don Brennan had a five-year career with the Yankees and Cincinnati Reds between the wars.[3]

Over its history, New Brunswick baseball remained closely connected to Maine. American border towns like Presque Isle, Caribou, Houlton, and the Loring AFB in Limestone were part of a larger transnational baseball network. St. Stephen Kiwanis, the dominant cross-border club of the interwar years, drew players from the interconnected communities of Calais, St. Stephen, St. Croix and Milltown and from communities on both sides of the St Croix River. St. Stephen was a frequent finalist in the Maritime senior championship as well, facing off against its Nova Scotian rivals the Yarmouth Gateways, Middleton Cardinals, Springhill Fencebusters and Liverpool Larrupers.[4] St. Stephen and Milltown won nine consecutive New Brunswick championships in the thirties and copped seven Maritime titles. They were as good as any semipro team in greater New England. St. Stephen was again a dominant club in the late 1950s playing in a cross-border league that included the independent Presque Isle Indians, who fielded an import-laden squad. The Woodstock Elks also played across the line. In 1960 St. Croix won the Border League pennant, knocked off Chatham to win the New Brunswick title, and defeated Amherst to capture the Maritime championship.

The College Conundrum: Independent versus Minor League Baseball

Few baseball historians have given serious attention to the game's history in the northeastern borderlands, assuming it an inferior product. Chris Jensen rightly points out that only seventy-five players from Maine went on to play major league ball, and most of those played during or before the dead ball era.[5] Another observer suggests that Maine has had a "dubious" baseball history, mistakenly adding that the Portland Pilots of 1946 and 1947 were the only teams from the state ever to play Organized Baseball. Although it is unwise to overestimate the quality of baseball at that time, it is also important to appreciate the unique context in which baseball developed in the northeastern borderlands, in fact along the entire Canadian-American border. Weather constraints meant that baseball often began late in the spring, usually not before the end of May in Nova Scotia and New Brunswick. Because of that, college prospects already in good shape after spring baseball were available at just the right time. The downside of relying on collegians, however, was that teams often lost them at the end of August as they returned to school and the opening of football season. This meant that for most clubs in the northeast there was a three-month window available for competitive baseball. Affiliation with Organized Baseball was an alternative, but this would mean an end to college players. Together, the "college conundrum" and the absence of large urban centers meant there was little incentive to affiliate with baseball's minor league system. Mixing local players and collegians with veteran players who were no longer considered major league prospects—but still good ball players—was a sensible strategy.

This situation was replicated in other borderland regions across the continent. While a comprehensive analysis of Canadian-American borderland baseball has yet to be written, the most competitive semipro leagues outside of Organized Baseball—the Vermont Northern League, the Halifax and District League, the Maine–New

Brunswick League, the Provincial League in Quebec, Ontario's Intercounty League, the Man-Dak League and the Basin League—all straddled the Canadian-American border. For those interested in this history there are sites such as Jay Del Mah's attheplate.com and Christian Trudeau's Provincial League website https://sites.google.com/view/ligueprovinciale/home that offer detailed information about borderlands baseball in the west and Quebec. A. Galley's Maritime Pro Ball blog maritimebaseball.wordpress.com does the same for baseball on the east coast. Surprisingly, little attention has been given to the history of Ontario's Intercounty League, the longest continuing independent baseball league in Canada.

This is not to say that baseball along the Canadian-American border was completely disconnected from Organized Baseball in the postwar period. Three professional leagues operated with teams on both sides of the border in the late forties. Two Class C circuits, the Can-Am League (1936–51) and the Border League (1946–51), provided opportunities for players from the northeast to play professional baseball. Their demise along with that of the Vermont League at the beginning of the fifties enhanced the reputation of both the H&D League and the Maine–New Brunswick League. The Pony League, a class D league with teams in Pennsylvania, Ontario and New York continued to operate until 1956, with franchises affiliated with the Dodgers, Athletics, Phillies, Tigers, Cardinals and Braves, all of which considered the H&D League and the New Brunswick League a breeding ground for college prospects. The Boston Red Sox often started their young prospects at Oneonta, and the Yankees sent young hopefuls to Amsterdam of the Can-Am League. Fewer players from the Maritimes ended up in the Border League, except for a few veterans of the Halifax Defense League. The 1946 Kingston Ponies had five players with wartime connections to Nova Scotia: NHL hockey star George Gee, Niagara Falls native Jimmy Heximer, pitcher Stan Stenoff, first baseman and Halifax native "Red" Kane, and outfielder Joe Lay, who played two years in Kingston before hitting over .300 with Granby of the Provincial League in 1948. Lay returned to the H&D League after that.

In the immediate postwar years, the Vermont Northern and Provincial Leagues were more competitive than those in New Brunswick and Maine. Although the Northern League operated for six seasons before the war, it re-emerged in 1946 and lasted for another five years. Burlington, Montpelier, St. Albans, Rutland, Brattleboro, Bennington, and St. Johnsbury in Vermont; Tupper Lake, Plattsburgh, Saranac Lake, and Malone in New York; Claremont and Keene in New Hampshire; and Farnham, Quebec, all competed at some point. The Northern League's most recognizable postwar alumni included future big-leaguers Robin Roberts, Johnny Podres, Harry Agganis, Johnny Antonelli, Joey Jay, Ted Lepcio, Billy Loes, and Chuck Stobbs.

As we have seen, many Northern Leaguers would also end up playing in the Maritimes and Maine. Agganis and Lepcio were members of the Augusta Millionaires' prospect-laden roster in 1949. Turk Farrell ended up in Burlington in 1952 after being released by the Halifax Capitals. Former Middleton Cardinal "Sonny" Senerchia went to the Northern League in 1950 before graduating to the Pittsburgh Pirates in 1952. Many of those who played with the Keene, New Hampshire, Blue Jays, including Johnny Watterson, Hal Burby, Emil Krupa, Socrates "Soc" Bobotas, and Bill Brooks had lengthy careers in the H&D League. As many as sixty players moved back and forth between the Northern League and teams in Maine and the Maritimes during the late forties. In addition, Jake Kline, Ray Fisher, Doc Gautreau, Stuffy McInnis, Freddy Maguire, Don Maynard, Archie Allen, Bill Lefebvre and Stan Benjamin managed teams in the Northern League and would serve in the same capacity north of the border.

One notable player to move back and forth between the H&D League and the Northern League was Bruce Blount, a six-foot-three right-hander who came to the H&D League Wildcats in 1947. Blount was a basketball and baseball legend at the University of Rhode Island. Captain of both varsity squads in Providence, the young natural athlete was courted by most NBA and major league teams. Blount chose not return to Kentville for the 1948 season, however, and went instead to Burlington in Northern League. Blount was bucking a trend, since many Northern Leaguers were heading north at the time, worried that their college eligibility would be in jeopardy if they continued to play in Vermont. Three college stars from the Northern League Montpelier club, Jack Kaiser, Jim Arbucho, and Art Raynor, joined the 1948 Wildcats as Blount headed south.

After his college graduation Blount spurned offers to play in the minor leagues and chose a quite different career path. He joined the Army and eventually rose to the rank of lieutenant general. One of the highlights of his military career came early. During the Army-McCarthy hearings of the early 1950s Blount gained nationwide notoriety when he revealed that the anti–Communist "Senator Joe" had doctored photographic evidence to suggest Communist infiltration of the military. Blount's intervention was largely responsible for bringing the hearings to a close. Commenting upon Blount's appearance before the committee, Bob Kennedy of the *Portsmouth Herald* thought that Blount might possibly follow an athletic career. "Blount is major league timber and, if he does get out of the army, half a dozen scouts have been on his trail for some time."[6] Blount was committed to his Army career, however, and never gave baseball a second thought.

Gardner, Massachusetts, native Al Norskey was another player who spent time in both the Northern League and the H&D League. A standout quarterback in football and basketball player in high school, Norskey was chosen to play first base in the 1947 New England Hearst Foundation All-Star baseball game opposite future Red Sox star Harry Agganis. After two years at the University of Massachusetts, Norskey was signed by Yankees scout Ray Manarel, who sent him to the Northern League Keene Blue Jays. Since Johnny Watterson and other H&D Leaguers played at the beginning and end of the baseball season, Norskey was aware of the baseball scene north of the border. In 1949 the Yankees sent him to Class B Norfolk along with another blue-chip prospect, Bill "Moose" Skowron, and Norskey found himself shifted to third base.[7] Realizing that Skowron would always be ahead of him on the Yankees depth chart, and with the Northern League teetering on collapse, Norskey decided to concentrate on summer baseball in Nova Scotia after that, playing for four years with the Truro Bearcats. After his baseball career ended, he returned to Gardner and began a dental practice in 1958. I had the pleasure of spending a day with Hal and his wife at their home while doing interviews for an earlier book.

By 1950 the Northern League was in crisis and did not operate during the 1951 season. When the league re-emerged for a final time in 1952, it was no longer the preeminent summer league that it had been immediately after the war. Philadelphia Phillies scout Tom Flemming, for example, was dismissive of the league's decision to cap monthly salaries at $250, pointing out that players in Maine and New Brunswick were being paid considerably more. Flemming noted that he had sent Phillies prospect Moon Mullin to Saint John instead and was aware of the higher salaries that Ray Fisher's Blacks Harbour club were receiving as well.[8] In Nova Scotia, H&D League salaries were even higher than those in Maine or New Brunswick. The strategy of many Nova Scotian teams was to allow younger prospects to play a season in the Maine–New Brunswick League. If they performed to expectations, clubs would then bring them to Nova Scotia after that. This was the case with future bonus baby Tommy Gastall, who played a year in Presque Isle and then three years with the Liverpool Larrupers, and also with First-Team All-American Don Prohovich, who went to Edmundston in 1952 before three subsequent years with the H&D League Kentville Wildcats. Two future major leaguers who started their summer stints in the New Brunswick-Maine League before ending up in Nova Scotia were pitchers Dave Stenhouse and Ralph Lumenti.

Of course, teams in Nova Scotia had imported and paid players during the war and continued to pay top-drawer salaries equivalent to those at AA and AAA within Organized Baseball after that, but in Maine and New Brunswick the movement to paid players developed haltingly. It was not until 1949 that clubs in the Aroostook League began paying players. Instead, the Presque Isle Indians, Houlton Collegians, and teams in Bangor and Lewiston relied on local college stars willing to play for expense money. Colby College, Ricker College, Bowdoin College, Bates College, and the University of Maine all had solid baseball programs and competed against teams throughout the east, so this was a bargain for most town clubs like the Houlton Collegians of the Maine–New Brunswick League. But as players came from elsewhere in New England and from New York and Pennsylvania, there was a push toward paying imports. In 1949 six players on the Presque Isle roster received salaries, but all of the local players were unpaid except for playing coach Jim Dyer.[9] Fort Fairfield led the movement toward paid players that year with a weekly payroll of $760, but not all clubs were happy with this trend. The Houlton *Pioneer Times* reported at one point that a Caribou newspaper thought that Presque Isle and Fort Fairfield were ruining Aroostook County baseball by paying generous salaries.[10]

Veteran players with experience in the minor leagues expected compensation. One of the best Maine natives to play in the immediate postwar period was Hal Cheney, a star with Presque Isle in the thirties who entered the Red Sox organization in 1938 and went 6–5 with Hazleton of the Class A Eastern league. His best year was 1941 when he went 13–7 with a 2.77 ERA with Hagerstown in the Detroit organization, but war brought a premature end to his minor league career. As a member of the Aroostook All Stars, Cheney had pitched effectively in exhibition tilts against the Red Sox and Braves in 1935, and the following year went 12–2 for Presque Isle, the only two losses coming against the St. Stephen Kiwanis. He would receive compensation on a game-to-game basis after the war and was still effective in the postwar years.

One of the earliest teams along the border to go the pay-for-play route was the tiny sardine-canning community of Blacks Harbour, New Brunswick. The Brunswicks competed both in the St. Croix League and against teams in the Northern Aroostook League after the war, and they played a number of exhibition games against the Houlton Collegians, Fort Fairfield Flyers and Augusta Millionaires. The team recruited a mixture of collegians from Maine, New Hampshire, and Massachusetts. An exception was George Toepfer, a New Yorker who spent two seasons with the Brunswicks before signing with the Red Sox. Others came from around the Maritimes. Scott Harvey, who had played a number of years with Saint John, and St. Stephen outfielder Gordie Eastman were well known on both sides of the border. Third baseman Eddie Surette, with roots in the Acadian shore region of Nova Scotia as well as in Boston, was one of its early stars, as was fellow Acadian Lou Moulaison, who played a number of years in the H&D League. Surette hit well over .300 in a couple of seasons with the Brunswicks in 1948 and 1949. Ed Dobbins, an American from Woburn, Massachusetts, with three years' experience in the Braves system, arrived the following year and ended up living in Blacks Harbour for the rest of his life.

Blacks Harbour provides an interesting example of the shifting connections and sports alliances of clubs along the border. Sometimes the Brunswicks focused on linkages with Maine, at other times with teams in the interior of New Brunswick, and occasionally played teams from Nova Scotia. In 1949 and 1950 it played in the New Brunswick League, and its roster included two future major league catchers: Mike Roarke and Hal Smith. In 1951—the first year of Ray Fisher's three-year stint as Blacks Harbour's manager—the Brunswicks competed in the Southern New Brunswick League, which also included Nova Scotia's Springhill Fencebusters. For the third time in three years, another future major league catcher, Charley Lau, was behind the plate. The Brunswicks played for two more years before reorganizing after the 1953 season.

Although Blacks Harbour followed other New Brunswick border towns in seeking out competition in Maine, teams from elsewhere in the Maritimes sought out prospects further afield in Massachusetts, Pennsylvania, and New York to help them in their quests for the provincial and Maritime championships. In Moncton, two Springfield College products, Ed Juszcyk and Ed Steitz, were the first imports to arrive. Juszcyk, who had already played three years of minor league ball during the war, had been reinstated as an amateur, enrolled at Springfield and played in the Northern League for a couple of years. Steitz, a multi-sport athlete with little interest in a professional baseball career, completed his PhD at Springfield in 1948 and joined the college's physical education faculty, where he served as assistant baseball coach to Archie Allen. Steitz's primary interest was basketball. An important figure in the development of the game internationally, Steitz was enshrined in the Basketball Hall of Fame in 1984 and in the FIBA Hall of Fame in 2007. In 1948 a dozen or more players from Springfield and Amherst College ended up in New Brunswick where they suited up against local players from the province and Maine. Shortstop Lou Giammarino, who had played with the semipro Springfield Rifles, and pitchers Charles "Bud" Hagen and Medo Rios ended up in Saint John.

That same year, a dozen players from nearby Amherst College—twenty miles from Springfield—arrived to play in Nova Scotia's Central League and on occasion travelled to Moncton to face off against Steitz and the Moncton Cubs. Stuffy McInnis managed the Stellarton Albions that year and was still the head coach at Amherst before taking over at Harvard in 1949. Ivan Rosendale, Don MacNeish, Bob Butters, Richard Orcutt, John Lacy and Don Delpierre accompanied McInnis to Stellarton, but they failed to impress local fans and did not return to the Maritimes in 1949.

Over the years, more than forty players from Springfield and Amherst joined the parade to the Maritimes, among them the widely acclaimed Hank Tominaga, who spent the 1951 season in Blacks Harbour and another season with the Kentville Wildcats. The best prospect to come out of Hawaii in the postwar period, Tominaga first hit the headlines as a teenager in the Brooklyn versus the World Classic in 1946. In 1950 Tominaga went to Springfield to work on a degree in physical education and played on the frosh team. The following year he was the main reason that Springfield advanced to the final NCAA championship series. In his debut against American International he walked the first batter he faced before retiring the next twenty-seven for a no-hitter and 2–0 shutout victory! "Tominaga has a world of slow stuff and is one of the smartest southpaws I've seen in the college ranks," said his coach, Archie Allen. Although I was only nine years old at the time, I vividly remember hanging around the visiting dugout in Kentville and hearing Bill Brooks, the coach of the Stellarton Albions, complain that they were facing Tominaga. "It will be slow stuff all afternoon," Brooks mused. "I don't know how he gets us out, but he does!" When Springfield went to Omaha and finished in fifth place, Allen warned major league scouts to "lay off" of the young Hawaiian. Like many talented players of the day, he had another career in mind. He was determined to go back to Hawaii when he graduated to head up the island's physical education and recreation system and coach baseball whenever he could.

The Maine–New Brunswick League: 1950–55

Of all the summer leagues operating in New Brunswick and Maine in the 1950s, none was more committed to importing players than the Maine–New Brunswick League, which fielded import-studded lineups through 1955. At first, American teams in the Maine–New Brunswick circuit relied heavily on college players from Maine, while those on the Canadian side of the border cast a wider net. Four teams, Presque Isle, Houlton, Grand Falls and Edmundston, provided a solid operating base for the league, although at various times Fredericton, the air base at Presque Isle and Loring AFB joined for a season or two. After 1955 the league became a local operation for the most part, although occasionally there were teams like the Presque Isles Indians with collegians from around the state. It is fair to say that no other league in the Maritimes, except for the H&D League, offered up such an array of classy ballplayers in the early fifties.

The league began the new decade drawing heavily on collegians from the University of Maine, Colby College, Bowdoin College, Ricker College and Bates College. There was a solid pool of veteran position players available to complement the youngsters. Outfielder Jim Dyer, an erstwhile member of the U.S. national team who hit .300 year in and year out, was a perennial all-star; shortstop Pat Proulx from Waterville had played a couple of years of pro ball in Texas and anchored the Presque Isle Indians; Johnny Catallo, a five-year veteran of in the minor leagues, won the batting title in 1951 with a .345 average and thirteen home runs with Edmundston; and power-hitting Dick Cormier bounced back and forth between Houlton and Fort Fairfield, the latter a powerful team like the Augusta Millionaires and the equal of the Maine–New Brunswick league aggregations. Cormier had a brief stint in the H&D League as well. In 1949 he showed his slugging ability by winning a home run derby against members of the Birdie Tebbetts All-Stars before the visitors knocked off the locals 10–5 at the Northern Maine Fairgrounds. Vinal "Red" Russell, Cormier's teammate from the Fort Fairfield Wanderers, pitched four scoreless innings that day, giving up just one hit, a single by Johnny Pesky. University of Maine student Ralph Clark was a mainstay at third base with Fort Fairfield in 1949, and catcher George Wales won the Aroostook League batting title with Houlton, contributing thirteen round trippers. At Colby College, Wales shared catcher duties with Norm White, who played in the H&D League. Other notables, George Alusik, Mike Roarke and Dick Tettelbach—all of whom went on the major leagues—spent time in New Brunswick and Maine. Roarke was a student at both Bates College and Boston College. Alusik, a high school phenom from Woodbridge, New Jersey, played for Saint John of the New Brunswick League. After a season with Fort Fairfield in 1949, Tettlebach went to Rutland of the Vermont League in 1950. A Yale graduate, Tettelbach signed with the Yankees the following year and rose quickly through their minor league system before breaking into the majors in 1955.

Eight. Borderlands Baseball

There was a surfeit of pitching talent in Maine at that time, including those who flitted back and forth between the minor leagues and local clubs as their semipro seasons ended. Big Dick England, a lanky, hard-throwing right-hander already ensconced in the Phillies minor-league organization with Class B Wilmington, was one of those available in the late summer for playoff-bound teams. Just a week after Cherryfield native Carlton Willey signed a contract with the Boston Braves in September 1950, for example, England was called upon to fill the gap in the Bangor News Braves roster. Since the New England League had folded at the end of the 1949 season, moreover, crafty veteran Ed Hadlock was also available despite spending his summers in Nova Scotia and Quebec. Hadlock played four seasons with Liverpool of the H&D League between 1951 and 1956 but would return to Maine each September ready to fill in when called upon. Ad Norwood, another young prospect, signed a Red Sox contract in 1950 but returned to Maine a few years later after his two-year military hitch ended. He pitched occasionally for town teams before resuming his minor league career in 1954. And finally, Stan Coulling, an eight-year minor league veteran, played in Maine and the H&D League in the early fifties as his career wound down.

These veteran players complemented the many standouts from Maine's collegiate ranks in the league's initial years of operation. Colby College's Jimmy Keefe had an excellent year in 1950 with Houlton, and local boy Bob St. Pierre was named the league MVP with Presque Isle in 1951. Mac Andrews from Colby, Andy McAuliffe from Bates, and fire-balling Jim DiFrederico, an all-star in the Eastern Maine League in 1949 who spent five years in the Red Sox organization after starring with Houlton and Augusta, were standouts. McAuliffe, Coulling, DiFrederico and Norwood all played at some point in the H&D League. In addition, Roger Clapp from Milo, Maine, spent a season in Nova Scotia's South Shore League auditioning for a spot on the Liverpool Larrupers' pitching staff. Clapp went on to a nine-year minor league career which ended in 1963 with the AAA Toronto Maple Leafs of the International League.

The first year of operation for the Maine–New Brunswick League was successful, particularly for the Presque Isle Indians, who edged Edmundston for the league pennant and knocked off Grand Falls to win the playoff series. The champs had three players from Colby, one from Bates, two from the University of Maine and one each from Boston University and the University of Virginia. Don Rafford (.367), George Wales (.329), Johnny Moore (.316), Archie Armstrong (.310), and Pat Proulx (.308), all from the league champs, finished in the top ten in the batting race, and Jimmy Keefe led pitchers with a 9–2 record while sharing the mound in Houlton with young Andy McAuliffe. Slugging outfielder Gerry Duffy of Houlton captured the batting crown with a .390 average and hit seven homers in only 100 at-bats. Shortstop Ralph Manfridi (.307) and outfielder Johnny Catallo (.296) led the Edmundston Republicans at the plate. The Republicans drew heavily on players from Temple University and elsewhere in Pennsylvania. Saint John native Jimmy Fox, the old Red Sox farmhand with experience in the Quebec Provincial League, led Grand Falls with a .297 average, and fellow New Brunswicker Johnny Harvey anchored the mound staff.[11]

While teams operated for the most part with players from Maine and New Brunswick, the league expanded its horizons in 1951. The addition of the Fredericton Capitols created a five-team league. There was a notable uptick in the standard of play that year, as major league organizations sent young prospects northward. Boston University catcher and future bonus baby Tommy Gastall signed with Presque Isle. Shortstop Francis McElroy, who would go on to AAA in the Tigers organization, ended up in Grand Falls, and slugging first baseman and catcher Syd Goldfader joined a star-studded Fredericton Capitols lineup that included future First Team All-American Fred "Moose" Flemming, veteran pro Johnny Boston from Tufts University, and Detroit Tigers prospect Dick Bentfield. Fredericton also recruited National Hockey League veteran Roly McLenahan, arguably the best ballplayer in New Brunswick at the time. McLenahan finished the season hitting .416 but fell short of the batting title requirement of 100 at-bats. Catcher Don Johnson, a Fredericton native and veteran of the baseball wars in the province for years, was a workhorse, hitting .293 in more than 200 at-bats while handling a veteran pitching staff. Former St. Louis Cardinals farmhand Johnny Catallo was back with Edmundston for a second season and served as the Republicans' playing coach.

Elsewhere in the Maritimes, the 1951 season witnessed new connections involving Michigan and the Carolinas. With the Vermont Northern League shutting down, Ray Fisher took the core of his Michigan Wolverines squad to Blacks Harbour of the Southern New Brunswick League. In Nova Scotia, players from Wake Forest and the University of North Carolina ended up following Bill Brooks and Art Hoch to Stellarton. The Carolinian connection strengthened in 1952 as players from the Duke Blue Devils, Bill Werber, Gordon Clapp, Al Spangler, Stu Erickson, and Footer Johnson, made the H&D League their summer home. Duke also sent players to the Maine–New Brunswick League for the 1952 summer season. Big Joe Lewis signed with Edmundston which had a working arrangement with the Brooklyn Dodgers and was the league all-star right-hander. He had suited up with Blacks Harbour they year before as had his Duke battery mate Jake Tarr. Bill Cary and Dick Miller gave Lewis solid support in Edmundston's rotation. Maine native Dick Black from Lewiston turned in a solid season and turned out to be the Presque Isle Indians' most solid starter. Ricker College student Bill Wing and Yale's Bob Davis were standouts for Houlton, and Dave Stenhouse, Bob St. Pierre and Joe Dunn anchored the Grand Falls rotation. In general, the quality of pitching was higher than in previous years.

Outfielder Andy McGowan, a New Yorker, won the league's MVP award in 1952 with a .343 batting average, as players from outside of New England increasingly infiltrated league rosters. A Maine–New Brunswick League All-Star squad selected by the *Bangor News* included the following players; many of them came from New York and New Jersey. Jersey boy Charles Schaffernoth, whose brother spent three years with the Chicago Cubs, won league honors, but Arlan Barber, a young Maine resident who spent three seasons with Presque Isle before entering the Cardinals' minor league system in 1955, was also in the mix. Bowdoin College star Jack Cosgrove was at first base, Presque Isle's Harry Hewes at second, Brooklyn native Vince Vane was the shortstop, and New Yorker Bob Webber was the third baseman. Sherm Kinney and Buzz Barry flanked McGowan in the outfield. Other notables, Holy Cross shortstop Don Prohovich and Springfield College outfielder Alvin Griggs, played in Edmundston that year before heading to the H&D League for the 1953 season. Webber went east to join the Liverpool Larrupers, Kinney and Vane went to the Class C Provincial League, McGowan went to Macon in the Sally League, and Schaffernoth went to the Wisconsin Rapids of the Wisconsin State League.

In 1953 catcher Jack Kurty won the Maine–New Brunswick League's most valuable player award, nosing out second baseman Grover "Deacon" Jones for the batting title. A standout at Penn State, Kurty played two earlier summers with Stellarton and Kentville in the H&D League before heading to Presque Isle as player coach. A recent inductee into the Maritime Sports Hall of Fame, Kurty won a second straight league batting crown in 1954. With Ray Fisher no longer at the helm in Blacks Harbour, the Brunswicks now turned to younger prospects from Massachusetts, signing four members of the 1953 Milford High School state champions in 1953: future Washington senator Ralph Lumenti, pitcher Bob Stoico, shortstop Bob Pagnini, outfielder Ed Ryan, and Dick Grant. Lumenti and Stoico were considered the best high school pitchers of the decade in Massachusetts and played a number of years in the Maritimes. Dick Grant, the "most talked about Maine high-schooler of the year" in 1954, had a good year with Edmundston, signed a contract with the White Sox and played seven years in the minor leagues.

The 1955 season began on an optimistic note with six teams ready to compete in the cross-border circuit, much to the delight of local sportswriters. "Haunted by major league scouts ... the loop is rated on a par with ... Class B circuits and has had its share of bonus babies," said one proud columnist, predicting a banner year for the league. In addition to Houlton, Presque Isle, Grand Falls and Edmundston, two military squads, Loring AFB and Presque Isle AFB, signed up for league play. Paced by hard-throwing future major leaguer Earl Francis, who racked up 81 strikeouts in just 58 innings pitched, Loring made it through the season despite being outclassed by clubs dominated by college prospects. Presque Isle AFB soon tired of losing one-sided matches and threw in the towel in mid-season, however. When the Houlton Collegians also folded in August, apparently facing mounting financial deficits, the league limped home with only four teams. The dismantling of Houlton that season and the club's subsequent decision not to operate in 1956 dealt the league a fatal blow. With only three teams willing to operate, the Maine–New Brunswick League was reorganized on an independent basis.

Despite having fallen on hard times in 1955, the cross-border circuit had an impressive array of talent in that final year. Future major leaguer Angelo Dagres, outfielder Dave Sime, and first-team All-American Bud Getchell finished one-two-three in the batting race. For the most part, pitching dominated. Norwalk, Maine, native Bill Thurston led the pitching parade with a 1.27 ERA, followed closely by Larry Bossidy and future New York Yankee Bill Kunkel, both of whom gave up less than two earned runs per game. Warren Hodgdon, Charles Seymour, Ralph Lumenti and Ron Perranoski also finished in the top ten. All of them had major league arms. This was Bossidy's third different summer league in a row, having played earlier in southern Minnesota and in Quebec's Laurentide League. In addition to Thurston and Perranoski, Edmundston's five-man staff also included Leo Gillis, Eugene Maier and Charles Symeon. Pitching was a problem for Houlton, but young Warren Hodgdon nonetheless had a good season. Subsequently signed to a contract by the Boston Red Sox, Hodgdon spent five seasons in the minor leagues.

Ron Staples, another Maine native already on Boston Red Sox radar, didn't sign a pro contract until 1958. Instead, he took the advice of the Bosox and joined Kentville for the 1957 season, where he joined two other Maine natives, first-team All-American Neil Stinneford and Bob Flynn of Lewiston. Flynn had already spent five seasons with Pittsburgh, and Staples would subsequently put in four years in the Red Sox organization. After his year in the H&D League, he was sent by the Red

Sox to play for former H&D League star Jack Kaiser in the Nebraska State League. A number of other prospects who played that final season in the Maine–New England League sought future summer opportunities in the H&D League. Pitcher Jim Farino, catcher Ed Czerniakowski, and outfielders Charlie Mellen and Al Fantuzzi all joined the Halifax Citadels in 1956. Outfielder George McCafferty and pitcher Charlie Symeon signed with Truro. Clearly, the H&D League now had its pick of the most talented players from Maine.

With the future of the Maine–New Brunswick League in doubt, John Winkin, coach at Colby College and future baseball icon at the University of Maine, reflected on what he considered the decline of competitive community baseball across the state. A decade earlier, he recalled, baseball in Maine was flourishing. "I can remember when I was in college [at Duke]," he told *Bangor Daily News* columnist Owen Osborne. "Everyone talked of playing summer baseball in Maine. Now they go to Wisconsin, Minnesota, or Canada. That league in eastern Canada [the H&D League] is a fine one." When Osborne pointed out that the Maine–New Brunswick League was "the last of the good circuits left in New England," Winkin agreed that "it certainly is," but there was an unspoken assumption that Maine was a second choice for many future prospects to playing in Nova Scotia, and this became obvious when the five-year experiment with the import model in the Maine–New Brunswick League came to an end.[12]

Five years earlier, baseball was flourishing. Teams like the Auburn Asas, the Augusta Millionaires, the Fort Fairfield Indians, the Farmington Flyers, and those on the Canadian side of the border were the equals of the best semipro teams in greater New England and the Maritimes. In 1949, for example, Farmington defeated the touring Kokomo Clowns, the Boston Colored Giants, the Boston Hoboes, the Original House of David, and the Santurce All-Stars, and had victories over New Brunswick's Fredericton Capitols, Grand Falls Cataracts and Marysville Royals. Augusta had future major leaguers Haywood Sullivan, Harry Agganis and Ted Lepcio on the roster that year along with a number of future pros like Larry DiPippo and Billy Porter. Fort Fairfield was led by Dick Tettlebach from Yale, who later played parts of three seasons with the Yankees and Washington Senators. The four-team Maine–New Brunswick League was a vestige of that earlier era; only the H&D League would continue to operate at that elevated level in the late fifties. As we shall see, however, the H&D League shrank from six teams to four in 1957 and eventually succumbed to the same perils that had already led to the contraction of minor league and small-town baseball across all of North America.

Nine

Troublesome Times
1955–57

In many ways the half-dozen seasons from 1949 to 1954 were the glory days of the import era. Nurtured by the Carolinian connection and NCAA stars from high-profile college programs, baseball became summer's staple on small town diamonds across the region. Yet, while the product on the field was top drawer, small-town baseball remained a financial crapshoot. Clubs struggled to meet payrolls rising with the expectations of local fans awaiting the new crop of young major league prospects every year. Looking back, it is easy to see the perils of a process that saw talented local players, so instrumental in the earlier growth of the game, pushed to the sidelines. Locals were increasingly taken for granted, often employed at the beginning of the season as placeholders for players arriving from the United States or at playoff time when collegians hurried back to campus in time for fall football practice.

Although some observers continued to concentrate on the exploits of local players, they were in a sense swimming against the tide. Most were infatuated by young Americans arriving in town at the beginning of the season, brimming with sophistication and self-confidence and stylishly adorned in khaki pants, buttoned-down collars, and sleeves with side pockets. Growing up in a house that was often a meeting place for visiting players, Brian Pulsifer became attached to many of them. Like me, Brian followed the currents of popular music, carefully recording the top ten songs of the week on television's *Hit Parade* in a neatly columned scrapbook. At one point when he and his family ventured off to Boston for a few weeks of vacation, he asked Jack McGowan, a young outfielder and third baseman from Trinity College boarding with them at the time, to carry on the project. "McGowan was a cool guy," Brian remembers, and no doubt enjoyed having the home all to himself since he was dating a local girl at the time. McGowan played three years in the H&D League before signing a minor league contract with the Baltimore Orioles.

There were many summer romances, of course. According to Jeannette Leblanc, who grew up in Grand Falls and followed the local Cataracts, the American boys seemed "so good-looking" and intriguing. Now and then, as was the case with the daughter of a local hotel operator, Gemma Leblanc, and a young second baseman from the States named "Buzz" Barry, the end result was marriage. Buzz and Gemma were not alone. Sil Cerchie, a young Italian American who billeted at the Pulsifer home in 1956—the "older brother I never had" (according to Brian Pulsifer) and one of the few players to have his own car—met and married local girl Annette Longmire. Another Wildcat, New Hampshire, native, Chris Tonery, did the same, tying the knot with Kentville's Doris Aymer. Cerchie and Tonery each played multiple seasons with the Wildcats and played together as well on the 1952 Penn State Nittany Lions club that went to the final eight of the NCAA championship. Penn State's roster also included Jack Kurty, Joe Ruyak, Carmen Troisi and eventual All-American Ronnie Weidenhammer, all of whom played in Kentville at one point in their careers.

Two Stellarton Albion stars, Joe Fulghum and Meredith "Moe" Morhardt, also found soulmates while playing for the Pictou County club. Veteran sportswriter Hugh Townshend sometimes writes about these boy-meets-girl stories in his columns in the Pictou *Advocate*. Fulghum and his sweetheart Helen Murray tied the knot at home plate before a home crowd and right after leading his club to victory. Joe recalled hitting two home-runs that day, one against his opponents and the second when Helen said, "I do." Morhardt met Georgie Cochrane at an IOOC dance in New Glasgow and employed a similar baseball allusion. "There was a dance going on, and I noticed a girl in a black dress, dancing with practically everybody in sight. She seemed to know everybody in the place," said Moe. "It was a pretty good day all around. I had three hits and two walks in the game and we won in the last of the ninth inning." The couple were married at the Kirk Church in New Glasgow in October 1959 and have lived happily for more than sixty years.[1]

Financing the Import Model

Despite the fascination that Maritimers had with the young boys coming north, adherence to the import model brought continuing fiscal challenges, even in earlier years. In 1949, for example, Kentville's import-laden championship club in the Central League ran into financial difficulty. More imports and fewer local players meant a ballooning salary budget. Midway through the season, the club suspended radio broadcasts of its games to save money, but it still ended up $4,000 in the hole. The other mainland finalist that year, the Dartmouth Arrows, lost $2,000 on its operations.[2] Winning championships did not guarantee making money! Stellarton's deficit was slightly more than $3,000 even after various fundraising dances, bingos and lotteries. In search of more stability, the Albions introduced a check-off system that enabled miners to have a portion of weekly wages deducted in return for access to games without an admittance charge. Problems continued in 1950 when Truro temporarily suspended operations in mid-season, unable to meet a payroll that paid some players as much as $150 per week. Halifax journalist Ace Foley summed up the financial situation: "For the majority of clubs which compete in the H&D League, baseball will always be a losing venture, much like major hockey," he wrote. He predicted that only Kentville and Stellarton would finish the 1951 season with a surplus. The clubs losing big money would be Halifax, Dartmouth, Truro and Liverpool in that order.[3]

Over the years, I searched for records that would give a more precise rendering of the financial status of the various teams around the Maritimes. The only relatively complete set was for the Stellarton Albions from 1951 through 1958, which allows a relatively clear indication of the declining fortunes of the league over time. Ace Foley was right. The 1951 Albions ended up in good financial shape after drawing over 46,000 fans that summer. Regular season crowds averaged 1,400 per game and 2,500 during the playoffs. There was a slight drop-off in season attendance to about 40,000 over the next two years. What the records clearly show, however, was the importance of qualifying for the post-season playoffs. Making it to the final playoff round often meant the difference between breaking even or making an occasional modest profit versus incurring substantial losses that left clubs vulnerable as they faced the future.

Table 1. Stellarton Albions Home Attendance, 1951–1958

Year	Attendance	Average	Playoffs	Average	Total	Average
1951	30,974	1,100	15,516	2,217	46,310	1,323
1952	32,719	1,169	11,575	2,315	44,294	1,342
1953	24,535	909	15,309	2,552	39,844	1,207
1954	24,840	857	5,403	1,801	30,243	945
1955	14,742	567	None	None	14,742	567
1956	16,364	584	3,760	1,253	20,124	649

Year	Attendance	Average	Playoffs	Average	Total	Average
1957	12,520	522	2,939	734	15,459	552
1958	10,569	460	1,429	715	11,998	480

Source: Stellarton Albions' Financial Records (1951–1958)

Monk Raines and John Waselchuk: Stellarton's Savior Strategy

During the 1953 season it had become clear to Stellarton's management that not going deep into the playoffs would lead to a substantial deficit. The solution was to search for an impact player before the July 15 deadline who could lead them into the playoffs. Well-versed in the Southern baseball scene, Bill Brooks turned to a rubber-armed pitcher with a dominant record in the Carolinas named John "Monk" Raines. The year before, Raines had been a twenty-six game winner for Edenton in the Coastal Plains League, putting up a sparkling 2.05 earned run average over 268 innings pitched. His great season attracted attention from a number of organizations, including the Braves who invited him to spring training where he made appearances against the New York Yankees and Chicago White Sox. He was then assigned to Double-A Atlanta along with eighteen pitchers vying for jobs but won a starting role. After a half-dozen appearances, however, Raines asked for permission to return home for the birth of his first child. When his request was denied, he broke a cardinal rule in professional baseball and jumped the club. This was an age when owners held the strongest hand, and defiance of their rules was not tolerated. The Braves decided to set an example of Raines to other young players and sent him back to Edenton. Since the Edenton club had folded at the beginning of the season, however, he became a free agent. Enter the Albions, who offered Raines $600 a month to come to Stellarton, considerably more than he was making, and he was quick to agree.[4]

The signing of Raines was a big gamble for a number of reasons, not the least of which was that his salary was 50 percent higher than the rest of the players. Had he not lived up to expectations, his teammates would have been upset. Even if he performed well, others would expect to be better compensated in the future. Fortunately, Raines became a team leader down the stretch, winning four games in five decisions and continued to pitch well in the playoffs. The Als captured the fourth and final playoff spot. Raines was especially brilliant in the playoffs as Stellarton knocked off regular-season pennant winner Liverpool in the first round and Kentville in the final series. Bobby Lee Brown, a Wake Forest star who would go on to pitch in Double-A, and UNC stalwart Tom Harkey also contributed to the championship run.

In 1954 the Albions again faced the prospect of missing the playoffs and searched once again for a late season savior. The choice was six-year minor league veteran John Waselchuk, who had pitched for Macon of the Sally League for two seasons. Only five-foot-eight and 150 pounds, the twenty-six-year-old right-hander had a serviceable fastball, but according to Hank Aaron, his curveball was the best in the Sally League. A bulldog on the mound, Waselchuk never shied away from throwing inside in order to set up the curveball. On one occasion in the highly-charged racial environment in Georgia, he threw close to the head of future Braves infielder Felix Mantilla, and a bench-clearing brawl ensued. Waselchuk maintained that he was just throwing the pitches that his catcher was calling: Mantilla thought otherwise.[5]

To entice Waselchuck to leave pro ball, the Albions coughed up $700 monthly, and the upward pressure on the salary budget continued. Raines still hauled down $600 per month salary as he did the year before, and coaches Brooks and Edwards were both well paid. Of course, the Albions were gambling that the extra arm would get them into the final playoff series and that the increases in playoff gate receipts would cover the hefty salary load. Unfortunately, the Raines-Waselchuk combo didn't have the same magical results that Bobby Lee Brown and Raines had manufactured the year before. With player costs significantly higher for the 1954 season and attendance dropping by almost 10,000, the club ended up losing more than $10,000 and faced an uncertain future going forward.[6]

The significant losses run up by the Albions and the upward pressure on salaries caused great concern around the league. Although Halifax put a terrific ball club on the field in 1954, attendance was spotty and its accumulated debt doubled. Liverpool was down a bit at the gate despite making it to the playoffs. What made matters worse was that Halifax, Dartmouth and Kentville all had installed lights, hoping to attract larger crowds with later start times. At season's end, the *Chronicle Herald* reported that all six clubs had lost money: Kentville ($11,000) Halifax ($10,000), Dartmouth ($6,500) Liverpool ($6,000), Stellarton ($5,000), and Truro ($4,000).[7]

Attempted Retrenchment

Prior to the 1955 season, club officials from around the league met at the Carleton Hotel in Halifax to discuss a new fiscal framework.

Rattled by the substantial losses in Stellarton and Halifax and the collapse a few months earlier of the Maritime Major Hockey League, their intent was to prevent a similar fate from befalling the H&D League. Among those attending were Clarence Johnson, Alf Bruce and John Murphy of Truro; Danny Seaman and Jack Randall, Liverpool; J.P. McGrath and Keith Lockhart, Kentville; Bob Munro and Alex Semple, Stellarton; and Clem Hollett, Halifax. Dartmouth was not represented but made it clear that it thought that changes were in order.

The meeting adopted several resolutions that club officials hoped would limit operating expenses without seriously diminishing the caliber of ball being played. Payroll and roster construction were front and center. Over the years, veteran professional players had regularly joined college students around the league, but it was decided to stick essentially to college players. Clubs would be limited to a sixteen-man roster, only thirteen of whom could be imports: none could be ex-pros. A club could have a pro or ex-pro as coach, but he would have to be non-playing. In addition, a salary cap restricted salaries to $300 per month. Another requirement was to have at least three local players on the roster. If followed, this would mean an opportunity for at least eighteen local players across the league.[8] A year earlier there were only six locals playing regularly in the league: Danny Seaman and Mac Bowers in Liverpool; Don Boudreau, Billy Carter and Johnny Clark in Halifax; and Chook Maxwell in Truro.

Almost immediately, however, arguments arose over whether the resolutions were firm rules or mere guidelines. Some clubs proceeded as though nothing had changed, but Stellarton considered the agreements binding. Sticking closely to the agreement, the Albions severed the connection that had sustained it for five years. Bill Brooks, Joe Fulghum, Monk Raines, Jim Edwards and John Waselchuk were cut adrift, saving $3,000 from the salary budget. Gone as well were fellow Southerners Dave Baxter, Jack Turney, Cole Jacobs, Connie Hemphill and four-year veteran Kent Rogers. Turney ended up in Dartmouth in 1955, where he led the Arrows with a .289 average. None of the others returned.

With Brooks no longer in charge of recruitment, the Albions turned over the job of putting the team together to Yankees scout Ray Garland and instructed him to bring in younger high school players wherever possible as a cost-cutting measure. Most of his baby-faced recruits were from the New York area, resulting in savings in transportation over players who came from further south. In 1954 player salaries had ranged from a low of $350 per month to Waselchuck's $700. In 1955 nobody made more than $300 per month. Catcher Walt Brady, a highly regarded prospect who would go on to play at the Triple-A level in the Baltimore Orioles chain, was the highest paid. Other collegians were signed for $250 and high schoolers for $200. Coach Stan Benjamin, a former major leaguer who assisted in the development of young players in the Yankees system, received $400 a month, which was $200 less than Brooks had received the year before.

The slashing of the salary budget was both dramatic and counter-productive. In 1954 players had received a grand total of $18,793.37 in salaries, the most in club history, but with the failure of the club to advance to the second round of the playoffs, attendance dropped from 40,000 to 30,000. The club lost $10,000. In 1955, adhering strictly to the guidelines established at the league meeting in Halifax, player salaries were cut by more than half to $8,711.07. Without the familiar Carolinian contingent, the Albions drew only 15,000 fans, losing as much as they did in 1954. The accumulated deficit of $20,000 over two years wiped out the surpluses that had accrued between 1951 and 1953 and left the club in a precarious position looking forward.

Stellarton fans had become accustomed to a high-quality lineup, but the too-young-to-be-competitive 1955 Albions ended up in the basement, a game behind the woeful Dartmouth Arrows. Attendance plummeted. By mid–July, sportswriter Ace Foley was criticizing the impatience of Stellarton fans, suggesting in cheerleader fashion that the club was building a solid basis for the future. "Gone are the high-priced heavy-footed pros," he wrote. "The Als are short on experience but they have hustle.... Naturally the young men don't show the poise of the high-salaried veterans of other years, but they do have promise. The Als hope to live within a certain budget and still be in the pennant fight.... A community effort deserves the backing of the community.... Young people perk up when the crowds are there."[9]

Without question there were talented players on the roster. Charlie Mellen, a star outfielder at Boston College who had played three years in Maine and New Brunswick, led the team in hitting with a .300 average. In addition, the battery of pitcher Russ Henrichs and catcher Walt Brady, both of whom eventually rose to the Triple-A level, had solid years. Many of the rest—like eventual major leaguer Jack Lamabe—were so green that the club released them before the mid–July roster deadline. Twenty-seven players came and went over the season, as the Albions tried to find the right balance between on-field performance and fiscal management. Manager Stan Benjamin still had the skills necessary to help the club; but other than a couple of appearances in the outfield and as a pinch hitter, he decided to let the youngsters gain experience in a tough playing environment. The forty-one-year-old former

Nine. Troublesome Times

major leaguer had played a dozen years in Organized Baseball in the thirties and forties, five of them with the Phillies.

As the July 15 deadline approached, it was clear that retrenchment was a failure. It has always been puzzling to me why the club so doggedly adhered to bringing in inexperienced Americans rather than filling with local players. There were dozens of experienced ball players around the Maritimes who could have undoubtedly outperformed the youngsters. Only a few years before, talented homebrews Harry Reekie and Syd Roy had been considered stars. Spurned by the Albions in 1954, they headed to Ontario's Intercounty League. Roy began his Ontario stint as a relief pitcher but worked his way into a starting role. Other local area players with the H&D League, like Leo Fahey who had played in the Cape Breton Colliery League and with Kentville and Stellarton over the years, and catcher Frankie Prozenor would have provided experience and leadership to the youthful Als.

As the 1955 season spiraled downward, and with other teams circumventing the prohibition against minor-league veterans, the Albions made one concession. They signed former Yankees farmhand Leo Parent, a native of Lowell, Massachusetts, who doubled as catcher and starting pitcher and provided badly needed veteran leadership to the kiddie corps. Parent would continue to play in the league until it folded. He won the batting title in 1959. A former pitching prodigy in the Yankees organization, he was a solid performer on the hill with both Stellarton and Truro. Given his performance over the years, one can hardly fault the club's decision to sign him. Left unresolved was why clubs were so reluctant to return to balanced rosters that included both imports and locals.

As crowds continued to dwindle both in Stellarton and Dartmouth in 1955, the over-matched Albions and equally inept Arrows requested an emergency meeting near the end of the regular season to discuss a proposal that would allow all six teams to enter the playoffs. "The meeting realized the financial troubles by both clubs who stand to be eliminated," the *Halifax Herald* reported. "In Dartmouth gates are down, and in Stellarton the shaky economy of the area did not enhance the prospects of keeping the club out of the red."[10] The Arrows and Albions complained that other clubs had violated the understanding arrived at in the spring, which was indeed the case. Although sympathetic, the league voted down the proposal, pointing out that if all clubs were allowed to participate in the playoffs, it would render the regular season pennant race meaningless. It would also extend the season. Already, fans were disenchanted with collegians leaving their clubs before the playoffs in order to get back to school for football camp and the opening of the fall term. When the league refused to address their concerns, Bob Munroe and Alex Sample gave notice that they would not be involved in the operation of the Albions in the future.[11]

The Last Gasp of Import Baseball in New Brunswick

While conditions were uncertain in Nova Scotia, they were worse in the Maine–New Brunswick League. Already in the first half of the fifties, a number of independent teams had been caught up in the broader contraction of professional and semiprofessional baseball elsewhere in North America. It was just a matter of time before teams farther north experienced the same fate. Citing declining attendance and growing indebtedness, the Maine–New Brunswick League ceased to operate at the end of the 1955 season. It was not that the clubs did not have exciting and high-profile performers. Future Baltimore Oriole Angelo Dagres won the batting title hands down, followed by Duke University speedster Dave Sime of the Edmundston Republicans. Bill Thurston was the league's top pitcher with a 5–0 record and a sparkling earned run average, just ahead of Larry Bossidy and future big-leaguer Bill Kunkel, both of whom gave up less than two earned runs a game. Hard-throwing Ralph Lumenti, Maine native Warren Hodgdon, Charley Symeon of Holy Cross and future Los Angeles Dodger Ron Perranoski finished in the top ten. Catcher and third baseman Dave Ricketts struggled at the plate yet went on to play a number of seasons at the major league level.

The contrast between player talent and financial instability was obvious to many who followed the H&D League. Newspaper reporters commented alternatively on club revenue problems and on the ability to attract the best available prospects in eastern North America. "The H&D League has grown in stature over the years," wrote Alex Nickerson in the Halifax *Chronicle Herald* in April 1955. "There was a time when the outstanding college men played in amateur leagues near their home base. Those leagues no longer operate, so the H&D League gets the cream of the college crop."[12] At the same time, the surfeit of imports and the limited number of roster spots available to local players throughout the Maritimes meant that baseball in the Maritimes in the fifties was a risky operation. After the collapse of the import model in New Brunswick in 1955, the H&D League was the only one to continue to operate.

The Final Year as a Six-Team League

On Nova Scotia's diamonds, the 1956 season was billed as a bounce-back year, with all six H&D League teams back for another season. Initially there was concern that Halifax would not field a team, but the season was salvaged when the newly-formed Citadels worked out an affiliation agreement with the Philadelphia Phillies. The deal was struck after the folding of the Quebec Provincial League left the Phillies with no place to send prospects. Philadelphia reassigned manager Lew Krausse, an old major leaguer already under contract for the year, to Halifax.[13] Among the players accompanying Krausse east was his hometown buddy Meredith "Spud" Murray from Media, Pennsylvania, a Double-A pitcher on the Phillies disabled list rehabbing a sore arm. The thought was to bring Murray along slowly before he returned to the pro ranks. Murray became a fan favorite in Halifax, putting up an 11–3 record by depending on pitching smarts and control. In 1958 Murray signed on as batting practice pitcher with the Phillies; a few years later, he signed on as pitching coach with the New York Yankees, and he stayed with the latter for five years. Jokingly, he talked of his "lucky sore" arm that allowed him to win a World Series ring with the Yankees in 1962. A few years later, in 1965, he made an appearance in the Florida Instructional League where he was coaching Yankees pitching prospects. In three innings he gave up four hits and a walk but held his opponents off the score sheet.[14]

Another important member of the Phillies organization was thirty-one-year-old Eddie Lyons, who was sent to Kentville as player coach. Lyons knew how to pitch and was respected for his ability to develop young prospects. His daughter Beverly remembers that Eddie's life mission was working with young players. "He was a teacher, an instructor, a coach—somebody who moved a lot of young lives forward." Beverly recalled how his mentoring of young ballplayers in Nova Scotia, Quebec, Kentucky, Tennessee, Pennsylvania, and New Jersey kept them on the move. "People ask me where I grew up," she told Jackie Friedman of the New Jersey *Star-Ledger*, "and I always say 'in the back of a station wagon on the way to some baseball game.'" In Kentville, Eddie and his wife Kay became good friends with the Buckler family and continued to stay in contact over the years. After Kentville, the Phillies sent him to manage Johnson City in the Appalachian League. He also coached young prospects in both the Florida Winter Instructional and Cape Cod leagues and was eventually inducted into the latter's Hall of Fame.[15]

The 1957 Wildcats sported a number of youngsters of interest to the Phillies. Ed Czerniakowski and Larry Rancourt shared the catching duties, and each played in the outfield when the other was behind the plate. Czerniakowski finished fourth in league batting with the Phillies' Halifax affiliate in 1956. Equally impressive was second baseman Tommy Morgan from Lafayette, a great defensive player who entered the Phillies' minor league system after a year in Kentville. He began his career with Tulsa of the Texas League in 1958. The pitching corps that year featured Lyons, Hal Deitz, Bob List, and Bob Krop, a right-hander with a mid-nineties fastball. Pitcher-first baseman and Kentville native Billy Wade won four of five decisions and hit .300 in a limited number of plate appearances. Rancourt, Deitz, List and Krop all went on play Triple-A ball. Czerniakowski and Morgan topped out at the Double-A Level.

Stellarton returned to its former roster strategy, having repudiated the failed retrenchment policy. Apparently, nobody had swallowed Ace Foley's claim that the 1955 season created a nucleus for future success! The only returnees from the year before were battery mates Russ Henrichs and Leo Parent. More significantly, the club restored the Carolinian connection that had sustained the club for years. Wake Forest grads Joe Fulghum, Jack Stallings, and Jack McGinley were back to lead an experienced group of Southerners. Unfortunately, a winning fiscal formula remained elusive. Growing dislocations in the coalfields and a further precipitous drop in attendance in 1957 hindered the effort. In 1957 neither the Citadels nor the Larrupers fielded a team. Only four teams operated in the H&D League from that time forward.

Despite financial woes, the league still attracted standout performers. In Halifax, Jim Raugh turned in top-flight performances over three seasons, notching twenty-six victories against fifteen losses. Equally impressive was Prince Edward Islander Don Macleod, a star at Boston College who spent two years in Liverpool before moving to Truro in 1957. MacLeod played five years in the Milwaukee organization after that. Three other youngsters, Kentville's Jim Bailey, Liverpool's Dale Willis, and Stellarton's John Boozer would end up in the majors after a single season in Nova Scotia. Boozer was the most successful, putting together a solid seven-year major-league career, winning fourteen of thirty decisions and posting a 4.09 career ERA as a member of the Philadelphia Phillies. He also had a reputation for flaky behavior, chewing and spitting tobacco, eating insects of various kinds, cleaning the pitching rubber with his fingers and then licking them to get them clean and dusting off his armpits with the resin bag.[16]

Elsewhere in the league, the Truro Bearcats had an array of stars in 1956 and 1957 led by future big leaguers Moe Drabowsky, Ken McKenzie and Ralph Lumenti. The mound staff also included Charlie Symeon,

Bob Wedin, Bob Dunn and Bob Ritacco. Ritacco would eventually settle permanently in Nova Scotia. Two local players, Springhill native Carmen Noiles who had a brief trial with the Red Sox affiliate in the Pony League in 1956, and hometown boy "Chook" Maxwell who broke the .300 barrier for the first time in 1956, were standouts. In addition, Sal Ferrara, one of the finest performers in league history, captured the batting title with a .345 mark, nosing out Jack Kubiszyn of the Liverpool Larrupers.

Stars of 56 and '57: Jack Kubiszyn, Sal Ferrara and Ray Looney

Jack Kubiszyn played three years in Nova Scotia, two in Liverpool under manager and local baseball legend Danny Seaman and the third with Kentville in 1957. I was in Victoria that summer, and since Jack billeted with my grandparents, I heard stories about him as a wonderful player and person. My cousin Bev remembers passing time fielding grounders on the front lawn with Jack, and my aunt Shirley helped him with his university correspondence courses. Through it all, he pined for his Alabama sweetheart back in Tuscaloosa. Every Friday, Jack and Lucy would talk on the telephone, something of a luxury since long distance calls were quite expensive at the time. "I was just so much in love," he told me. Despite enjoying his summer in Kentville, he couldn't wait to get back home.

In 2009 Lucy published a biography of husband Jack titled *When a Star Fell on Alabama: The Jack Kubiszyn Story*. It follows his college years as a basketball and baseball star at Alabama and Jack's journey through the minor leagues to the big-league Cleveland Indians. It is also a story of frustration with the politics and broken promises of professional baseball and the premature end to his career when beaned by Joe Shipley.[17] When I talked with Jack at his home in Tuscaloosa, the beaning was front and center in the conversation. "Shipley threw at me," Jack told me. "I know he threw at me." While in a hospital bed fearing that he might lose his eye, Jack was sustained by his faith. A deeply religious man who had grown up Catholic in Buffalo, Jack spent time praying and trusting in God that he would recover. Recover he did, but it was the death knell of his career as a professional ballplayer.

Although Jack's experience in professional baseball was a mixture of accomplishment and disillusionment, he had good memories of his collegiate career and of the H&D League. He had traveled north in 1955 on the recommendation of Boston Red Sox scout George Digby, who

Jack and Judy Kubiszyn, March 22, 1991. A three-year star in the H&D League, equally well-known for his basketball exploits at the University of Alabama, Jack Kubiszyn went on to play parts of two seasons with the Cleveland Indians (author's collection).

considered the H&D League "one of the top semipro leagues in existence." In fact, many highly rated prospects were unable to cut it: if they didn't perform well in the first few weeks, they were sent home. "I never thought they could send me home. I didn't realize that some good ballplayers were being sent home. In retrospect it's a good thing I didn't know," Jack recalls. "Nova Scotia was a wonderful place to play ball. It was a great league, and many big-league ballplayers got their start in this league. Living expenses were cheap. Our room rent was $20 a month. The food was good. We ate a lot of blueberry pie and a T-bone steak that cost only $1.25."[18]

After leaving the Wildcats, Jack played a number of years in the Cleveland organization, along with other H&D League stars Sal Ferrara, Ty Cline, and Gene Lary. He was a superior defender at third base and shortstop, winning a Silver Glove as the best defensive third baseman anywhere in the minor leagues one season. He later played at the major league level in 1961 and 1962. Gene Lary, another Alabama grad, was a good friend. "Gene would have loved to play major league ball," Jack told me. Despite his 19–7 season at Mobile in 1956 and three successful years at Triple-A, the Indians never gave him a major league shot.

Ferrara was a particularly talented player who could play any infield position except catcher. He was a .300 hitter everywhere he played, including his three minor league seasons with the Indians. Both Ferrara and Kubiszyn ranked in the top ten H&D League players in career batting average for players with more than 200 at-bats.

Power-hitting Ray Looney, a first baseman outfielder with Dartmouth, was another offensive star that year. A starting quarterback at George Washington University and a major league baseball prospect, Looney grew up around Pittsburgh and while in high school attracted interest from the Pirates, who gave him a standing invitation to work out with Hall of Famer Harold "Pie" Traynor whenever the Pirates were on the road. Traynor knew Nova Scotia well since his father Jimmy was a long-time resident of Halifax. After high school Looney decided to play for Bill Rinehart at George Washington University. A good friend of Art Hoch's, Rinehart recommended Looney go to Dartmouth to play summer ball. He roomed with Jim Raugh at the Robinson family's home on Dawson Street. "It was a terrific experience," he told me, "my first time away from home. I think I got $400 a month my first year and then a pay cut to $350 in 1957. It was an excellent league with the best college players in the East, but also a fine education—living in a different country." He made a lot of lasting friendships. Ken Mackenzie, who became Yale's pitching coach, was a close companion and racquetball partner; John Stokoe, who became chief cross-check scout for the Baltimore Orioles after hanging up his spikes; and infielder Bert Muench, who played with him in the Pirates system, were among his closest buddies.

During Looney's final year with the Arrows, the Baltimore, Washington, and Pittsburgh teams were dangling bonus offers. He chose his hometown Pirates and went to spring training with them in 1959. Unfortunately, a seriously dislocated shoulder while playing in the Carolina League in 1960 led to shoulder surgeries in 1961 and 1963. After another spring training, the Minnesota Twins held out hope that his arm would recover and that he could advance to the majors. After sitting out the 1963 season and testing his arm again with Atlanta, he retired at the end of the 1964 season. It is a story replicated over and over in baseball history, a player with obvious major league talent having the dream end as a result of a disabling injury.

Looney was disappointed, but when I talked to him, he expressed no bitterness. "I got $30,000 from the Pirates," he said, "and that allowed me to get three boys through college." All three of his sons played baseball and hockey, including Brian who went to Boston College hoping to play both sports. His hockey coach forced him to choose one or the other. When he chose baseball, his hockey coach told him he was making a mistake, that at 5-foot-10 and 180 pounds he would never make it as a pro ballplayer. A few years later he led the Expo organization in strikeouts and was the opening day starter for the Expos' Triple-A farm club in Ottawa in 1994. He played parts of three seasons in the majors. His hockey coach at BC motivated him. "I'll show that son of a bitch," he said.

Despite young stars like Kubiszyn, Ferrara, Looney and others who would make their way to the big leagues, the H&D League in 1957 was different than it had been in its glory days. Now a four-team league, it would continue as such until its demise after the 1959 season. Outfielder Jack Kaiser's final year in Nova Scotia was 1957. When Liverpool's fabled Larrupers withdrew from the league at the end of the season, Kaiser shifted his attention westward, sending his young charges at Saint John's University to the Basin League. Players like Ted Schreiber, a Brooklyn boy who went on to play in the majors, would almost certainly have accompanied Kaiser to Nova Scotia before that. One year later when Wake Forest star Art Hoch was unable to land a coaching job in the scaled-down circuit, he ended up in Pierre, South Dakota.

By that time the loss of a single franchise would spell the end of the league's fifteen-year history. In fact, when Stellarton withdrew in 1959, the league was only saved when the Boston Red Sox decided to establish a team in Halifax. Boston sent veteran minor leaguer Joe Camacho to look after its young prospects and act as playing-manager. Halifax had not fielded a club in 1958, and this would be its last gasp. This was the precarious situation that the league confronted and one that I didn't fully understand when I returned to Kentville from British Columbia for the last two summers of the league's existence.

Ten

Playing Out the String
1957–59

Most of us have memories of a treasured time. Mine was the summer of 1958. I was still living in British Columbia, eagerly anticipating the end of the school year and heading to Nova Scotia for the summer. My grandfather had visited Victoria earlier, and the plan was to travel cross-country by bus, meeting relatives in New York and Boston before making our way to the Maritimes. The adventure began with a little hop in a DC-3 across Puget Sound from Victoria to Seattle, my first plane trip. We picked up our bags at the airport luggage carousel and then walked a quarter of a mile—suitcases in hand—to a bus stop on Highway 5. For four days and seventeen hours, our home was the same Trailways bus. Only the drivers changed as we rolled through Portland, Denver, Omaha, Kansas City and Chicago on our way to the Big Apple. Luckily, as the first ones to board, we grabbed the front seat across from the driver and never relinquished it, giving us an unobstructed view of the changing landscapes and major cities along the way. This was my second coast-to-coast trip—my first by train from Halifax to Vancouver occurred a few years before—but you saw more by bus, especially in the cities. One vivid memory was passing by the stadium in Cleveland where the iconic and controversial Chief Wahoo logo of the Indians (now the Guardians) stared at us from above the main gate. Another was threading our way through upper Manhattan, watching people hanging out of tenement windows and kids playing stickball as we drove by.

Fenway Park: My First Big-League Game

Arriving at New York's 34th Street terminal, we were met by my uncle, the former Wildcat who was teaching in the small town of

Wallkill at the time. My grandfather, who had worked on a railway mail car all his life, stepped off the bus energetically. I was exhausted, but after taking it easy for a few days, we were off again, this time to Boston and looking forward to seeing the Red Sox at Fenway Park. I could hardly contain my excitement. Approaching Fenway, I remember nodding at a young guy about my age hawking programs. My intent had been friendly, but he responded with a withering—even venomous—glare, obviously disdainful of a lucky and seemingly big-feeling "rich kid" going to the game. I have often considered it an educational moment, forcing me not only to reflect on my own good fortune but also upon the pain and resentment that social and economic inequality generates. I still wonder how his life turned out.

In any event, we entered the stadium and found our seats high up above the third-base line with a clear view of the "Green Monster." Before long, my grandfather asked an usher to deliver a note to Dick Gernert in the Red Sox dugout. "Impossible," the guy said, having no intention of leaving his section unattended. My grandfather persisted, passing the note back with a $5 bill attached. Five bucks was a lot of money in those days, and suddenly the usher thought it a great idea. Not too much later—although it seemed an eternity to me—he was back, reporting with obvious surprise that he had been asked to guide us to the dugout. It would be a quick visit since umpires frown on fraternization, but shaking my idol's hand and saying a few words was an unforgettable experience. Looking beyond Gernert and into the dugout, I saw Pete Runnells and Jimmy Piersall in the foreground. A few feet further along stood Ted Williams, who momentarily took his gaze off the field and looked our way. I like to think that his slight smile was intended for us. Given that he vacationed on the Miramichi River in New Brunswick to fly-fish for salmon on a regular basis, it would have been only right.

The Red Sox won handily that day. Ike Delock went the distance, giving up eight hits and three earned runs, and Williams, Frank Malzone and Gernert collected three hits apiece. In the third inning, Williams launched a towering drive deep into the seats in right field, putting the Sox up 2–0. Later, Malzone singled and Gernert sent a rocket into the gap and into the quirky little jog in the outfield around the bullpen that scored another run. The usher—now our buddy—came over gushing. "Looks like you brought him good luck," he said. Later when Gernert made a fine left-handed grab of a shot down the line and threw to second to start a sharp 3–4–3 double play, he was back again. "Not too many would have made that play," he exclaimed.

Ten. Playing Out the String

The 1958 Wildcats: Manly Johnston, Norm Gigon and Lee Elia

After spending a few days with relatives outside Boston where I got to play pick-up ball games with American kids my age, we hit the road again. Before I knew it, I was in Kentville, standing at Memorial Park's waist-level fence beside the third-base dugout watching the Wildcats work out. Towering over most of his teammates was Manly Johnston, a six-five, 220-pound outfielder from Dothan, Alabama, who would make the majors as a right-handed pitcher with the Chicago White Sox but never saw any on-field action. Nicknamed "Shot" by his father—a shortened version of "hot shot"—Johnston had an audacious quality. In warm-ups he would often confound teammates by throwing knucklers and laughing when they had difficulty catching them. Despite his potential as a big-league pitcher, scouts at the time were interested in his raw hitting power. One weekend Chicago White Sox scout Chuck Ward sat in the grandstand at Memorial Park as Johnston raked the ball to all fields and for prodigious distances. Although he hit only .264 as a Wildcat, his performance in front of Ward was enough to convince the White Sox to sign him to a $50,000 bonus contract. Johnston left Kentville soon after that.

Despite Johnston's hitting close to 100 home runs in his first four minor league seasons, twenty of them in 1962 with Lynchburg in the Sally League in just 179 at-bats, the White Sox toyed with turning him into a pitcher. He became what Mark McCarter described as "the first two-way superstar of the modern Southern League."[1] Johnston won thirteen games for Lynchburg that season. Invited to spring training in 1963, he dominated with his blazing fastball and slider and the occasional knuckle-curve. In one appearance against the Phillies, he struck out Don Demeter, Tony Taylor, Ruben Amaro, Wes Covington, and Don Hoak—all of them regulars—and in another appearance, he struck out the side in the ninth inning for a win.

In 1964 Johnston dominated the Southern League both as a pitcher and hitter and is a central character in former minor league ballplayer Larry Colton's marvelous *Southern League: A True Story of Baseball, Civil Rights, and the Deep South's Most Compelling Pennant Race*. This was the year of the infamous church bombing in Birmingham and extraordinary racial brutality across the segregated south. Not surprisingly, racial animosities carried over to the baseball diamond. Johnston was in the middle of it all and reputedly threw at black players. Colton's gripping account of that year's pennant race focuses on the rivalry between Lynchburg's Johnston and John "Blue Moon" Odom of the Birmingham

A's, a talented young black pitcher destined for future big league stardom. Johnston's teammates with Lynchburg included outfielder Danny Murphy and first baseman Deacon Jones, both former members of the Truro Bearcats. After winning eighteen games at Triple-A Indianapolis in 1966, Johnston was unable to respond to a September call-up because of arm soreness. He called it quits at age twenty-seven.[2]

I always wondered what Jones, a black ball player, thought about all this, what he went through playing in the south and how he got along with Johnston, his teammate for three or four seasons. "Manly Johnston, 'my lawdy boy' Manly," the Deacon exclaimed, as he talked about playing in Lynchburg. Deacon had experienced the worst of Southern racism, once hiding all night from the Ku Klux Klan in Columbus, Georgia, and another time having a guy point a gun in his face at a rest stop. In Greenville, South Carolina, one night "a bunch of rednecks were on my ass, calling me all kinds of names and using the 'n' word," he recalled. Then someone insulted his mother and he lost it, charging over to the chain link screen, screaming at them, even as his knuckles were being bloodied. His detractors warned that they would be waiting for him at the end of the game. When Deacon got back to the dugout and told of their threats, "Manly says 'I know how to handle them local boys. Everybody grab a bat.'" The team left the stadium in two lines, bats in hand, and Deacon walked up the middle, "just like going down the aisle at a wedding."

In addition to Johnston, the 1958 Wildcats had a talented roster. Behind the plate, Armand Sabourin acted as the defensive quarterback and team leader. Ron Liptak from Bridgeport, Connecticut, had a solid year at shortstop and sparkled defensively in his second year in the league. Future major leaguer Lee Elia shared third base with New Hampshire native Ray Stebbins, but moved to the outfield after Dick Berardino signed a $30,000 bonus contract with the Yankees. Berardino was hitting well below the Mendoza line (baseball jargon for a sub-.200 batting average) when he left town. Few people even remember seeing him that year. He spent a number of good years in the Yankees system but made his major league debut with the Red Sox in 1989 as a member of their major league coaching staff.

The Wildcats outfield for the last half of the season had Jack Mac-Gowan in left, Norm Gigon in center, and Elia in right. Gigon was unquestionably the team's best player, finishing fourth in the league batting race with a .304 average. The Phillies later signed him and turned him into a second baseman. With the big league Chicago Cubs, he was a solid utility player who could play first, second or third base and both corner outfield positions, and he even volunteered to fill in behind the plate if needed. Gigon's big break came in spring training in 1967 when regular third baseman Ron Santo was injured. He went on a tear for a couple of weeks and hit close to .400. "He's some kind of player," Leo Durocher told the *Chicago Tribune*. A reporter asked why Gigon had remained at AAA for so long. "Once in a while," Durocher smiled, "a player comes out of the pickle vat."[3]

Elia was Gigon's double-play partner for a number of years in the minors. After a twenty-nine home run season in Triple-A, Elia broke into the majors in 1966 with the Chicago White Sox as a replacement for injured shortstop Ron Hansen. In Kentville he was playing out of position and many considered him a journeyman ballplayer. What they overlooked was the mental toughness and tenacity of a hard-working, Eddy Stanky–type of competitor determined to make it to the big leagues by force of will. A student of the game, Elia had a twelve-year career as a player and another eight years as a manager, including stints with the Phillies and the Cubs.[4]

Stellarton's Last Hurrah

Nineteen fifty-eight was Stellarton's final year in the H&D League. Declining attendance and economic dislocations in coal country doomed an illustrious franchise that began the fifties with three successive league championships. Catcher Emmett Dietz, second baseman Joe Cooper, and two University of Connecticut outfielders, Ken Cullum and Moe Morhardt, led the club in its final year. A vicious left-handed pull hitter with enormous potential, Cullum had an unfortunate reputation as a heavy drinker and bad influence on younger players while playing in the Braves organization in the early sixties. In his celebrated baseball memoir, *A False Spring*, Pat Jordan had this to say about his teammate with the McCook Braves in the Nebraska State League. "There was a rumour ... that after Ken Cullum drank 20 or so bottles of Falstaff, he'd go outside on particularly hot nights and fall asleep on the lawn waking in the morning to find himself covered with dew and still wearing only his white boxer shorts emblazoned with red cupids." Although Jeff Jones had signed Cullum after watching him in Nova Scotia, Jones had concerns about Cullum's behavior and warned Jordan to keep his distance. "He's too mature for you," said Jones. Cullum spent four seasons with the Braves, but even after a breakout year with Boise of the Pioneer League in 1961 where he hit over .300, clubbed fifteen home runs, and stole nine bases, his reputation impeded his development. The organization would not advance him beyond Class C.[5]

Moe Morhardt was more successful. Playing with Stellarton in

1958 and the Truro Bearcats in 1959, Morhardt was a left-handed first baseman and All-American at Connecticut. After signing with Lenny Merullo and the Cubs, he impressed with his speed and line-drive hitting, and Chicago moved him quickly through the minors. A September call-up in 1961, he played seven games at first base, hit .278 and earned an invite to spring training with the Cubs the following spring where he hit .389 and beat out a half-dozen other first basemen. A highlight was his bases-loaded single off Dick Radatz in a tenth inning 5–4 victory over the Red Sox.[6] At the time, however, the Cubs had decided to give the shortstop job to Andre Rogers and shift thirty-one-year-old Ernie Banks to first. According to the *Chicago Tribune*, Morhardt was a "good left handed batter" who simply had the misfortune of being crowded out of the regular lineup by the shift of Banks to first base.[7] Although the Cubs told him that they planned to keep him on the roster all season and wouldn't send him to the minors, Morhardt was unhappy and in late May asked the club to send him somewhere so he could play every day. Despite his solid season in the Texas League, the Cubs never asked him back to the big leagues.

Another future major leaguer with Stellarton that year was Prince Edward Islander Vern Handrahan. After a year in the Charlottetown city league, Handrahan wrote to H&D League clubs offering his services and received invites from both Stellarton and Truro. He chose the Albions and headed to Nova Scotia with two other Islanders, Bobby Lund and Roger MacLeod, appearing in fifteen games as a reliever. After Stellarton's final game of the year, Jeff Jones approached him with an offer to turn pro with the Braves. This was the beginning of a twelve-year professional career that included stints with the Kansas City Athletics in 1964 and 1966.[8] Stellarton's staff also included Ithaca College stars Bob Graham and Basil Curry, both of whom advanced to Double-A San Antonio, and Jim Hannan, an eighteen-year-old from Notre Dame. Hannan had a wicked fastball but walked more than a batter an inning. Youthful statistics are often deceiving, however. Hannan amazed his teammates and major league scouts with his power arm, throwing 100-foot pop-ups one after another during team practices. He went on to a lengthy career in the big leagues, winning forty-one games with Washington, Detroit and Milwaukee.

Art Hoch and the Dartmouth Arrows

If 1958 marked the final year for Stellarton, it was also Dartmouth playing coach Art Hoch's swan song after eight summers. The Arrows had his characteristic Southern touch. Accompanying Hoch north were fellow North Carolinians Mike Ricigliano, Jack Turney, Don Hafer and Harry Lloyd and two Clemson University stars, Ty Cline and Hal Stowe, who would later play in the majors. Stowe was the ace of the Dartmouth squad, while Cline played first base and in the outfield and chipped in with a .278 average. Bob List, Jim Farino, Tom Bujnowski and Emil Viola from Saint John's University were the other imports on the pitching staff, and local boy Eric Parsons was solid in seven appearances. The following spring, Washington invited Viola to Double-A Chattanooga, which was loaded with Maritime baseball graduates Ralph Lumenti, Don Damiano, Dick Harris, Art Brophy and Wayne LeNeave. After a three-inning scoreless outing in which he allowed only one baserunner, Viola demanded that the Senators increase their contract offer. That a rookie would be so presumptuous angered the Washington brass. They released him at the end of spring training.[9]

By contrast, Stowe signed with the Yankees and moved rapidly up the minor league ladder, posting an excellent 15–3 record with Amarillo of the Texas League. A favorite of Casey Stengel, Stowe was a September call-up in 1960 and a candidate for a big league job the following spring. Cracking the World Series champion Yankees lineup was a tall order—former Halifax Red Sox pitcher Rollie Sheldon defied the odds in making the jump from Class D Augusta 1961—but Stowe received the most outstanding young pitcher award in spring training, holding opponents to just four hits over seventeen innings. Despite outpitching Sheldon, Stowe had a strained relationship with new Yankees manager Ralph Houk. Stowe made the big league roster and stayed until the trading deadline, but Hoch never once used him before sending him down. "At the time, I felt as if I were a big-league pitcher," Stowe told Kevin Czerwinski, "and Casey thought so, too." Houk's behavior was puzzling. "I guess I wasn't his type of pitcher. I had no idea why. A lot of people asked me that question, but I never knew why."[10]

I remember looking forward that year to a possible playoff match-up between Stowe and Kentville's Hal Deitz, but it was not to be. Truro knocked off Hoch's Arrows in eight games, setting up a Bearcats versus Wildcats finale. The teams split the first six games with fine pitching performances by Deitz, "Buzz" Bowers and Jack McCracken offset by Truro's Bob DeFino, Ed Willey and Johnny Graham. In the deciding game, Truro gave the ball to DeFino, one of dozens of Holy Cross Crusaders to play in the H&D League during the fifties. Although Johnny Graham remembers DeFino as having mediocre stuff, a mid-eighties fastball and a "winkle curve," he always seemed to get batters out, and he did so again that day. Led at the plate by Leo Parent's two-run homer and great defensive plays in the outfield by "Chook" Maxwell, the Bearcats won the league championship.

I missed most of that series on another cross-country bus trip, this time accompanied by my good friend Donny Brown. We were so very young: I had just turned fourteen, and Don was but a few months older. A couple of kids traveling on their own without cell phones or email connection seems unimaginable today, but it didn't seem that big a deal at the time. After a brief stop in New York, we jumped on a Trailways coach for another four-day junket. Don was living in LA at the time, so we would travel together only as far as Portland. He headed south to LA and I went north; we promised to see each other the following summer.

One Final Season

I returned to Kentville by train in 1959, accompanied by my mother and two brothers. Although they spent a lot of time at a family cottage at nearby Medford Beach, baseball kept me in town most days, playing for the Valley Drive-Ins during the day and watching the Wildcats at night. I pitched now and then and played in the infield, and my performance—like my golf game today—was mostly mediocre with occasional flashes of incompetence. Happily, my coach Frank Fillmore drafted me for the second straight year to play alongside more talented guys like Doug Forbes at first base, Johnny Lockhart in centerfield, and Loris Keizer behind the plate. Fillmore's son Nick was a pretty good pitcher who later played junior ball for the provincial champion Canning Habs.

I remember Frank as a coach with a real interest in the development of young kids and a broader commitment to social justice. Later, as an historian interested in working class history and protest movements in the post–Confederation Maritimes, I learned more about the Fillmores, including Frank's father Roscoe, a renowned horticulturalist and socialist visionary. As a Communist Party of Canada member during the 1930s, Roscoe had travelled to the Soviet Union to study collective agricultural practices. Decades later, long-time socialist Charley Murray would host an annual Roscoe Fillmore picnic, attended by large crowds of social activists and uninvited members of the RCMP (Royal Candian Mounted Police), who nosed around surreptitiously checking license plates. By then, earlier warnings from my grandfather not to be swayed by the "crazy ideas" of Roscoe—I didn't quite understand them at the time and later thought my grandfather's advice unnecessary—came into focus. Frank and Nick ran an alternative newspaper called the *Fourth Estate* in Halifax for a few years, and Nick became a highly-regarded journalist, CBC (Canadian Broadcasting Corporation) producer and environmental activist.

Another constant companion in those two summers in Kentville was my cousin Bev. We shared a room; hung out with buddies Cyril White, Wayne Sangster, and Len Huffman; and played ball every day. My older cousin Jim was around occasionally, but not as much as he liked since he was often out of town catching for the Intermediate Hantsport Shamrocks. Along the line he came to the attention of and received tryout offers from the Braves and Tigers, but since he was interested in a military career, he didn't follow up on them. Now fifteen, I hoped to compete on equal terms with Bev, who was a year and a bit older. One afternoon we faced off as opposing pitchers at Memorial Park. "It was the only time we actually pitched against each other," Bev remembers. Usually, our games were at the smaller field next door, but that day at least we imagined ourselves as big-time Wildcats, especially since a number of them were lounging in the grandstand and watching us play. Not surprisingly, Bev was the better pitcher: Frank Fillmore took me out after four innings. Bev had a great day, at one point nailing my teammate Brian Conway when he tried to steal home. He also struck me out on a curve ball that I thought was a few inches off the plate but was called a strike by umpire Peanuts Mahaney. I had learned earlier never to argue with Peanuts. In an earlier game, I thought I had struck out Johnny Warden, one of the better hockey and ballplayers in town. Johnny had tried to check his swing, but I knew he hadn't and Peanuts called a ball. "Hey, he swung at that," I said. Before I knew it, Peanuts was in my face. "Listen, kid," he said, "never question me like that. You're not big enough!" On the next pitch, Johnny lined it back at me and up the middle, missing my head by a foot or so. When I looked over at first base, he was standing there laughing his head off.

That season the H&D League operated again with four teams. After a two-season hiatus, Halifax had returned with a team of prospects selected by the Boston Red Sox, averting the league's collapse. Joe Camacho was playing coach. A veteran minor-leaguer, director of the Ted Williams Baseball Camp, and later a member of Williams' Washington Senators coaching staff in 1969, Camacho had a solid pitching staff led by future major leaguers Ed Connolly and Rollie Sheldon and eventual minor league stars Charley Bunker and Gerry Glynn. Unfortunately, the club, including Camacho, was anemic at the plate. Speedy second baseman Tony Zash, a Maine native, was the best of the position players. Two local standouts, Billy Carter and Jimmy Beckman, made valuable contributions at times. One of the finest local players of the late fifties —like Cape Breton pitcher-infielder Mike Roberts—Beckman was a perpetual MVP with the Hantsport Shamrocks in the 1960s and later in the decade hit .300 in the import-laden Quebec Provincial League. Roberts spent two seasons in the Braves organization.

The standard of play in 1959 was disappointing, perhaps because of a new NCAA regulation that restricted college-level players to those in their senior year. As a result, some fans turned their attention to the recently-established Eastern League, filled with emerging local stars such as Howie Spears, Bobby Burchell, Darrell Hurley, Joe Mercer, and Joe Power. Convinced that his sons Howie and Jerry were more than good enough to play for Camacho's Red Sox, Gerald Spears suggested that they might even play for nothing. Camacho's hands were tied, however. Boston determined who they wanted on the roster, and the club was not willing to purchase extra injury insurance for the boys. When Spears suggested an exhibition game with the Red Sox, the answer again was no. "You might beat us," said Camacho, "and where would that leave us?"

Although I heard similar grumblings about the level of play, I wasn't overly concerned. Our buddy Armand Sabourin had returned for another year and was ensconced in a downstairs bedroom. Unfortunately, he suffered a fractured hand and returned home to Massachusetts. This was disappointing. So were the shrinking crowds. Armand's replacement was playing-coach John Turk, who was sent to Kentville by the Phillies to help develop their young prospects. A barrel-chested power hitter, Turk was a veteran of four years in the Phillies chain. Among the remaining position players, first baseman Ron Overcash, a future Silver Glove winner in the minor leagues, long-striding centerfielder Paul Hughes, and shortstop Karl Frantz were standouts. Jim Craig, Bob Russell, Bob Meckwood and Jack Moltenbrey made up the pitching rotation. Just seventeen, Moltenbrey was a big kid at 6-foot-2 and 200 pounds, with a blazing fastball. John Lockhart remembers him as "really big and really quick," no one was surprised when he signed with the Phillies. In Moltenbrey's first minor league season, he went 13–8 with 211 strikeouts in only 178 innings. Like many hard-throwing youngsters before Tommy John surgery, however, elbow troubles brought an untimely end to his career.

No stranger to arm trouble himself, Halifax native Wilson Parsons, whose elbow had popped five years before with Kansas City of the American Association, returned to Nova Scotia midway through the season. Parsons was a standout at the Maritime juvenile finals in 1950 and was offered a tryout by Dartmouth Arrows coach and Yankees scout Bob Decker. Decker, Parsons and catcher "Stu" O'Brien met up behind the stands at Dartmouth's "Little Brooklyn." "I threw three or four pitches and he [Decker] said 'is that as hard as you can throw...? I want you to throw hard so I can see how you throw.' So I wound up and threw one to Stu. Stu says 'time' and went and got the mask and the shin guards and his chest protector." After finishing the season with the Arrows, Parsons barnstormed Newfoundland on a team organized by Gerry "Gabby" Regan, later the premier of Nova Scotia. Parsons noted, "I pitched just about every game over there against all of the American bases.... We played in Corner Brook, we played in Grand Falls, we were over there for a couple of weeks. We won every game." Upon his return, two contract offers awaited him: one from the Boston Red Sox and the other from Lee McPhail, the Yankees' director of scouting and later president of the American League. Parsons chose New York.

In Parsons' first two years with the Yankees, he and Johnny Kucks were the top two pitching prospects in the entire New York system. "Whoever you talked to knew the two of us had the town," Parsons remembers. "Johnny Kucks and myself. We were doted on at every turn." The Yankees even signed one-time great Brooklyn Dodger catcher Mickey Owen for the sole purpose of catching Parsons and developing his knowledge of the game. Promoted to Triple-A, Parsons opened the

Bill Dickey, Mickey Owen, Jerry Lynch and Wilson Parsons. Halifax native Parsons and Johnny Kucks were the Yankees' top two pitching prospects of the early fifties (Halifax Municipal Archives, CR67-5-2012.01.242).

1954 season in Kansas City with a complete-game seven-hitter. A few weeks later on a cold and rainy night in Charleston, South Carolina, he said, "I tore everything out of my elbow, one pitch. The catcher, he heard it, ran to the mound. By the time he got there that elbow was like a softball." Parsons spent months after the injury consulting with Dr. Sydney Vanier in New York, and although they "wanted to go in there I wouldn't let them." Instead, he worked with a Yankees trainer rehabbing the arm. "When my arm was like this," he told me, showing me a crooked arm, "he got it so it would straighten.... The things we would go through every day to heal, but it never came back. The least bit of cold weather and it would just flame up." He continued for another five years in the Yankees system. In Birmingham or Richmond during the heat of the summer he was fine, but in Denver where it was cold in the spring he would struggle.

When the Yankees loaned Parsons to the Baltimore Orioles for the 1959 season, he decided to return to Nova Scotia and join his brother Eric with the Arrows. "I called Herm Kaplan in Dartmouth and said, 'Herm, do you suppose the Arrows would need a pitcher for the summer?' He said 'Why?' I said, 'I've just quit.'" Dartmouth's coach, Bill Wilhelm, a veteran minor league catcher and baseball coach at Clemson University, was happy to have him. Parsons won seven of nine games and another three against Kentville in the playoffs. "It was strictly experience," he told me, "knowing what to do with the ball, even though I am sure there were a lot there, say 75 percent ... who could throw better than I. They just didn't know what to do with the ball." According to Burton Russell, "not since Philip 'Skit' Ferguson's 18–1 season with the 1946 Truro Bearcats, Jack Halpin's history-making summer with the 1948 Halifax Capitals and Monk Raines' great playoff heroics with the 1953 Stellarton Albions, had provincial baseball followers been treated with such pitching mastery as that displayed by this former pro."[11]

While Parsons' career was winding down, the career of another local boy, Johnny Graham, was just beginning. The young Truro product, in his second season with the Bearcats, was one of the most exciting and best all-around players in the league in 1959. He went 6–4 with a 2.45 ERA in the regular season, won another couple of games in the playoffs, and played in the outfield, hitting .304 on the year. A natural athlete who grew up playing marsh hockey and pick-up baseball, he didn't play on an organized baseball team until he was eighteen. Johnny had a good season in 1958, highlighted by an inside-the-park home run. "It was in Kentville against Hal Deitz who had a terrific sinking curve ball," Johnny recalls, "and the center fielder was playing in, probably thinking that I was a pitcher and had little power. I hit it over his head." The ball went all the way to the fence in center field, 408 feet away. I was in the stands that day and watched him motor around the bases and finish with a head-first slide. In 1959 Johnny was joined by fellow lefthander and local boy Carmen Noiles from Springhill. Noiles was known for throwing a heavy ball, while Johnny's fast ball sat around ninety miles an hour with zip and movement. According to Howie Spears and Mike Thomson who played against him, Graham was "sneaky fast." As for Noiles, "Carmie threw so effortlessly," Graham remembers. "He once pitched two games in a row and I asked him how he was doing." "I'm just getting warmed up," was the reply. Graham also threw a no-hitter against the 1959 Halifax Red Sox, the only one by a Nova Scotian in the history of the H&D League.

The third local player with the Bearcats in that final year was Chook Maxwell, a mainstay in the outfield since 1954. Every year, Maxwell was among the league leaders, outperforming many of the young collegians who later went on to play in the big leagues. He was also a great teammate, never one to dwell on his own successes, unlike many of the cocky young prospects from the States who failed to live up to expectations when they came here. "Not only was Chook as good as any," says Graham, "but he was just a good person and so easy to get along with." This was a common sentiment. Charlie Wambolt, who grew up in Dartmouth and spent a lot of time watching H&D League games, found Chook "so personable and such a good person. I often played golf with him and his brother Darrell." Devin Maxwell remembers his uncle's humility. He was just a regular guy "sitting on the couch in his underwear and watching ball games on TV and never going on about his accomplishments." Johnny Graham deserves a final word about a down-to-earth guy with a great sense of humor. "I went into the hospital to see him just before he passed away," he recalls, "and he looked up and said to the nurse 'what's that old has-been doing here? I taught him everything he knows.'"

One notable player on the Bearcats roster that final year deserves mention as well. Pitcher-outfielder Danny Murphy, a sixteen-year-old from Beverly, Massachusetts, had already attracted the interest of every club in the major leagues before arriving in Nova Scotia. A high school star with Danvers St. John's Preparatory School, Murphy hit almost .500 and won eleven pitching decisions without a defeat. Coming to Truro on the recommendation of Jeff Jones, Danny hit a solid .280 but demonstrated plus power and a bullet-like arm. The June 27, 1960, issue of *Sports Illustrated* featured Danny on its cover. Roy Terrell wrote that "Danny was playing Little League with boys 10, 11, and 12 when he was only 7.... Last summer, at 16, Danny was home run champion in the very fast Nova Scotia semipro league." Scouts couldn't wait for the youngster's graduation and lined up at his home to make their pitch to the Murphy family; Terrell gave a minute-by-minute record of the negotiating process. Murphy's father gave each club a half-hour to come in and make their offer. There would be no second round of bidding. Most of the scouts at the Murphy home that day had followed him in the H&D League, among them Jeff Jones of the Braves, Neil Mahoney of the Red Sox, Lenny Merullo of the Cubs, Harry Hesse of the Yankees, Joe Cusick of the Orioles, and Bill Enos of the Kansas City Athletics. After receiving a promise that he would go directly to the majors, Danny signed with the Cubs for $100,000. He had two stints in the majors, the first as an outfielder with the Cubs, the second almost a decade later as a relief pitcher with the White Sox.[12]

As the 1959 playoffs began, I was on the train on my way back to Victoria. At the very same time, a number of college players around the league headed south to take part in fall football camp. This had been an enduring problem for the league over the years. In 1958, for instance, the Wildcats played the final playoff round with just ten players and a couple of pitchers; Norm Gigon, Lee Elia, and Armand Sabourin had already gone home. In the final game that year, the Wildcats used first baseman Dick Keating as a relief pitcher. Almost alone in the stands watching the final game at Memorial Park, Burton Russell—the league's most loyal fan over its fifteen-year existence—had serious misgivings. "Very few friends were in attendance as school was starting, cottages were being closed and thoughts of work and study were major concerns.... I regrettably realized that the handwriting was on the wall and that the dismal fate of this high-classed circuit with its many expenses was all but written."[13] I would not return to Nova Scotia again until the end of my first year in college in 1962. I was happy to be back, but the loss of H&D League baseball created an empty space that has been never truly filled except in the world of memory and reminiscence that is at the heart of this project.

Eleven

Post-Game Reminiscences

A couple of years ago I received an invite to a reunion for the 1963 Maritime champion and the 1964 Kentville Junior Cardinals from long-time friend Russell Fox. Since I hadn't seen Russell or his twin brother Charlie for a number of years, I was excited to reconnect with Kentville's "hard ball kids" from the late fifties and early sixties. Baseball historian Burton Russell was there that day as well, and he drew from his impressive collection of scrapbooks to present the journey of the Eddie Gillis–coached Cardinals to the regional championships and then onward to Montreal. Despite leading 2–1 going into the bottom of the ninth, the 1963 Cardinals lost in a final game to a Montreal all-star team by a single run. The Cardinals would return the following year, knocking off the Quebec representatives at Jarry Park before losing in the semi-final to the Toronto Leasides.

It was great to mingle with members of the team like Russell and Charlie, Paul Althouse, Wendell Wambolt, Sonny Gibson, George "Whitey" Smith, Mike Kenney, Peter Goucher, and Loris Keizer. Wendell was one of two pick-ups for the trip to Montreal; the other was Glenn Matheson from Brookfield, who wasn't there that day. In *Fox Tales: Recollections from Moments in Time*, Charlie offers up a detailed and humorous recollection of the Cardinals' championship journeys and their trip to Montreal, where the underdog kids became fan favorites and were praised in the columns of the *Montreal Gazette*.[1] A bunch of kids from a town of about 5,000 people facing an all-star team drawn from a population of more than a million people was a classic David versus Goliath encounter. Goliath prevailed, but only by the slimmest of margins. "We learned from this," said Johnny Lockhart, "how much can be accomplished when you believe in yourself."

For my part I had just returned to Halifax from Victoria in the summer of 1963 after a four-year hiatus from Nova Scotia. Being in Halifax and working during the week, I played only a few exhibition games

Peter Goucher (left) and Burton Russell at the 1963 Kentville Cardinals reunion in 2018. Russell was a respected educator and baseball historian, and Goucher was one of the top first basemen in the history of Nova Scotian baseball (courtesy Charles and Russell Fox).

with the Kentville guys on weekends and was never a Cardinal. On one memorable occasion, though, a group of guys including Doug Forbes, one of the classiest first basemen of the time; Dave Landry, a personable guy with a great sense of humor; and many of those who played with the Cardinals, jammed into a couple of cars for a game on the south shore. Dick Roop, the long-time team manager, who worked with a local car dealership and bore the brunt of too many practical jokes over the years, was at the wheel of a brand-new vehicle chugging along Route 12 from Kentville to Chester. "Faster, Dick, faster," the guys said, egging him on. Sitting in the back seat, probably as petrified as Dick was, I cringed as he reluctantly pushed the gas pedal further down. At one point I saw his face in the mirror with tears running down his cheeks. Fortunately, we arrived in one piece.

    I had only returned to Nova Scotia a few days earlier, and, not having my own uniform or cleats, I was outfitted in what was left over and available. Swimming in a uniform much too big for me and with cleats so big that I had to string the laces around my ankles, I nonetheless remember getting a hit and scoring a run that day. It wasn't easy since my ankles turned over every four or five steps. When I got back to the bench just feeling good having crossing home plate, Landry looked up with an impish grin and asked, "hey, what kept you?" It was one of the things I liked about baseball. You could never get a swelled head before someone brought you back to earth. I was only twenty at the time and never played on an organized team after that, yet I learned many simple truths and gained so many friends along the way. Charlie's chapter title sums it up. "Team Mates.... Forever" he calls it.

In the years since I had last been in Nova Scotia, the baseball scene had altered dramatically. Gone were the imports and college prospects. The return to local players had a two-fold effect: in the first place, it created a new context for the development of good players throughout the Maritimes and brought back a number of stars from previous seasons who had hung up their spikes earlier. At the same time, the lower standard of play meant that games were played before a mere handful of fans in most places. Gone were both the paid players and the large deficits that accompanied them, as players were now recruited on the basis of community loyalties and were only occasionally given travelling expenses. Although it was no longer "NCAA North," senior baseball in the Maritimes was nonetheless a good foundation for competitive play. A number of players would go on to the minor leagues or had the ability to do so. Young Murray Cook from Sackville, New Brunswick, who was the general manager of the Montreal Expos in the eighties, played four years as a shortstop in the Pirates organization, while Phil Doroin in nearby Moncton was probably the best player in the region at the time and was a member of Team Canada at the Pan-Am Games a few years later. Doroin was also a hockey star, teaming up with Oscar Gaudet, another multi-sport athlete and a good ballplayer who eventually played for the NHL Chicago Blackhawks. When former major league pitcher Bill Lee, who had a lengthy career with the Red Sox and the Expos, ended up in Moncton a couple decades later, he observed that he had never seen a place where so many AA-level players were kicking around. In a nod toward first baseman Pete Goucher, he said, "and there is a guy who is a AAA ballplayer."[2]

Among the best players in the immediate post–H&D League era were those who had played for those clubs in the fifties or in the other leagues around the Maritimes. Cape Breton's Colliery League had developed a number of excellent players, none better that shortstop/pitcher Mike Roberts, who was signed by Braves scout Jeff Jones in 1958 and sent to McCook of the Nebraska State League, where he hit over .300 as its starting shortstop. He played for the Braves in 1959 but returned home after that and was a mainstay on the diamond for a number of teams. Elsewhere, Eric Parsons, Johnny Graham, Art Leggatt, Eugene "Farmer" White, Carson Ellis, Donny Cormier, Carmen Noiles, power hitter Denny Clyke, outfielder Dave Crabbe—who also played football for the Calgary Stampeders, Mister-all-everything Jimmy Beckman, second baseman Hal Murray (the brother of songstress Anne Murray), Liverpool pitchers and future pros John Hagen and John Foley, and Yarmouth's durable Keith Bridgeo all demonstrated skills that would have served them well in the H&D League if it had continued to operate. So, too, Lyle Carter, an NHL netminder in the 1970s and a four-time All-Canadian softball player at third base who won nine batting titles with the Brookfield Elks.[3] Carter also played senior baseball. In New Brunswick, there was no better player in the sixties and seventies than Marysville's Scott Harvey, Jr., a hard-hitting third baseman and perhaps an even better pitcher. Harvey still holds the highest single-season batting average in New Brunswick senior baseball, played three years of pro ball in the Dodgers and Cardinals organizations, and in one sparkling pitching performance in the mid-seventies held the visiting Cuban national team to a single run in a heartbreaking 1–0 loss.[4]

A while ago I had a lengthy conversation with Mike Thomson, who was a central figure in baseball in Dartmouth after the H&D League Arrows closed up operations. Thomson was a playing coach through the sixties and a regional scout for the Montreal Expos after that. In more recent years, Dartmouth has been an enduring force in senior baseball in the Maritimes, building upon Thomson's legacy. Under coach and Cape Breton native Bobby Gillis, who was a star pitcher for the Toronto Maple Leafs of the Ontario Intercounty League in the 1970s and guest pitching coach one year with the Blue Jays in spring training, the Dartmouth Moosehead Dry have represented the province year in and year out at the Canadian nationals, where they have won gold three times. A few of Gillis' players have gone on to play minor and major league baseball, among them former Toronto Blue Jay Vince Horsman, Steve Nelson, Dave Detienne, Darren Doucette and most recently New York Yankees draftee and top-thirty prospect Jake Sanford. Now and then I fill in as an alternate on Gillis's regular foursome at Oakfield Golf Course, where we get a chance to talk baseball as well, although many of our conversations fall outside the scope of this book.

Mike Thomson was one of Darmouth's most prominent players of the sixties, winning senior batting titles on a couple of occasions. A good all-round athlete, he grew up in Dartmouth and lived just over the hill from where I lived on Sinclair Street. Although he was a couple of years ahead of me in school, I remember being in his house a couple of times. Mike followed the H&D League Arrows and went to games, sneaking into the park as we did as kids in Kentville. As a player he often played above his age group and at one time played midget, juvenile, junior and senior at the same time. He would play one night against pitchers who struggled to hit 70 mph and then face a fireballer like Bob

Ritacco the following day. By then, Ritacco, an ex–H&D Leaguer from the States, was a student at Dalhousie, and like Ray Slivocka, an American who played both with Stellarton and in the Pittsburgh organization, would take up residence in the province for the rest of his life. Thomson was a good enough player to attract the attention of major league scouts. At one point he was offered a chance to go to spring training with the Washington Senators. The club had done its due diligence and knew that gout ran in the Thomson family and asked him to go to the Victoria General Hospital to get his legs checked out before agreeing to pay his airfare back and forth. Mike's father was opposed to his going and emphasized his need to get an education instead. Mike enrolled at Saint Mary's University, where he played football and basketball.

During his time at Saint Mary's, Mike played linebacker and was a teammate of quarterback Dick Loiselle, who had recently arrived in Halifax via Manchester, New Hampshire. Loiselle, whose then-wife Pat Connolly was a colleague of mine at Saint Mary's, made Halifax his home up until his death a decade ago. In Manchester, Loiselle was a star both on the gridiron and on the diamond; after signing a contract with the Milwaukee Braves in 1959, he played three seasons with Wellsville, Boise and Cedar Rapids. Assigned to AAA Vancouver in 1962, he was slowed by a sore arm which ended his big league hopes. Although he hoped to go back to college to play football, his pro ball career left him ineligible to play in the NCAA, so he made the decision to come to Nova Scotia, where he was eligible in the CIAU (Canadian Interuniversity Athletics Union) since he hadn't played professional football. His pitching arm improved enough for him to resume playing baseball, and in the summer he and Thomson headed to Valley to play for the 1962 Kentville Braves alongside hometown products Don Fox, Frank Barteaux, Bill Buntain and Billy Wade. Brian Pulsifer, whose conversations with me have added so much to this project, also played with the Braves but got tired of sitting on the bench and gave it up as a result.

Loiselle was a tough, hard-nosed competitor, as evidenced in an encounter with the veteran H&D League player "Hum" Joseph. Always fiery and vocal in razzing his opponents, Joseph had been taunting Loiselle as a "big-feeling American," and, in response, Loiselle vowed to hit him between the shoulder blades the next time he came to bat. When Hum eventually stepped into the batter's box, there were two guys already on base, and Thomson thought, "he can't hit him this time," but Loiselle didn't care about the game result and threw a pitch that cracked Hum's shoulder. The hot-tempered Joseph rushed the mound bat in hand but had second thoughts as Loiselle, who loomed over his smaller opponent, headed toward him. When about ten feet away, Joseph threw his bat at Loiselle but Loiselle kept on coming and bloodied "Hum's nose" and knocked him down. While flat on his back, the "Hummer" began kicking upward. "Loiselle had spike marks up and down his legs," Thomson laughed.

Beginning in the late '70s, Mike was named a Montreal Expos regional scout working with Pictou-born Bill MacKenzie, a catcher whose career in the Detroit organization ended after a home-plate collision and broken shoulder. Looking at baseball in the sixties, Mike was most impressed by Dartmouth native John Hines, a first baseman that he thought was better than either Pete Goucher or Darren Doucette. He also thought later that long-time Dartmouth Moosehead Dry second baseman Greg Marquis was a fine player, good enough to have turned pro. Thomson also signed Halifax outfielder Kevin Umlah, a solid hitter and all-around good athlete who spent a couple of weeks with the Expos team in the Gulf Coast League until an incident at the batting rack where he had taken out his frustrations led to his early release. Star players at the local level, of course, were often forgiven for similar indiscretions, but things were different when they went away and played against the best players from across the continent.

In 1985 Kentville played host to the Canadian senior baseball championships; once again the little Valley town would meet the best from across the country. I hadn't been to a game at Memorial Park in years, but I took in the entire tournament. It brought back memories of the old H&D League. At one point I ran into my teenage buddy Cyril White who, caught up in the moment, gushed, "isn't this great? We haven't had crowds like this at Memorial Park in twenty-five years." The Wildcats had two brother acts, the Van Blarcoms (Sandy, Kirk and Barney) and the Moshers (Ian and Monty), as well as Doug Forbes' son Kevin, the talented Pete Goucher, second baseman Kevin Poirier and pitcher Bob Oakley. They had been strengthened with the addition of national team member Kevin MacLeod, who later played four seasons in the Oakland A's organization and reached AA Huntsville, and four other Cape Bretoners: Chet Boudreau, Robbie Mann, George MacLean and Jim McEachern. The coaching staff was led by Goucher, with Eddie Gillis, John MacDonald and McEachern as assistant coaches. Bruce Ross, who had managed Kentville in earlier years, was out of the province at the time.

The Marysville Royals represented New Brunswick with an equally talented roster, having twice knocked off the Wildcats earlier in the season during the Maritime championship series. During the round robin, they outlasted Kentville with a fourteen-inning 4–3 victory that lasted into the wee hours of morning. Marysville had a baseball history that rivaled that of Kentville or Dartmouth, and local alumni such as Matt Stairs and Paul Hodgson went on to major league careers. The Royals, led by their long-time pitcher and coach Billy "the Buzzard" Saunders, had won the 1981 Canadian senior baseball championship, another gold for New Brunswick in 1983, silver in 1984, and ended up undefeated in the round robin phase in 1985. Saunders later teamed up with Bruce Ross to scout talent in the Maritimes for the Yankees. In the playoff round, Marysville lost to Ontario's Tecumseh Green Giants in the semi-finals and then to Manitoba in the bronze medal game. "It was very disappointing," Saunders recalls, "but we didn't have the pitching depth that year.... We were happy at the same time to see Kentville do well."

Just prior to the tournament, Saunders had signed future big-leaguer Rheal Cormier as a pick-up. Although Cormier's registration was complete, in the meantime the Woodstock juvenile/junior squad enticed him to go with them to the nationals in Central Canada, where he thought he would get more exposure in front of big league scouts. In addition, Bill Lee had been declared ineligible for playing in the national championship in 1984 despite having done so for Quebec in 1982 or he would have been in Kentville as well. Those two additions would likely have had a positive influence on the team's chances as would have the addition of former Toronto Blue Jay Paul Hodgson, who had played for the Royals in 1984 but was unavailable due to work commitments. Shortstop Mark Healey, third baseman Len Munro, catcher Dan Estey and pitcher Josh Corlette were standouts for Marysville throughout the tournament.

After knocking off Manitoba in the semi-final round, the Wildcats advanced to the finals against Ontario's Tecumseh Green Giants. Few of the people who filled the stands for that final game—even the players, for that matter—would have recalled the close linkages that had developed between the Detroit-Windsor area and the H&D League almost forty years before, when Jimmy Dumeah, Bernie Parent, John and Jim Wingo, Paul Oleynik, Nik Nikita and others suited up with the Middleton Cardinals. Tecumseh was a town of about 20,000 people just ten miles down the road from Windsor, and the Tecumseh Green Giants along with the powerful Windsor Chiefs were a mighty force in Canadian senior baseball throughout the 1980s. Between 1981 and 1989, Windsor-area teams won six gold medals, including two by Marysville, and on this evening, Kentville would do what it could to add a national championship to its history as a leading baseball center in the Maritimes.

What transpired was a classic "story book" finish that serves as a particularly appropriate ending to this history of Maritime baseball in the postwar era. The Green Giants, led by power-hitting David Cooper who was something of a legend in Ontario baseball, took an early lead roughing up Kentville's starter Chet Boudreau, a fire-balling Cape Bretoner who had been added to strengthen the Wildcats roster. Cooper hit two home runs, and Jamie Struthers contributed another, as Tecumseh took a six-run lead and chased Boudreau from the box after five innings. After that Bob Oakley held the Ontarians scoreless. In the bottom of the eighth, everything changed as the Wildcats went on a roll, scoring run after run. My daughter Heather was with me that night, and I remember saying, "There's a good chance they're going to win this." At the end of the eighth inning, the score was knotted at six and stayed that way into the bottom of the ninth. With runners at second and third, Ian Mosher hit a routine fly ball to left that popped out of Struthers' glove and allowed the winning run to score. I really don't believe in destiny, but this seemed to me as close as it gets. However we describe it, it capped off forty years of my love affair with baseball. My only regret is that it took me another thirty-five years to complete this story of baseball in the postwar Maritimes.

Twelve

Great Performers, Great Performances
A Statistical Retrospective

In the years following the demise of the H&D League, my recollections of baseball in the fifties were kept alive by collecting statistics for those who played in the Maritimes and often went on to future careers in Organized Baseball. At first, this research was undertaken as a hobby, a minor component of my broader interest in baseball history, but I subsequently found the information useful in preparing for interviews for my first baseball book. Not long before that, statistical research on baseball had been revolutionized by the pathbreaking work of sabermetrician Bill James, who demolished the myth that there was no connection between minor league and major league player performance. Instead, James provided a formula for determining major league equivalencies (MLEs) across different levels of competition, comparing major league and minor league performance and adjusting for park dimensions, age levels, and various run-producing environments. James continues to believe that quality of competition (QUOC) indexes for any league between 1900 and today—professional, semipro or amateur—can be calculated even if it would require considerable effort. "It should be possible," he recently observed, "to create a common standard, assign every league since 1900 a QUOC score, a common standard number for the quality of competition."[1]

James' insights have led to all kinds of elaborate performance measurements that are increasingly employed by major league organizations in roster construction, selecting prospects in the amateur player draft, salary determination, trade negotiations and the fleshing out of organizational depth. The new analytics at once supplement and in some cases supplant more subjective assumptions about player quality that tended in the past to value major league experience more highly than minor league performance. Former gold standard measurements of player abilities—batting average for hitters and earned run averages for pitchers—have been eclipsed by a host of new statistical measurements including OPS (on-base percentage plus slugging), WAR (a player's wins above replacement value), BABIP (batting average on balls in play) and other acronyms ranging from WHIP (walks and hits per innings pitched) to FIP (fielding independent pitching).[2] In addition, there are other indexes that border more on the arcane than useful. In 1993, Michael Lewis' book *Moneyball: The Art of Winning an Unfair Game* brought the utility of the new metrics into clear view, chronicling how Oakland's general manager Billy Beane used statistics as a way of getting the most out of the team's limited salary budget. The 1998 movie of the same name cast Brad Pitt as Beane and dramatized the tension between the new analytics and traditional judgments about player quality based upon player reputation and recognizability.

As mentioned earlier, I had many discussions about this with Art Hoch, an eight-year veteran and playing coach in the fifties with Stellarton, Truro, and Dartmouth who spent a few more years in the semi-pro Basin League after the H&D league folded. More often than not, our conversations ended with him commenting "you know statistics, but I know baseball" or something to that effect. Although a keen observer of baseball over the years, I do not presume to know the game on the field as well as Hoch or many of the scouts, players and managers that I spoke to in the course of this research. I respect their knowledge and have been guided by their subjective judgments on individual player abilities at the plate or specific recollections of a pitcher's selection of pitches, control, command, and temperament. Their insights are important in identifying the great performers and performances in the history of the league.

It is also important to note that the statistical analysis of player performances in this chapter may not rise to the level of sophistication of some sabermetricians. For one thing, Maritime statistical data over the years has been uneven and often incomplete, especially for certain leagues. Sometimes, the only calculations provided were for at-bats, hits and batting average. While extra-base hits numbers were relatively complete during the 1950s, they were occasionally absent. Rarely were base-on-balls included in final league statistics. The H&D League and Maine–New Brunswick League records are the most reliable, although for some reason final tabulations for the 1951 H&D League season were never completed. I have reconstructed that season through day-by-day tabulations from box scores. It is also worth mentioning that in certain

Twelve. Great Performers, Great Performances

years, final statistics were for regular season play only, while playoff statistics were included for other years. In many cases, the final tabulations did not include players who were left off the roster after the July 15 player deadline for playoff eligibility. Finally, complete season fielding averages exist for some seasons and remain absent for others, as is true of stolen bases.

Pitching statistics are similarly inconsistent, varying with the whims of the league scorer each year. The choices of what was tallied nonetheless provide an indication of what was considered important at the time. Won-lost records are pretty complete as well as records for runs allowed, but occasionally, earned run averages were not calculated, perhaps because of the effort involved. Most seasons have strikeout and base-on-ball totals. WHIP numbers were never provided but are easily constructed. Since we have solid runs-per-game totals for both teams and leagues in the fifties, moreover, we can construct a good picture of league run-producing environments. This is an essential component in establishing a QUOC index for both the H&D League and the Maine–New Brunswick League through the 1950s. Park factors can be estimated as well and can be nuanced by knowledge of the peculiar dimensions of a number of the ballparks throughout the region.

Earlier I mentioned my interest in assessing the level of the competition for the H&D League and the Maine–New Brunswick League. In discussions with knowledgeable baseball people over the years, a consensus emerged that the level of play was similar to that of Class B or A leagues in Organized Baseball. (This was before a restructuring of the minor leagues in 1962, which saw some Class A leagues, like the Eastern League, reclassified as Double-A, and Class B leagues would resemble Advanced A leagues today.) The statistical approach employed by James and other sabermetricians provides a more effective comparison and should allow us to confirm or modify more subjective judgements that are based upon the remembrances of scouts, coaches and players who played with or against each other at various levels. Later in the chapter, I provide test cases of fifty ballplayers, most of whom moved from the Maritimes to Class A and B teams within Organized Baseball from one year to the next, and some who went in the reverse direction. These comparisons help establish workable QUOC indexes for teams in the H&D League and the Maine–New Brunswick League; those indexes can be used for the eventual calculation of major league equivalencies.

If you ask anyone familiar with the H&D League about its players, certain names will jump to mind as standout performers: Dick Gernert, who spent two years with Kentville and went on to a ten-year career in the majors is one; Zeke Bella, who had two stints in the H&D

League—the first in 1948 and 1949 and a second in 1954—is another. Springhill native Buddy Condy was in many minds the equal of both Bella and Gernert, and Liverpool's Danny Seaman was a perennial all-star with a major league bat. In later years, infielder Jack Kubiszyn, his future Cleveland Indian teammate Ty Cline, and Maine–New Brunswick leaguer Angelo Dagres distinguished themselves as first-rank stars in the Maritimes and Maine. Heading the list of pitching greats in the region are imports Moe Drabowsky, Dave Stenhouse, "Turk" Farrell, Ron Perranoski, Art Ceccarelli, "Smokey" Jim Heller, Jack Halpin, and Rollie Sheldon and local boys Skit Ferguson, Wilson Parsons, Jackie Bowes, Billy Harris, Syd Roy, Moon Mullen, Johnny Graham, Vern Handrahan, and dozens more.

What follows is an analysis of player performance based upon available statistics. Appendix 1 includes the career batting statistics and major league equivalencies (MLEs) for prominent players with at least 200 at-bats between 1946 and 1959. Appendix 2 lists the best single-season batting performances between 1948 and 1957. Appendix 3 provides career records of twenty well-known pitchers. Appendix 4 includes NCAA affiliations for a number of prominent players who performed in the region. Appendix 1 lists the top-ten career performers ranked by batting average as follows: Dick Gernert, who spent two seasons in Kentville in 1948 and 1949, led the hitting parade with a .383 career average and 27 home runs in 347 at-bats. Next in line was Roly McLenahan, a New Brunswick native and NHL hockey player with the Detroit Red Wings, who hit .381 over five years. McLenahan played summer baseball all over the Maritimes and Maine and was well-known in both sports in Ontario's Nickel Belt region. "Bustin" Buddy Condy of the Halifax Capitals and big Joe Fulghum with Stellarton had almost identical career totals in some 1000 at-bats, finishing third and fourth, respectively. Considered the best Nova Scotian player of the postwar era, Condy hit .364, nosing out Joe Fulghum, who averaged .361 over eight years. In fifth place was Angelo Dagres, a top performer in the Maine–New Brunswick League, posting a .347 batting average over two summers. First baseman Roger Rada, who spent a couple of years with Kentville, was next at .341, and Herb Rossman, who held down second base for Halifax Shipyards in 1948 and 1949, occupied the seventh spot. Rounding out the top ten were H&D League veterans Jack Kubiszyn and pitcher-outfielder Leo Parent who were tied for seventh with identical .325 averages, just ahead of local product Pat Proulx with Presque Isle of the Maine–New Brunswick League. Kentville's Steve Korcheck, Stellarton's Gair Allie and Dartmouth's Ty Cline were also among the top twenty career performers who went on to play major league ball.

Twelve. Great Performers, Great Performances

In addition to the above, there is data that allows us to compare home runs per at-bat and slugging percentages for a number of players. Dick Gernert was the most prolific in this regard with a home run every 13.5 at-bats, followed by Angelo Dagres 1 in 14, Gair Allie 1 in 15.3, Ray Looney 1 in 17, Barney Teliszewski 1 in 18.4, Leo Parent 1 in 21, George Lewis, 1 in 21, Danny Murphy 1 in 22, Syd Goldfader 1 in 23 and Al Ware 1 in 23. Notably Gernert, Dagres, Allie, and Parent were among the top fifteen performers in career batting average. Unfortunately, career slugging statistics are unavailable or incomplete for Joe Fulghum and Buddy Condy and Zeke Bella. Condy twice led the H&D League in home runs, however, clubbing eight in 190 at-bats in 1947 and ten more in 212 at-bats in 1950. In four seasons when home runs were included in league statistics, Condy hit 40 round trippers.

Seen here with the championship trophy, Springhill native Buddy Condy led the H&D League in batting average for three successive seasons from 1949 to 1951 (Halifax Municipal Archives, CR67-5-996.178.01).

Appendix 2 tabulates the best single-season batting performances and includes many who fell short of the 200-at-bat limit necessary for inclusion in Appendix 1. The top performer was Chris Tonery, a Penn State student and big league prospect who hit .461 with the 1949 Wildcats of the Central League. Unfortunately, broken legs in 1950 and 1951 turned him from prospect to journeyman. While anchoring the Fredericton infield in 1948, Roly McLenahan hit at an equally jaw-dropping .455 clip. Three years later with the same club, McLenahan hit .416 in the Maine–New Brunswick League. However, since his 77 at-bats did not qualify for league honors that year, I have not included the 1951 season in Appendix 2. Following McLenahan in the list of outstanding performances was future New York Yankee Zeke Bella, whose .419 average in 1954 was the highest in H&D League history. Following closely behind Bella, Stellarton's Joe Fulghum and Halifax's Buddy Condy hit .418 and .411, respectively, in an exciting H&D League batting race in 1951. The only other player to exceed .400 in a single season was Presque Isle's Angelo Dagres, whose dominant summer in 1955 led directly to a stint with the major league Baltimore Orioles that same September. Following these six were Al Ware, whose .399 average led the 1949 Cape Breton Colliery League, and the Kentville Wildcats dynamic duo of Dick Gernert and Jack Kaiser, who put up .396 and .392 averages, respectively, in 1948. Hal Buckwalter followed with a .390 average in the 1949 Central League., Maine star Gerry Duffy had identical numbers the following year playing in the Maine–New Brunswick but only had 100 at-bats and is not included in Appendix Two.

It is important to note that some players appear more than once in the top 25 single-season performances. Buddy Condy had three such finishes between 1948 and 1951. Joe Fulghum had a second appearance on the list when he finished runner-up to Zeke Bella in the H&D batting race in 1954. Jack Kaiser and Dick Gernert repeated their H&D League dominance in 1948 with top performances in 1949 as members of the Central League Wildcats. Between them Condy, Gernert, Kaiser, and Fulghum occupy seven of the top fifteen single-season performances over the postwar years.

One thing that jumps out from this data is that averages in the 1940s were considerably higher than those in the 1950s, especially from 1952 onward. Performances in both the Cape Breton and the Central League in the 1940s, moreover, had higher run-producing environments than the H&D League. These differences were evident to observers at the time. Sportswriter Alex Nickerson of the *Halifax Herald*, for example, often commented on a difference that seems obvious at a glance. When the *Herald* published the Central League batting statistics for the

Twelve. Great Performers, Great Performances 169

1949 season, for example, Nickerson wrote that "certainly the pitching hasn't been distinguished in the Central League.... Nineteen batsmen had over .300 averages." He questioned in particular Chris Tonery's league-leading batting average. "How much lower would Tonery's average be if he were batting in the H&D League?" he asked.[3] Of course, this is the very question that sabermetricians try to answer when they attempt to calculate major league equivalencies.[4]

Another Central League star, Clark Wojtowicz, would likely have been included had the final batting statistics for 1948 been released. Indeed, *The Sporting News* reported on March 2, 1949, that "the Yankees are bringing up an outfielder named Wotowicz [sic] ... with a .410 batting average last season" from what it called "the Nova Scotia independent league."[5] Whether this is accurate or not, most observers had raved about the strong-armed young outfielder with speed and good batting skills.

Taking into account the inflated run-producing environments of the Central League and Cape Breton Colliery League, and more generally performances between 1946 and 1951 in comparison to the later H&D League and Maine–New Brunswick League, helps in determining more reliable major league equivalencies. Adjusting for these differences provides more effective comparisons with player performances over time. As a result, Gernert's .396 average in the 1949 Central League resulted in a lower MLE than did his .357 in the H&D League the year before. MLE's are included for all players in Appendix 2, and where possible they are compared with those provided in *Out of the Park Baseball*'s historical simulations.

The experience of Jack Kaiser, *Varsity Magazine*'s College Player of the Year in 1949, provides an indication of the different competitive environments of the 1940s and 1950s, as well as performance levels in the Central and H&D Leagues. Kaiser had two stints in Nova Scotia, the first with the Kentville Wildcats in 1948 and 1949, then as the playing coach of the Liverpool Larrupers from 1954 through 1957. In between he spent four years in the Red Sox organization. Kaiser was a dominant player in the Central League with Kentville in 1949, putting up numbers equivalent to teammate Dick Gernert, albeit with more limited power. As we have seen, Kaiser's .392 batting average in 1949 ranks in the top ten single-season performances of all players in the Maritimes over its fifteen-year history. After his initial two years in Nova Scotia, Kaiser maintained those numbers in the Canadian-American League in 1950, had solid seasons in Roanoke in 1951 (.301) and another with Albany of the Class-A Eastern League in 1952 (.284). After he returned to the H&D League, his performance reflected the more competitive run-production environment of the fifties, hitting .289 with 19 home runs in 640 at-bats, about .100 points below his numbers in the previous decade.

Quality of Competition (QUOC): Comparative Individual Performance

The following case studies of fifty-three players, equally divided between position players and pitchers, provide insights into competition levels by comparing players' performances in the Maritimes with their initial season in Organized Baseball. For the most part, these studies include statistics for players moving directly from the H&D League to Class B or A leagues. A few went directly to Double-A. A handful of veteran players with careers at the professional level before coming to the Maritimes are included as well. In some cases—like Kaiser—players had two stints in the Maritimes, before and after their sojourn in Organized Baseball. Players who began or ended their professional careers at Class D were not included in this sample because they are too numerous to mention.

Position Players

Dick Ballestrini was a five-year veteran minor league catcher in the Dodgers organization who came to Kentville in 1954 from the Carolina League. His numbers were almost identical at both levels.

	AB	H	2b	3b	HR	Ave	OPS
1953 Carolina B	138	35	9	0	3	.254	
1954 Kentville (H&D)	172	44	9	3	6	.256	

John "Zeke" Bella played in the H&D League in 1949 and 1950 before signing with the New York Yankees. He returned to Halifax for another season in 1954. In five AAA seasons he compiled a .316 average and had brief appearances in the majors in 1957 and 1959.

	AB	H	2b	3b	HR	Ave	OPS
1949–50 Dartmouth H&D	428	117				.273	
1951 Class C Can-Am	233	89	12	8	2	.382	1.026
1951 Class A Eastern	63	20	3	0	0	.318	0.723
1954 Halifax H&D	212	87	18	5	9	.406	
1955 Class A Eastern	372	138	24	7	10	.371	1.021

Twelve. Great Performers, Great Performances

Hal Buckwalter, a second baseman out of Temple, had a monster season with Amherst of the Central League before turning pro with Oneonta of the Class C Can-Am League. He was the youngest regular in the AAA American Association in 1952.

	AB	H	2b	3b	HR	Ave	OPS
1949 Amherst (Central)	164	64				.390	
1950 (Class C Can-Am)	505	165	27	7	2	.327	

Ty Cline played with the Dartmouth Arrows in 1958 and 1959. An All-American at Clemson University, he began his professional career in 1960 with Mobile of the Southern Association and went on to play twelve years in the majors. His numbers in the H&D League and at AA were almost identical.

	AB	H	2b	3b	HR	Ave	OPS
1958–59 Dartmouth (H&D)	205	63	14	5	4	.307	
1960 Southern AA	379	118	20	8	9	.311	.836

Ed Czerniakowski was a power-hitting catcher with Kentville and Halifax before being signed by the Philadelphia Phillies and sent to their AA Texas affiliate in 1958. He put up similar numbers at both levels.

	AB	H	2b	3b	HR	Ave	OPS
1956–7 Halifax-Kent H&D	272	72	19	4	5	.264	
1958 Texas League AA	211	54	7	0	4	.256	.632

Harry Durkin was Notre Dame's starting shortstop and home run leader in 1951[6] and an all-star shortstop with Halifax in 1949. His performance in his first minor league season was superior to his previous three years in the Maritimes.

	AB	H	2b	3b	HR	Ave	OPS
1950–2 H&D/Me-NB	532	140	18	5	6	.263	
1953 CARL B	293	82	10	6	6	.314	.848

Stu Erickson spent three years (1949–51) at Class C and B, hitting .284 in over 1000 at-bats with power. He joined Art Hoch's 1952 Truro Bearcats, put up identical numbers, and played a few years in the H&D League before going to Nova Scotia's South Shore League as player coach.

	AB	H	2b	3b	HR	Ave	OPS
1949–51 Class C/B	1059	301	54	13	46	.284	.952 (1949)
1952 Truro H&D	200	57	13	2	6	.285	

Sal Ferrara is one of the most underestimated players to play in the Maritimes despite winning the H&D League batting title in 1956. He was twenty-four years of age when he turned pro, which may explain why this .300 hitter at all levels did not advance further.

	AB	H	2b	3b	HR	Ave	OPS
1955–56 H&D	398	125	8	10	15	.314	
1957 Carolina B	231	71	3	3	3	.307	.734
1957 Eastern A	167	53	8	3	0	.317	.780

Bob Flynn was a five-year veteran in the Pirates organization when he was released in the middle of the Eastern League season in 1956. He struggled in the H&D League as well that year.

	AB	H	2b	3b	HR	Ave	OPS
1956 H&D	117	22	2	0	0	.188	
1956 EAST A	130	23	0	1	4	.177	.597

Wendell Forbes played with the Middleton Cardinals and Fredericton Capitols before signing with Saint Louis in 1951. In four minor league seasons he hit .284 with limited power.

	AB	H	2b	3b	HR	Ave	OPS
1949–50 H&D/NB	266	74				.278	
1951 Class B	310	82	8	3	3	.265	.685

Alvin Griggs played two seasons in the Maritimes at Edmundston and Kentville. His statistical line was almost identical to his first stop in the minors with Williamsport (Eastern) in 1954.

	AB	H	2b	3b	HR	Ave	OPS
1953 H&D	245	61	5	2	12	.249	
1954 Eastern A	192	47	6	3	2	.245	.658

Dickie Harris, a Wake Forest product and son of major league player and manager Bucky Harris, played two seasons in Nova Scotia before signing with the Washington Senators in 1954.

	AB	H	2b	3b	HR	Ave	OPS
1952–3 H&D	262	63	7	4	3	.241	
1954 CARL B	287	74	14	7	3	.258	.747

Grover "Deacon" Jones played two years for coach Ray Fisher in Blacks Harbour and Truro with dramatically different results. Jones hit .353 in New Brunswick in 1953 and .243 in the H&D League in 1954. He had two brief stops in the majors with the Chicago White Sox.

	AB	H	2b	3b	HR	Ave	OPS
1953–54 Me-NB/H&D	364	105	27	11	12	.286	
1955 Three-I League B	267	85	11	7	9	.318	.978

Jack Kaiser had two outstanding years with Kentville before entering the Red Sox system in 1950. He retired before the 1954 season and was playing coach and Red Sox scout at Liverpool for four more seasons.

	AB	H	2b	3b	HR	Ave	OPS
1952–53 Eastern A	759	207	32	4	14	.273	
1954–57 H&D	640	185	34	8	19	.289	

Steve Korcheck was a highly regarded catcher who put up similar numbers to his H&D League performance in his initial season at Class A Charlotte. He struggled at the plate in future years at the major league level.

	AB	H	2b	3b	HR	Ave	OPS
1953 Kentville H&D	215	68	9	9	7	.316	
1954 Sally A	167	48	8	2	4	.287	.770
MLB	7	1	0	0	0	.143	

Ray Looney was a power-hitting first baseman from Pittsburgh who played two years in Nova Scotia. An obvious big-league prospect, his career was derailed by shoulder injuries early in his minor league career. Looney's son Brian later pitched for the Montreal Expos.

	AB	H	2b	3b	HR	Ave	OPS
1956–57 H&D	328	91	16	6	19	.278	
1958 Class B-A	459	132	23	12	23	.288	.935

Eugene "Bucky" Luck played two years for the Liverpool Larrupers before signing with the Detroit Tigers. An outfielder with good range, his minor league career numbers at Class B Durham and Class A Knoxville closely matched those in the H&D League.

	AB	H	2b	3b	HR	Ave	OPS
1954–55 H&D	491	140	25	4	9	.285	
1956 Carolina B	373	101	19	5	4	.271	.712

Tom Morgan was a second baseman out of Lafayette University who was known more for his defensive skills than his bat. After spending the 1957 season in Kentville, he performed for a couple of years in the Phillies chain before retiring from baseball.

	AB	H	2b	3b	HR	Ave	OPS
1957 H&D	142	37	5	3	0	.261	
1958 Texas AA	152	33	4	1	0	.217	.592

Danny Murphy was the most sought after high-school prospect of the late 1960s and signed a $100,000 bonus after a year with Truro. He played sparingly in the big leagues in his first year of pro ball but put up similar numbers in the Texas league to those in Truro the year before. Initially an outfielder, he was turned into a relief pitcher and made a second trip to the majors a number of years later.

	AB	H	2b	3b	HR	Ave	OPS
1959 Truro H&D	153	43	8	1	7	.281	
1960 Texas AA	177	52	11	2	8	.294	.904

Bob O'Donnell was another good-field, no-hit shortstop whose bat kept him from advancing beyond the Class A Eastern League. After four minor league seasons he returned to the H&D League in 1957 for a final year of summer ball.

	AB	H	2b	3b	HR	Ave	OPS
1953 Class C-B	488	118	11	7	3	.242	.662
1951–52/1957 H&D	682	188	25	10	7	.264	

Don Prohovich was a basketball and baseball star at Holy Cross. A talented shortstop, Prohovich went on to play a number of years in the Chicago White Sox system. He began his four-year stint in the Maritimes with Edmundston in 1952 before moving to Kentville for the next three seasons.

	AB	H	2b	3b	HR	Ave	OPS
1952 NB 1953–55 H&D	544	136	21	8	14	.251	
1956 Western Class-A	236	67	14	0	1	.284	.900

Larry Rancourt, another of the many Holy Cross collegians to play in the H&D League, played for Kentville in 1957 before signing a minor league contract with the Cincinnati Reds. He began his five-year pro career with Savannah in the Sally League, reached as high as AAA and went to spring training with the Reds in 1962.

	AB	H	2b	3b	HR	Ave	OPS
1957 H&D	164	43	8	2	3	.262	
1958 Sally A	200	49	8	0	3	.245	.682

Dick Santaniello, from Holy Cross, played first with Grand Falls and then with Truro in the mid-fifties. The Baltimore Orioles considered him one of the finest defensive outfielders in their system.

	AB	H	2b	3b	HR	Ave	OPS
1954–55 H&D/MeNB	385	99	14	10		.257	
1956 B/A	225	56	7	2	3	.249	

Matt Sczesny, a Brooklyn native, was a .260s hitter in his only year in Nova Scotia and replicated that at every level he played at in his subsequent minor league career. Sczesny went on to spend fifty-five years with the Red Sox as player, manager and scout.

	AB	H	2b	3b	HR	Ave	OPS
1953 H&D	164	44	10	5	3	.268	
1954 CARL B	140	37	6	2	0	.264	.703
Eastern A	48	12	1	0	2	.250	

Al Spangler, one of a number of talented outfielders from Duke who played two seasons in Halifax, went on to a twelve-year career in the majors with Milwaukee and Houston.

	AB	H	2b	3b	HR	Ave	OPS
1952–53 Halifax H&D	302	89	9	4	2	.295	
1954 Class B-A	191	54	9	5	1	.283	.752

Don Stafford was a feared hitter in the minor leagues and was sometimes referred to as a "doubles machine." He was a minor league Silver Bat trophy winner in 1952. In 1955 he joined the Carolinian contingent in the H&D League as a member of the Halifax Cardinals.

	AB	H	2b	3b	HR	Ave	OPS
1954 Carolina B	344	105	23		17	.305	.909
1955 Halifax H&D	195	57	8	4	11	.292	

Performance Comparisons for Position Players

Performance trajectories of position players in back-to-back seasons were analyzed to determine if they were able to replicate the previous season's results. Offensive player performances were sorted into three categories: maintained, underperformed and overperformed. Batters were categorized on the basis of batting average, but in marginal situations may have been adjusted if their slugging averages were markedly different from the previous year. A difference of less than 10 percent in offensive output was considered to have replicated previous performance; differences of more than that were classified either as underperforming or overperforming. The vast majority of comparisons involved the H&D League and the Maine–New Brunswick League and Class B or Class A levels within Organized Baseball. In a few cases the comparisons involved performance at Class C or Class AA. In addition to players going from the Maritimes to the minor leagues, there are a few instances of players moving in the opposite direction.

Of the twenty-six players in the sample, twenty-one maintained their previous year's level of performance. Three of them (Cline, Murphy and Czerniakowski) maintained at Class AA, eight maintained at Class A, and seven others did so when going from the H&D League to Class B. Three players who came to the Maritimes from Class B Leagues maintained their earlier offensive output numbers as well. Of the four remaining players, Don Prohovich outperformed his H&D League career at Class A Colorado Springs and Harry Durkin improved on his H&D League numbers in the Class B Carolina League. Tom Morgan underperformed in the AA Texas League, as did Bob O'Donnell at Class B. In general, the results of the above comparisons suggest a relatively seamless transition for H&D League and Maine–New Brunswick League players moving to either Class B or A.

Pitchers

Jim Arbucho bounced back and forth between the H&D League and the minor leagues in 1949 and 1950 with somewhat similar results. His pitching stats from the Central League in 1949 are unavailable

	W	L	ERA	IP	H	R	BB	K	WHIP
1949 Central Lg				not available					
1949 Norl C	5	6	3.35	102	95	46	38	71	1.304
1950 H&D	5	2	2.59	52	49		20	30	1.353
1950 ISLG B	3	5	3.70	56	52	42	36		1.571

Charles "Buzz" Bowers, a Michigan State product, began his minor league career at Triple-A in 1950 and spent his later years in the Eastern League. In 1958 the Phillies tabbed him to be the player-coach of the Kentville Wildcats of the H&D league. He was the club's leading reliever that season before embarking on a lengthy scouting career with the Red Sox and Dodgers.

	W	L	ERA	IP	H	R	BB	K	WHIP
1957 Eastern A	14	8	2.93	135	134	50	63	79	1.459
1958 H&D	3	4	3.06	47	50		15	33	1.382

Twelve. Great Performers, Great Performances

Jack Bowes. Along with Billy Harris and Wilson Parsons and Vern Handrahan, Jackie Bowes ranked at the top of the Maritime-born players during the 1950s. After pitching for McAdam and Saint John in 1949 and 1950 and Guelph of the Intercounty League in 1951, Bowes signed a minor league contract with the Indians. He had an outstanding season in 1953 in the Quebec Provincial League.

	W	L	ERA	IP	H	R	BB	K	WHIP
1949–51 NB Lg				not available					
1951 Guelph	7	3	2.27	83	53	33	36	65	1.194
1952 IIIL B	9	14	3.87	186	159	90	122		1.511

Bobby Lee Brown was one of the many Wake Forest collegians to play for the Stellarton Albions in the early 1950s and was an important cog in their Maritime championship team in 1953. He went on to pitch for a number of years in the Washington Senators organization.

	W	L	ERA	IP	H	R	BB	K	WHIP
1953 H&D	6	6		85	57	40	54	46	1.305
1954 TRIS B	10	12	4.30	138	123	82	70	76	1.399
SALL A	2	3							

Dick Bunker spent three years with the Kentville Wildcats between 1953 and 1955 before being assigned by the Philadelphia Phillies to their Eastern League affiliate. After a dominant rookie year, he played a number of years at the AAA level.

	W	L	ERA	IP	H	R	BB	K	WHIP
1953–55 H&D	16	17		306	241		224	152	1.519
1956 East A	17	8	2.09	202	163	61	95	143	1.277

Ron Cote, from Holy Cross, played three years in the Maritimes before turning pro and eventually rising to the AAA level.

	W	L	ERA	IP	H	R	BB	K	WHIP
1953–5 H&D	16	15		275	238		163	202	1.458
1956 Class B-A	2	6	4.20	75	76	44	49	40	1.666

Jim Craig played three years in the H&D League with Kentville and Halifax, winning twenty-two games against just five defeats.

	W	L	ERA	IP	H	R	BB	K	WHIP
1957–59 H&D	22	5		235	203		140	239	1.459
1960 CARL B	2	7	4.89	92	84	57	56	61	1.446

Hal Deitz spent two years with Kentville before starting his pro career with York (Eastern) in 1959. His 0.946 WHIP ranks as the best ever in the history of the H&D League.

	W	L	ERA	IP	H	R	BB	K	WHIP
1957–58 H&D	11	5	2.23	185	133	60	42	152	0.946
1959 Eastern A	8	9	3.44	136	144	63	17	71	1.184

Jim DiFrederico was one of many young prospects from Maine who played in the Maritimes before and after his five-year minor league career in the Red Sox organization. After three solid seasons as a starter in the Piedmont League, he came to the H&D League in 1954 with the Liverpool Larrupers.

	W	L	ERA	IP	H	R	BB	K	WHIP
1953 PIED B	6	6	3.49	80	87	47	41	25	1.600
1954 H&D	3	2	4.+	44	53	25	23	26	1.730

"Turk" Farrell came to the Maritimes as a sixteen-year-old with the 1951 Springhill Fencebusters. In 1952 he played briefly with the Halifax Capitals and broke into pro ball the next season with the Phillies in the Class A Eastern League.

	W	L	ERA	IP	H	R	BB	K	WHIP
1951–52 NB H&D	4	2	3.+	65	57	37	43	45	1.538
1953 East A	7	3	3.39	93	88	47	47	65	1.452

John "Four Eyes" Forizs was a high-school phenom from Bridgeport, Connecticut, who was sent to Kentville by the Dodgers in 1951. Forizs rose to the Triple-A level, but his major league aspirations ended with arm troubles.

	W	L	ERA	IP	H	R	BB	K	WHIP
1951 H&D	4	3	2.67	64	36		27	67	0.984
1952 Class C	20	8	2.04	216	137	65	123	252	1.203

Gerry Glynn played the 1959 season in Halifax. Signed by the Braves, he began his four-year minor league career with Austin of the Texas League. Although his WHIP at AA was almost identical to that in Nova Scotia, his ERA was elevated.

	W	L	ERA	IP	H	R	BB	K	WHIP
1959 H&D	4	5	3.39	77	65	41	58	59	1.597
1960 Texas AA	2	9	5.49	77	82	51	42	38	1.610

Twelve. Great Performers, Great Performances

Charles Heerlein was a first team All-American in 1954 at Saint John's University after winning eleven games for Liverpool the previous year.

	W	L	ERA	IP	H	R	BB	K	WHIP
1953 H&D	11	4		78	71		28	27	1.269
1954 Eastern A	1	1	3.83	54	53	30	21	17	1.388

"Smokey" Jim Heller was a veteran right-hander and two-time 20-game winner in the minors. A favorite of Yankees scout Bob Decker, Heller was a dominant pitcher through the later forties and into the fifties.

	W	L	ERA	IP	H	R	BB	K	WHIP
1948 WTMN C	20	9	4.55	251	299	162	110	137	1.629
1949 H&D	14	2	2.22	142	101		27	110	0.964
1950 H&D	9	7	2.81	126	111		29	78	1.111
1951 GULF B	20	5	4.42	218	238	107	78	118	1.450
1952 GULF B	8	10	3.71	148	141	71	51	75	1.297
1952 H&D	5	1		56	34		12	39	0.821

George Heller, brother of "Smokey" Jim, was a veteran minor leaguer who rose to AAA in the Giants organization in 1950 and 1951. He spent a season with the Dartmouth Arrows in 1954 before returning to AA the following year. (He over-performed at Class A.)

	W	L	ERA	IP	H	R	BB	K	WHIP
1953 WL A	4	8	4.12	118	117	82	95	67	1.797
1954 SALL A	4	5	2.65	78	66	28	48	48	1.462
1955 H&D	1	2		31	29	19	12	17	1.322
1955 Eastern A									

Bob Krop, who impressed in 1957 with a high-90s fastball, rose quickly through the Cincinnati system. A lack of command and persistent wildness kept him from making the big leagues.

	W	L	ERA	IP	H	R	BB	K	WHIP
1957 H&D	3	4	4.02	31	30	14	28	32	1.903
1958 NORW B	9	6	2.75	134	100	50	78	138	1.328
PCL AAA									

Gene Lary was another H&D Leaguer who made it to the cusp of the major leagues. Brother of big league star Frank Lary, Gene had a rocky season with Truro in 1954 but followed that with a number of solid seasons in the minors.

	W	L	ERA	IP	H	R	BB	K	WHIP
1954 H&D	1	4		39	60		19	26	2.062
1955 East A	9	4	4.21	92	84	47	39	55	1.337

Joe Lewis, a mainstay of the Duke University Blue Devils pitching staff in the early fifties, had a standout season in the New Brunswick Maine League in 1952 before beginning his minor league career in the Carolinas.

	W	L	ERA	IP	H	R	BB	K	WHIP
1952 Me-NB	7	6	2.52	109	83		71	129	1.431
1953 CARL B	8	8	3.18	119	108	59	71	106	1.504

Bob List played on the Brooklyn Dodgers rookie squad while in high school before coming to Nova Scotia in 1956. A big league prospect, his career was derailed by a serious car crash while pitching in the Cardinals organization.

	W	L	ERA	IP	H	R	BB	K	WHIP
1956–58 H&D	12	16	3.+	250	218		143	212	1.442
1959 B-AAA	6	1	2.94	52	57	23	13	36	1.346

Vance Long, from Richmond, Virginia, spent the summer of 1953 in Nova Scotia before three years in the Yankees organization. Although he performed reasonably well in the minors, he did not advance beyond A ball.

	W	L	ERA	IP	H	R	BB	K	WHIP
1953 H&D	2	3	4.+	36	43	24	8	21	1.417
1954 C-B	7	9	3.42	137	131		71	105	1.474

Ken MacKenzie, from Gore Bay, Ontario, was a teammate of Moe Drabowsky in Truro and the Bearcats ace in 1957. Signed by Braves scout Jeff Jones, he went directly to AA in 1958. Later he was a member of Casey Stengel's hapless 1961 New York Mets.

	W	L	ERA	IP	H	R	BB	K	WHIP
1956 Truro H&D	10	4	3.26	97.1	96	44	26	63	1.253
1957 SOUA AA	14	6	3.26	204	174	82	64	147	1.166

Wilson Parsons, perhaps the most talented local pitcher to come out of Nova Scotia in the fifties, joined the New York Yankees organization in 1952. A serious arm injury with AAA Kansas City in 1954 derailed his big league dreams, but he continued to pitch at the Triple A Level through 1959. He returned to Nova Scotia that year for one final season.

	W	L	ERA	IP	H	R	BB	K	WHIP
1951 H&D	3	4	3.69	68	46	28	41	54	1.294
1952 PIED B	9	1	3.53	130	91	62	128		1.685
1958 IL AAA	2	6	3.63	72	74	36	48	33	1.694
1959 H&D	7	2	2.36	88	82		23	97	1.193
1959 Miami AAA	2	0		11	10	7			

John Patula was a journeyman pitcher who had a good year in Liverpool in 1952 before signing a Red Sox contract. His numbers in the Class B Carolina League closely resembled those in the H&D League.

	W	L	ERA	IP	H	R	BB	K	WHIP
1952 H&D	7	3		87	76	38	61	61	1.575
1953 CARL	8	9	3.93	126	98	69	98	79	1.556

Jim Raugh won eight games for Halifax in 1956 and entered the Detroit Tigers' system the following year. A product of the University of North Carolina, Raugh spent five years in the minors, winning thirty games against only thirteen defeats.

	W	L	ERA	IP	H	R	BB	K	WHIP
1956 H&D	8	1	4.01	199.1	112	56	46	79	1.330
1957 CARL B	6	4	2.05	101	82	38	34	66	1.153

Hal Stowe was runner-up in the H&D League pitching derby in 1958. He had a successful minor league debut the following year. A favorite of Casey Stengel, he experienced a personality conflict with Yankees manager Ralph Houk that limited his big league career to a single inning.

	W	L	ERA	IP	H	R	BB	K	WHIP
1958 H&D	7	3	1.81	75	59	23	31	83	1.200
1959 NORL C CARL B	5	4	2.75	95	81	35	33	90	1.232

Don Swanson had three seasons in the H&D League and three subsequent years in the Cubs organization. He played parts of two seasons in the Texas League and had a brief appearance with Los Angeles of the Pacific Coast League.

	W	L	ERA	IP	H	R	BB	K	WHIP
1955–57 H&D	23	9	3.+	250	197		102	170	1.196
1958 III B	12	11	4.33	183	201	108	86	124	1.568

Phil Tarpey was a hard-throwing righty out of the University of Massachusetts who played in the Maine–New Brunswick League and with Halifax of the H&D League. He spent two years at Class B Burlington of the Three-I League in the Cubs organization.

	W	L	ERA	IP	H	R	BB	K	WHIP
1953–54 Me/H&D	10	5		152	148		90	81	1.552
1955 III B	5	3	3.55	71	63		39	37	1.310

Performance Comparisons for Pitchers

The results for the twenty-seven pitchers included here suggest a higher rate of variability than for position players. This is to be expected. Pitching statistics are more difficult to assess, given that year-by-year performances are more commonly affected by arm injuries, the development of new pitches, or changes in usage from starter to reliever. This is perhaps why Bill James focused more on batting performance in establishing equivalencies, and less on the development of a formula for analyzing pitching performances from year to year. Of the twenty-seven pitchers included below, most went directly to Class A or B clubs and a few made the jump to AA for their initial minor league season. As with position players, their performances are categorized as maintaining, outperforming or underperforming their previous year's record. My approach was initially to compare walks and hits per innings pitched (WHIP) with secondary emphasis on earned run averages and after that won-lost records. The various variables associated with pitching performance are reflected in the mixed performance results of those included in this sample.

Eleven pitchers maintained their H&D League or Maine–New Brunswick League performance levels as they began their professional careers. Two of those players (Glynn and MacKenzie) did so at Class AA, four replicated their earlier success at Class A, four more at Class B, and another at Class C. Five players put up better records in their first pro season than in their previous stints in the Maritimes, and nine others underperformed, all of the latter at Class B through AAA. In some circumstances, underperformers still put up respectable seasons, but they could not approximate the superior results that they put up earlier. One such example was Hal Deitz, whose 2.23 ERA and 0.946 WHIP with Kentville over two summers gave way to a 3.44 ERA and 1.184 WHIP with Class A York of the Eastern League in 1959. Although he was ranked as underperforming, his first season in pro ball was nonetheless a success and led to his promotion to AA the following year. He continued his progression to AAA in 1961.

Determining QUOC

There are many things to consider in establishing a quality of competition (QUOC) index for the H&D League and the New Brunswick League in the 1940s and '50s. One important element is the way players moved from one level to the next in the same or subsequent years, thus the fifty-three case studies presented above. According to Bill James, position players moving from AAA to the majors lose about 18 percent of their run-producing output. From this assumption he calculates two factors: an M factor and the square root of M, which he calls m. In the case of AAA players, M is .82 and m is .9. For my purposes I have used these factors to compare levels from AA through Class D. If batters performed at .82 of their major league run-producing ability at AAA, then Class A players would lose a similar 18 percent of their AAA effectiveness, i.e., .18 × .82 = or 14.7 percent. This would continue in the same fashion downward, classification by classification. The resulting adjustment for different levels of competition and M and m factors is included in the table below. One should bear in mind, however, that the classifications within Organized Baseball represent only a general indicator of quality of competition. Some Class C Leagues were as competitive as the average Class B League—"hitting above their weight," so to speak. According to Christian Trudeau, this was the case for the Quebec Provincial League from the late forties through the mid-fifties—while the differences between Class B and A leagues at the time were not always clear. In 1951 Rip Sewell observed that most teams in the Class B Florida International League were superior to those in Class A.[7]

	M	m
Major League Baseball	---	---
Triple A	.82	.905
Double A	.67	.819
Class A	.55	.741
Class B	.45	.678
Class C	.37	.608
Class D	.30	.550

After considerable reflection I have developed QUOC indexes for the five most prominent leagues in the postwar Maritimes: the Halifax and District League, the Central League, the Cape Breton Colliery League, the Maine–New Brunswick League, and the New Brunswick League.

		M	*m*
Halifax and District League	1946–8	.37	.608
	1949–51	.42	.648
	1952–6	.55	.741
	1957–9	.52	.721
Central League	1947–9	.33	.574
Cape Breton Colliery Lg	1949–50	.30	.550
New Brunswick Lg	1946–8	.33	.574
	1949–50	.37	.608
Maine–New Brunswick Lg	1950–1	.41	.640
	1952–5	.45	.678

A final adjustment comes by comparing run-scoring environments of specific leagues. A comparison of the runs-per-game statistics with those of MLB by year allows for the calculation of major league equivalencies. Appendix 3 includes statistics for a number of prominent pitchers. Finally, I relied on these calculations to select an all-star team of great performers (and honorable mentions) from Maritime baseball in the postwar era.

The Best of the Best

Earlier on I referred to the important work that Nova Scotian Burton Russell did in chronicling Maritime baseball history. His publications, often encyclopedic in nature, have provided a solid point of reference for this study. One of Russell's preoccupations—along with his celebration of local idols Johnny Clark and Buddy Condy—was the selection of his personal all-star teams, derived from witnessing play on the diamonds across the region for some seventy years. Russell's all-time H&D League All-Star selections were as follows. His catcher was Steve Korcheck of the 1953 Kentville Wildcats. Another Wildcat, first baseman Dick Gernert, anchored an infield that included "The Westville Flash" Johnny Clark at second base, Stellarton's Gair Allie at short, and Jack Kubiszyn, who played for both Liverpool and Kentville, at third base. His outfield was composed of Joe Fulghum in left field, Zeke Bella in center, and Buddy Condy in right. Left-hander Skit Ferguson and right-hander Jim Heller were his selections on the mound. The statistical evidence contained in this chapter is not a challenge to his choices, but rather is another indication of the great performers and performances of the postwar era. Furthermore, it expands Russell's focus on the H&D League to include the exploits of players in New

Twelve. Great Performers, Great Performances

Brunswick and in the Maine–New Brunswick League. What follows is my Maritime All-Star selections, grounded in sabermetrics: Burton Russell meet Bill James!

All-Maritime All Stars 1946–60

First Team			Honorable Mention
Catcher	**Leo Parent**	Stell/Truro	(Steve Korcheck, Jack Kurty)
First Base	**Dick Gernert**	Kentville	(Hal Buckwalter, Roger Rada)
Second Base	**Roly McLenahan**	Fredericton	(Herb Rossmann, Deacon Jones)
Shortstop	**Sal Ferrara**	Truro	(Gair Allie)
Third Base	**Jack Kubiszyn**	Liv/Kentville	(Al Ware)
Left Field	**Zeke Bella**	Hfx/Dart	(Danny Seaman)
Center Field	**Angelo Dagres**	Presque Isle	(Ty Cline)
Right Field	**Buddy Condy**	Halifax	(Fred Flemming, Al Spangler)
DH	**Joe Fulghum**	Stellarton	(Herb McLeod)
Utility	**Johnny Clark**	Truro/Hfx	(Norm Gigon)
RHP	**Moe Drabowsky**	Truro	(Jim Heller, Hal Deitz)
LHP	**Ron Perranoski**	Edmundston	(Hal Stowe)
	Skit Ferguson	Truro/Hfx	(Jack Halpin)

Not surprisingly, available statistics tend to reinforce more subjective judgements about the great performers in the Maritimes and Maine, but they also suggest some interesting refinements. I recognize, of course, that statistical performances always need to be contextualized, as eight-year veteran playing coach Art Hoch emphasized in our many conversations. Indeed, if I were to include a slot for coach/manager among the all-star selections above, Hoch would be my choice. Selected as the 1946 First Team All-American shortstop on the National Baseball Congress' sixteen-man squad, he became a household word in Nova Scotia in the 1950s. He put together teams year after year, drawing on the best young players in the Carolinas along with veteran minor leaguers. Hoch gained respect wherever he played and coached, from Stellarton to Dartmouth to Halifax, and he inserted himself in the lineup wherever he was needed on the diamond. In over 1500 at-bats during the fifties, Hoch hit .258. His best season was in 1951 before taking on coaching responsibilities that he thought distracted from game readiness.

As for the position players, there were three leading candidates for all-star honors at the catcher's position—Leo Parent, Steve Korcheck and Jack Kurty. My choice was Parent, a five-year veteran of the H&D League who ranked ahead of the others in batting average, showed solid power, and demonstrated his versatility with a number of excellent pitching performances over the years. Korcheck put up good numbers, but the future big-leaguer's H&D League career was limited to a single summer. Kurty was a two-time batting champion in the Maine–New Brunswick League, but his three years in the H&D League fell a bit below that standard. Dick Gernert, who played two years for the Kentville Wildcats, was a hands-down selection at first base, nosing out veteran minor leaguer Roger Rada, who had two excellent years in the H&D League, and Hal Buckwalter who deserves mention for a superior season at Amherst in 1949. One of my biggest surprise performers was New Brunswicker Roly McLenahan, an NHL hockey player who finished second in both the career and single-season batting average tabulations. An infielder who was more accomplished with his bat than his glove, McLenahan edges out Halifax's Herbie Rossmann and two-year veteran Deacon Jones as my selection at second base. At shortstop there was a flat-out tie between Sal Ferrara and future major leaguer Gair Allie. Ferrara hit for a higher average, Allie with obvious power: both were consummate defenders. At third base, Jack Kubiszyn, who played two seasons in Liverpool and a third in Kentville, was an unrivalled performer at the hot corner. Al Ware deserves honorable mention for his outstanding season in the 1949 Cape Breton Colliery League.

In the outfield there was little difficulty selecting Buddy Condy, Angelo Dagres and Zeke Bella as the all-star trio. Big Joe Fulghum was their equal at the plate, but given his defensive limitations I include him here as a Designated Hitter, despite there not being such a thing at the time. Another defensively challenged outfielder, Springhill's Herbie McLeod deserves honorable mention as DH, given his consistency at the plate. Two others, infielder-outfielders Johnny Clark and future big-leaguer Norm Gigon, join my all-star selections as utility players. In the outfield, Liverpool Larruper standout Danny Seaman, Halifax's Al Spangler, New Brunswick native Fred Flemming, and Dartmouth Arrows Ty Cline all deserve honorable mention.

The selection of the all-star right-handed and left-handed pitchers had its own challenges, given the many remarkable performances over the years. Moe Drabowsky was a relatively easy choice, given his two excellent summers in Truro and his ability to go directly to the major leagues, where he immediately assumed a starting role in the Chicago Cubs rotation. Two other righties were outstanding performers. Jim Heller, twice a twenty-game winner in the minors, had a 41 and 16 record in the H&D League, just one win below all-time league leader and Nova Scotia native Neil "Ozark" Staples. Heller's 1.098 WHIP followed closely behind Don Eason at 1.020 and Drabowsky's 1.021. Equally deserving Hal Deitz put up a career WHIP of 0.948 in

Twelve. Great Performers, Great Performances

Zeke Bella was one of the best all-around ballplayers in the H&D League in the late forties and early fifties. He played parts of two seasons in the majors with the Yankees and Athletics (Halifax Municipal Archives, CR67-5-989.01.45).

his two years in Kentville, the best of all performers spending two or more seasons in the league. The choice of all-star left-handers was far more challenging. There were many possible choices, but Ron Perranoski's two years in Edmundston in the mid-fifties gave an indication of his future long-term career with the Los Angeles Dodgers. If one focuses on performers from the 1940s, however, Philip "Skit" Ferguson and Jack Halpin were standouts and equally talented. Halpin won forty games against only eighteen losses, and his career WHIP of 1.124 ranks fifth behind Heller and the others. Ferguson was unrivalled in the opening year of H&D League play and continued to perform well after that until arm problems cut short his career. I have decided to differentiate Halpin and Ferguson from the forties and Perranoski and future Yankee Hal Stowe from the fifties, but singling out great performers and performances is always subject to debate. The statistical information included here nonetheless provides a further way to compare different stars at different times in the history of postwar Maritime baseball. Hopefully, this research will contribute to the continuing conversation involving quality of competition indexes for Organized Baseball and the many summer leagues that straddled the Canadian-American border after the Second World War.

"Two of the H&D League's finest left-handers, Skit Ferguson and Jack Halpin, square off with two young boys on their backs and League President Harry Butler in the background." (Halifax Municipal Archives. CR67–989.01.80).

Appendix 1
Career Batting and Major League Equivalencies: Maritimes and Maine

Names in **bold** indicate individuals who went on to play in the major leagues.

Year	Name	Team(s)	AB	Hits	2B	3B	HR	B.Ave	MLE	OOTP
1948–49	**Dick Gernert**	Kentville	361	138			27	0.383	0.247	(51).249
1947–51	Roly McLenahan	Middleton/Fred	588	224			7	0.381	0.245	
1947–55	Buddy Condy	Halifax	1196	432			40	0.364	0.242	
1950–57	Joe Fulghum	Stellarton	975	352	50	8	35	0.361	0.241	
1954–55	**Angelo Dagres**	Presque Isle	245	85	6	3	17	0.347	0.237	(56).235
1955–56	Roger Rada	Kentville	376	128	20	4	2	0.341	0.233	(54).255
1948–49	Herb Rossman	Halifax	240	80			7	0.333	0.222	(50).205
1955–57	**Jack Kubiszyn**	Liverpool K'ville	593	193	35	3	20	0.325	0.244	(59).205
1955–59	Leo Parent	Truro Stell	597	194	34	8	28	0.325	0.244	
1950–53	Pat Proulx	Presque Isle	207	67	9	4	4	0.324	0.242	(49).222
1949–54	**Zeke Bella**	Halifax	640	204				0.318	0.241	(56).280
1949–51	Stu O'Brien	Dartmouth	451	143			20 est.	0.317	0.239	
1953	**Steve Korcheck**	Kentville	215	68	9	9	7	0.316	0.235	(54).189
1947–49	Socrates Bobotas	Kentville	731	231				0.316	0.225	
1955–56	Sal Ferrara	Truro	398	125	8	10	15	0.314	0.235	(58).256
1946–51	Herb McLeod	Central/H&D/NB	434	136				0.313	0.234	(50).264
1951	**Gair Allie**	Stellarton	289	91			19	0.312	0.234	(54).204
1958–59	**Ty Cline**	Dartmouth	205	63	14	5	4	0.308	0.231	
1949–53	Chris Tonery	Kentville	494	151			6	0.306	0.225	
1951–52	Fred Flemming	Fredericton	233	67	12	4	4	0.301	0.224	(54).247

Appendix 1

Year	Name	Team(s)	AB	Hits	2B	3B	HR	B.Ave	MLE	OOTP
1953	Eugene Schiller	Liverpool	196	59	8	6	8	0.301	0.224	(55).231
1950–52	John Catallo	Edmundston	318	95	13	6	18	0.299	0.222	
1946–52	Danny Seaman	Liverpool	985	294				0.298	0.222	
1952–53	**Al Spangler**	Halifax	302	89	9	4	2	0.295	0.222	(54).211
1953–55	George Lewis	Houlton-Livpl	572	169	34	7	28	0.295	0.222	(56).276
1951–52	Francis McElroy	Grand Falls	262	77	13	4	2	0.294	0.221	(54).211
1947–51	Doc Acocella	Dartmouth	1062	312				0.294	0.221	
1950–54	Jack Kurty	Stell-Kent-PI	758	226	30	4	10	0.291	0.219	
1953–56	Charles Mellen	Ho'tn-Dart-Hfx	659	191	32	4	23	0.289	0.218	
1954–56	Jack Kaiser	Liverpool	640	185	34	8	**19**	0.289	0.218	(52).228
1951	Dick Bentfield	Fredericton	211	59	7	0	1	0.289	0.218	
1953–54	**Deacon Jones**	NB-Truro	364	105	27	11	12	0.286	0.216	
1954–55	Bucky Luck	Dart-Liverpool	491	140	25	4	9	0.285	0.216	
1953–55, 58	Jack Turney	Stell-Dart	703	199	35	6	10	0.283	0.215	
1954, 56–58	Jim Edwards	Dartmouth	435	123	24	7	9	0.283	0.215	(56).209
1956	Dean Robbins	Halifax	228	64	11	0	3	0.281	0.214	(58).213
1952–59	Billy Carter	Dart-Halifax	796	224	29	14	16	0.281	0.213	
1954	**Tommy Carroll**	Halifax	218	61	10	0	7	0.281	0.212	(56).209
1946–51	Leo Woods	Halifax	1140	321				0.281	0.211	
1956–57	Ray Looney	Dartmouth	328	91	16	6	19	0.278	0.209	(59).178
1954–55	Dave Sime	Hfx-Edm'ston	270	75	8	7	3	0.278	0.209	
1953, 56–58	Harry Lloyd	Dart-Truro	780	223	38	18	6	0.278	0.209	
1954–59	Chook Maxwell	Truro	1065	293	26	18	12	0.276	0.208	
1946–55	Johnny Clark	Truro, Hfx	1400	384				0.271	0.204	
1951–53	Syd Goldfader	NB-Dartmouth	455	122	18	4	20	0.267	0.202	(56).204
1957–58	Ron Liptak	Kentville	286	76	18	1	11	0.266	0.201	
1950–52, 56	Bob O Donnell	Liverpool	682	188	25	10	7	0.264	0.199	(60).224
1951–54	Al Norskey	Truro	945	245	35	6	18	259	0.196	
1951–58	Art Hoch	Hfx-Stel-Tr-Dt	1520	392	52	20	21	0.258	0.195	
1958–59	**Moe Morhardt**	Stellarton	167	42	5	1	7	0.254	0.191	
1952–55	**Tom Gastall**	Liverpool-NB	511	129	21	9	5	0.251	0.188	
1952–55	Don Prohovich	Kent-Ed'ston	544	136	21	8	14	0.251	0.188	(59).191
1952–53	Bill Werber	Stellarton	327	129	11	6	7	0.248	0.186	(56).205
1949–52	Dave Kiley	Saint John	403	100	15	1	6	0.248	0.186	(54).220

Appendix 2

Single-Season Batting and Major League Equivalencies: Maritimes and Maine

Name	Year	Team	AB	H	2b	3b	HR	B.Ave	MLE/Ave
Chris Tonery	1949	Kentville H&D	141	65				0.461	0.273
Roly McLenahan	1948	Fredericton NBLg	121	55				0.455	0.269
Zeke Bella	1954	Halifax H&D	212	87	18	5	9	0.411	0.284
Joe Fulghum	1951	Stellarton H&D	210	86			7	0.409	0.287
Buddy Condy	1951	Halifax H&D	215	85	15	7	1	0.407	0.285
Angelo Dagres	1955	Presque Isle Me-NB	128	52	2	3	13	0.406	0.289
Al Ware	1949	Colliery League	188	79			8	0.399	0.224
Dick Gernert	1949	Kentville Central Lg.	207	82			19	.396	0.221
Jack Kaiser	1949	Kentville Central Lg.	194	72				0.392	0.217
Harold Buckwalter	1949	Amherst Central Lg.	164	64				0.390	0.216
Soc Bobotas	1948	Kentville H&D	219	85				0.388	0.214
Joe Fulghum	1954	Stellarton H&D	234	89	15	1	8	0.383	0.275
Jack Turney	1953	Stellarton H&D	173	57	10	2	2	0.380	0.261
Jack Kaiser	1948	Kentville H&D	167	65				0.379	0.266
Buddy Condy	1949	Halifax H&D	212	78			10	0.368	0.246
Joe Lamonica	1949	Stellarton Central Lg	125	46				0.368	0.209
Roger Rada	1955	Kentville H&D	193	71	8	4	1	0.368	0.252
Jack Kurty	1953	Presque-Isle	121	44	7	1	4	0.364	0.245
Chuck Arnold	1955	Halifax	135	49	12	2	8	0.363	0.247
Deacon Jones	1953	Grand Falls Me-NB	138	50	14	2	5	0.362	0.244

Appendix 2

Name	Year	Team	AB	H	2b	3b	HR	B.Ave	MLE/Ave
Buddy Condy	1948	Halifax H&D	260	93				0.358	0.238
Dick Gernert	1948	Kentville	157	56			8	0.357	0.257
Jack Kubiszyn	1957	Kentville	163	58	10	2	7	0.356	0.262
John Hafeneker	1949	Truro Central Lg.	161	57			10	0.354	0.201
Johnny Clark	1950	Truro/Hfx/Dart	222	77				0.350	0.224
Herb Rossmann	1948	Hfx Shipyards	123	44				0.348	0.233
Paul Bulger	1948	Middleton	219	76				0.347	0.232
Johnny Catallo	1951	Edmundston	166	58	5	3	11	0.345	0.232
Sal Ferrara	1956	Truro	203	70	6	5	12	0.345	0.238
Andy McGowan	1952	Houlton	143	49	9	3	3	0.343	0.231

Appendix 3
Career Pitching

Name	Years	Teams	W	L	IP	Hits	BB	K	ERA	WHIP
Tom Bujnowski	51–2, 55, 58	Halifax	29	18	442	370	150	361		1.176
Ron Cote	1953–55	Liverpool	16	15	275	238	163	202		1.458
Bob Davis	1951–2, 54	H'tn/HFX	19	8	238	192	127	176		1.340
Moe Drabowsky	1955–56	Truro	12	10	188	73	119	183		1.021
Don Eason	1953–55	Truro	23	13	298	229	75	219		1.020
Jim Farino	1956–58	Hx/Dtm/Ken	16	13	238	206	145	136		1.474
Johnny Graham	1958–59	Truro	9	8	147	114	90	145	2.65	1.387
Ed Hadlock	1952, 54–56	Liverpool	28	22	424	391	111	288		1.183
Jack Halpin	1948–51	Halifax	40	18	555	415	209	489		1.124
Jim Heller	1949–50, 52–4	Hfx-Dart	41	16	481	403	125	320		1.098
Ron Jirsa	1952–53	Liverpool	22	8	207	143	104	138		1.193
Ralph Lumenti	1955–57	PI/Liv'pl/Truro	7	14	195	145	153	223		1.528
Don MacLeod	1955–57	Liv-Truro	20	12	234	193	165	178		1.529
Jack McGinley	1956–57	Stellarton	16	15	270	257	141	198		1.474
"Spud" Murray	1956–57	Halifax	16	9	204	190	125	62	3.49	1.544
Leo Parent	1955–59	Truro-Stellarton	24	26	318	268	226	171	est 3.10	1.553
John "Monk" Raines	1953–54	Stellarton	9	6	155	134	66	112		1.290
Syd Roy	1950–1952	Stellarton	22	10	291	288	125	117	3.86	1.391
Neil Staples	1946–52	Dart/Liv/Hfx	42	25					est. 3.75	
Dave Stenhouse	1952–54	Me-NB/Kentville	22	11	210	130	147	255		1.248

Appendix 4
Players from Major NCAA Programs

Auburn, Alabama, Clemson, Elon, Florida, Florida State, Georgia, Lenoir Rhyne, LSU, Maryland, Virginia, Rollins College: (25) Bob Barnes, Doug Baxendale, Jerry Boxer, Art Brophy, Bill Cary, Ty Cline, Luther Conger, Jack Crouch, Al Fantuzzi, Sherrill Hall, Hank Hamrick, Bill Hardy, Bill Hearn, Jack Kubiszyn, Manly Johnston, Gene Larry, Vance Long, Ron Overcash, Wyn Overstreet, Ron Pavia, Don Stafford, Harold Stowe, Paul Susce, Art Swanson, Fred Twomey

Duke University: (24) Bill Bergeron, Tom Blackburn, Dick Brewer, Johnny Carroll, George Carver, Gordon Clapp, Andy Cockrell, Frank Dale, Bob Davis, Stu Erickson, Johnny Falwell, Harley Fatsinger, John Gibbons, Ralph Kehoe, Bob LeClerc, Jack McGuire, Joe Lewis, Tim Powers, Fred Sheppard, Dave Sime, Leroy Sires, Al Spangler, Dave Traynor, Bill Werber

Holy Cross: (30) Dick Berardino, Jackie Brennan, Paul Brissette, Ron Cote, Harold Deitz, James Farino, Matt Forman, Joe Frechette, Dick Hogan, Bill Lefebvre, Matt Foreman, John Fortunato, Joel Liebler, Ron Liptak, Gene Malinoski, Gordon Massa, Art Moossmann, Pete Naton, James O'Neil, Larry Rancourt, Bill Rochford, Lou Panella, Dick Parisi, Ron Perry, Billy Porter, Don Prohovich, Dick Santaniello, Eugene Schiller, Bill Spanswick, Jackie Whalen

East Carolina, North Carolina State, University of North Carolina: (28) Carroll Bolick, Frank Caradonna, Bill Cline, Gaither Cline, Roger Craig, Fred Dale, Connie Gravitte, Don Hafer, Cecil Heath, Ed Hooks, Ed Horbelt, Bob Kennel, Jim Kuykendall, Harry Lee Lloyd, Bill Lore, Don Marbry, John Motsinger, Joe Morgan, Joe Pazdan, Chalmers Port, Jim Raugh, Carman Santoli, Sam Stell, Jack Turney, Hal Workman, Carl Wyles, Johnny Yvars, Jack Yvars

University of Maine, Colby, Bates, Bowdoin, Ricker College, Vermont: (37) Phil Archibald, Lou Audet, Dick Black, Ralph Clark, Jim DiFrederico, Gerry Duffy, Gus Folsom, Norm Gigon, Ed Hadlock, Ed Jasinski, Jimmy Keefe, Dave Kuhn, Andy Lano, Chick Leahy, Tony Lupien, Lloyd MacDonald, Don Maynard, Andy McAuliffe, Ad Norwood, Tubby Raymond, Don Reimer, Tom

Pierce, George Rodin, Ted Shiro, Dave Sneddon, Ron Staples, Bob St. Pierre, Neil Stinneford, Brud Stover, Tom Tierney, Blain Trafton, Frank Vecella, George Wales, Norm White, Red Wilson, Bill Wing, Tony Zash

University of New Hampshire: (11) Soc Bobotas, Hal Burby, Red Falco, Gerry Girard, Ray Guptill, Joe Kazura, Huck Keany, Emil Krupa, Hank Swasey, Chris Tonery, Johnny Watterson

George Washington, Providence College, University of Rhode Island, Connecticut: (35) Pat Abbruzzi, Art Aloisio, Tony Attanasio, Bob Anderson, Buzz Barry, Bruce Blount, Carl Buniva, Ken Cullum, Angelo Dagres, Don Demonge, Don Doiron, Tony Granger, Gordon Grolms, Tom Halliwell, Dick Howe, Steve Korcheck, Ted Kosior, Brad Leach, Ron Liptak, Ray Looney, Moe Morhardt, Bob Murray, Herb Nicholas, Jerry Paparella, Rolly Rabitor, John Risley, Joe Rosania, Bob Ritacco, Tom Saffer, Roland Sheldon, Dave Stenhouse, Bill Stevens, Frank Tirico, Bob Wedin, Art Weinstock

University of Massachusetts, Boston College, Boston University, Northeastern: (61) Harry Agganis, Bob Bagwell, John Bitetti, Mike Bobrowicki, Dick Boehner, Robert Boehner, George Boston, Charley Bunker, Leo Cassidy, Len Ceglarski, Ed Connolly, Chet Corkum, Len Dempsey, Don Eason, Ron Eason, Bob Flanagan, Ed Fontes, Tom Gastall, Gerry Glynn, Lou Gobeille, Gordon Grolms, Gerry Hamel, Dawes Hamilt, Fran Harrington, Bob Kroeck, Ted Larkin, Gerry Levinson, Ralph Lumenti, Bob Manning, Don MacLeod, Roger MacLeod, Charles Maloney, Pete Marchegiano, George McCafferty, Joe McCusker, Jack McGrath, Bob McManus, Jack McGrath, Charles Mellen, Len Merullo, John Moore, Joe Morgan, Bob Niemic, Lou Pollack, Bob Quirk, Mike Roarke, Leo Parent, Bob Pedigree, Lou Pollack, Don Russell, Bill Robinson, Armand Sabourin, Dick Siska, John Skypeck, Joe Spadafore, Steve Stuka, Don Swanson, Phil Tarpey, Bernard Teliszewski, Felix Wisniewski, Johnny Yurewicz

University of Michigan, Michigan State, Western Michigan, Ohio, Notre Dame: (38) Charles Bowers, Tom Bujnowski, Dick Bunker, Tom Carroll, Ray Collard, Jack Corbett, Gene Duffy, Harry Durkin, Don Eaddy, Ray Fisher, Johnny Gee, Jim Hannan, Bruce Haynam, Ed Hurley, Ron Jackson, Leo Koceski, Joe Kokos, Dick Krawczack, Richard Leach, Frank Lerchen, Paul Lepley, Ralph Nuzum, Ron Perranoski, Dick Peterjohn, Tubby Raymond, Jack Ritter, Frank Ronan, Bob Russell, Hal W. Smith, Herb Schroeter, Myron Stallsmith, Charles Symeon, Bill Thurston, Ken Tippery, Howard Tommelein, Felix Wisniewski, Marv Wisniewski, Joe Yaeger

Adelphi, Saint John's University, Fordham, Long Island University, Manhattan, NYU, Tufts, Wagner: (39) Art Beato, Walt Brady, Tony Blose, George Boston, Gene Caiafa, Bob Coccodrilli, Jack Curran, Dick Eichorn, Jim Felton, Rudy Fobert, Frank Franchesini, Tony Garin, Harry Guckert, Jack Hinfey, Ray Holland, Mike Imbriani, John Lang, Joel Kelfer, George Lewis, Don MacKenzie, Andy McGowan, Burt Muench, Dom Novak, John Kaiser, Joe Oliva, Bill Oster, Mickey Pinto, Lou Portocarrero, Creon Psome, Mike Ricigliano, Tom Scanell,

Bob Scariato, Charles Schmidt, Ray Tully, Emil Viola, Dick Wilkins, Bob Webber, Don Weiderecht, Art West

Springfield College: (34) Archie Allen, Arlan Barbour, Ed Bengston, Pete Berland, Steve Bilik, Bill Bushing, Bob D'Agostino, Bob Douglas, Duke Dukeshire (American International), Ed Dunn, Leroy Getchell, Alvin Griggs, Ray Jacobson, Paul Jordan, Ed Juszcyk, Sherm Kinney, Joe Kobuskie, Dick Maloney, Matt Maetoza, Dave Martens, Hugh Mendez, Frank Murgo, Bill Nordberg, Jim Pelcher, Tom Ruggiero, Jack Sanford, Ed Steitz, Bill Sullivan, Norm Swenson, Hank Tominaga, Dick Traynor, Bill Wade, Roger Wickman, Wayne Wilson

Temple University, Trinity College, Penn State, Seton Hall: (23) Phil Bracalante, George Case, Phil Cataldo, Jim Crossmore, Hal Buckwalter, George Case, Moe Drabowsky, Dick Gernert, Gardland Gingerich, Ron Kozuch, Jack Kurty, Roger LeClerc, Ted Lepcio, Jack McGowan, Jack Riley, Joe Ruyak, Syl Cerchi, Art Rees, Ray Reifsnyder, Charles Sticka, Chris Tonery, Carman Troisi, Ed Yeomans

Wake Forest University: (28) Gair Allie, Al Baker, Ken Batchelor, Bobby Brown, Bill Brooks, Tunney Brooks, Bob Coluni, Lowell Davis, Joe Fulghum, Art Hoch, Lynwood Holt, Gene Hooks, Jack Liptak, Jack McGinley, Luther McKeel, Rex McMillan, Doc Murphey, Vern Mustain, Jack Phillips, Bob Quinn, Kent Rogers, Jack Stallings, John Stokoe, Bill Walsh, Wiley Warren, Pat Williams, Rudy Williams, Woodrow Wrenn

Yale, Princeton, Colgate, Cornell, Dartmouth, Harvard, Ithaca: (26) Larry Bossidy, Bob Davis, Lou Davanzo, Bill DeGraaf, Don Fessler, Colin Gracey, Hugo Guidotti, Deacon Jones, Walter Judd, Don Kern, Ray Lamontagne, Al Levine, Bob List, Ron Mangini, Dick Meade, Phil Mathias, Ken MacKenzie, George Owen, Bill Pryor, Bob Quirk, Art Quirk, Bill Schifino, John Stoughton, John Sutton, Ted Thelander, Bob Thwaites

Essay on Sources

As a memoir, this book draws upon my life experiences over seven decades, watching and reading about baseball, collecting memorabilia, including baseball cards and photographs, following box scores, analyzing statistical data, and engaging in baseball simulations which have since evolved into a flourishing online industry. Today thousands upon thousands of baseball fans put together fantasy teams and re-create historical seasons using games such as *Out of the Park Baseball* (OOTP), *Pursue the Pennant*, and *Dynasty League Baseball*. All of these are grounded in baseball's fascination with statistics, performance measurements and the new analytics, and they create algorithms that factor in player potential, experience and development over time. OOTP, for example, allows gamers to include virtually anyone who ever played in the major or minor leagues and rates them on the major league standard 20–80 scouting scale.

In the days before computers, baseball simulations were available as board games with individual player cards, and results were a function of rolling the dice. Two of the earliest were Strat-o-Matic and APBA. Not only did I play both of these over the years, but on my travels across the country I visited their respective offices in Glen Cove, New York, and Millersville, Pennsylvania. Although neither published minor league card sets, the formulas they used were simple enough to replicate, and it was relatively easy to construct player cards for any player or league using available statistics. For minor league teams, one only needed the exhaustive *Official Baseball Guide* published annually by *The Sporting News*. I have used these guides extensively for this project, particularly for the period 1946–1965.

Over the last few decades, the *Official Baseball Guide* has been superseded—although not completely—by the online site www.baseball-reference.com and other searchable data bases such as Stathead Baseball (stathead.com/baseball) and Retrosheet (https://retrosheet.org). There are hundreds of online baseball sites too voluminous to mention here, but I have no doubt frequented most of them both as a hobbyist and in the development of this project. Among the most useful for me were the *Society for American Baseball Research* (SABR) (www.sabr.org) and *The Hardball Times* (https://tht.fangraphs.com). For baseball in Canada, see Hall of Fame journalist Bob Elliott's (canadianbaseballnetwork.com), Alan Galley's (maritimebaseball.wordpress.com), and Jay Del Mah's wonderful Western Canadian baseball site (www.attheplate.com). Christian Trudeau's searchable database of players in the Quebec Provincial League in the 1940s (http://sites.google.com/ligueprovincial/home) is another valuable resource, and I am indebted to him for providing access to it. Bob Dawson's essays at boxscorenews.com and the story of the Chatham Coloured All Stars found at cdigs.Uwindsor.ca/BreakingColourbarrier are important resources dealing with black baseball in Canada.

A subscription to SABR allows researchers to search issues of *The Sporting News* (TSN), which is indispensable for any baseball historian. I have used TSN extensively for the period 1945–1970 to follow the careers of players after they left the Maritimes. The SABR biography project and its oral interview collection provide an extensive and carefully sourced history of individual player lives which I have used here on many occasions in descriptions of those who played here. The Statistical Analysis Committee of SABR also publishes a newsletter and publicizes the work of sabermetricians interested in performance measurements. In addition, there are recorded interviews available on the SABR website and from a number of other sources. The ones pertinent to this project are noted at the end of this section.

Another essential tool in the collection of information on players and their exploits all across the continent was access to newspapers available at newspaper.com. I have accessed all available newspapers in major league cities and many in the minor league cities as well, especially for spring training reports and box scores that are not available elsewhere. I have also profited from working with newspaper collections at the Nova Scotia Archives and Records Management (NSARM), the New Brunswick Archives, the Maine State Archives, and the University of Arizona library. Staff at the Halifax Municipal Archives were helpful in accessing photographs for this project. Online searches of obituaries have also been useful in fleshing out player histories within the context of family life. The broader collections of the Nova Scotia Sports Hall of Fame, the Canadian Baseball Hall of Fame, and The National Baseball Library and the Baseball Hall of Fame in Cooperstown, New York, which I have visited on many occasions, have been important resources. When *The Sporting News* Archives was still located in St. Louis, then-archivist Stephen Gietscher was very helpful in making their collections available to me.

Another important source of baseball history involves the various conferences and associated publications that derive from them. Among the most important for me over the years was the annual conference of the North American Society for Sport History and its associated *Journal of Sport History*, which can be accessed through www.nassh.com. I also attended the annual Spring Training Conferences associated with the journal *NINE: A Journal of Baseball History and Culture*, organized initially by the late Bill Kerwin and more recently by Jane and Dan Ardell, who have been committed to bringing research and on-field experiences together each year. The other major conference is the annual SABR conference and satellite meetings around specific topics such as 19th-century baseball, the minor leagues, women's baseball, and black baseball. On a local level I have also profited over the years from interactions with and insights of newspaper columnists from across the

Maritimes, including "Ace" Foley and Alex Nickerson at the *Halifax Herald*, Hugh Townsend (Pictou *Advocate*), Charles Stevens (*Eastern Daily News*), Cal Best (The *Clarion*), and Lyle Carter (Truro *Daily News*).

This personal memoir is grounded in techniques associated with oral history, which I first employed thirty-five years ago while working on my book *Northern Sandlots: A History of Maritime Baseball* (Toronto: 1995). Along with Ken Clare, a professional librarian at Saint Mary's University, interviews were undertaken with sixty or so players who came to the Maritimes, and the H&D League in particular. There were also interviews with local players and others with reminiscences of baseball in the postwar era. Their assistance and insights are included here as recollections since, it is important to note, I did not commit to the present book project until my retirement from Saint Mary's in 2020. Many of these conversations, moreover, took place before more contemporary procedures regarding personal interviews were in vogue, and developed out of long-term friendships or within my extended family. Along the way I made people aware that I might write a book at some point, and I have been committed to employing their insights and conversations in an ethically appropriate manner.

I am indebted to the following people who along the way have shared their memories and insights and sometimes commented on the manuscript:

Gair Allie, Charlie Ambrose, Zeke Bella, Bill Bergeron, Paul Brissette, Charles "Buzz" Bowers, Alton Brooks, Bill Brooks, Don Brown, Bev Buckler, Hal Burby, Lyle Carter, Art Ceccarelli, Johnny Clark, Ty Cline, John "Twit" Clarke, Ted Cumming, Gerry Davis, Bob Dawson, Bob Decker, Moe Drabowsky, Robert Elias, Bob Ferguson, Jim, John and Bev Frizzle, Charlie and Russell Fox, Philip "Skit" Ferguson, Amby Foote, Joe Fulghum, Steve Gietscher, Norm Gigon, Bob Gillis, George Gmelch, Syd Goldfader, Johnny Graham, Art Hoch, Bill Humber, Clarence "Soapy" Johnston, Grover "Deacon" Jones, Danny Joseph, Herm Kaplan, Huck Keany, Steve Korcheck, Leonard Koppet, Jack Kubiszyn, Guy and Jeanette Leblanc, Roger LeClerc, Gerald Levinson, John Lockhart, Ray Looney, Ralph Lumenti, John Lutz, John "Brother" MacDonald, Don MacVicar, Darrell Maxwell, Devin Maxwell, Aylmer McKerlie, Herb McLeod, Johnny Mentis, Jack McCracken, Frank Mitchell, Moe Morhardt, James Morrison, Monty Mosher, Doc Murphey, Al Norskey, John Paris, Jr., Wilson Parsons, Ron Perry, Don Prohovich, Brian Pulsifer, Roger Rada, John Reid, Syd Roy, Kent Rogers, Burton Russell, Howie Spears, Armand Sabourin, Billy Saunders, Jack Stallings, Clyde Sukeforth, Mike Thomson, Bill Thurston, Christian Trudeau, Johnny Watterson, Ed Willis, Cyril White, Bill Young.

Interview References

The above interviews provided much of the information included throughout the manuscript. Specific usage is indicated below. Other references are included in the notes at the end of each chapter.

Preface: Interview with Ty Cline, Charleston, South Carolina (16 April 1991).

Chapter One: This chapter draws on interviews and follow-up conversations with the following informants. Interview with Brian Pulsifer, Kentville,

N.S. (November 15, 2017), and subsequent telephone conversations and email correspondence. Telephone interview with Cyril White, Kentville, N.S. (April 20, 2020). Interview with John Lockhart, Kentville, N.S. (July 2, 2018), and subsequent telephone conversations. Family conversations with John Frizzle, Chester, N.S., and Jim Frizzle, Middleton, N.S. Telephone interview with Jack McCracken (March 18, 2019). Interview with Armand Sabourin, Medford, Massachusetts (March 28, 1994), and subsequent telephone conversations. Interview with Clyde Sukeforth, Washington Corners, Maine (April 4, 1994). Telephone interview with Charles "Buzz" Bowers, Worcester, Massachusetts (April 7, 1994). Interview with Skit Ferguson, Dartmouth, N.S. (April 10, 1994), and subsequent meetings.

Chapter Two: Interview with Philip "Skit" Ferguson, Dartmouth, N.S. (April 10, 1994). Skit Ferguson's address to Nova Scotia Sports Heritage Center, "Brown Bag Series," (March 1992). Interview with Clarence Johnson, Fort Myers, Florida (March 18, 1994). Informal conversation with Danny Joseph, Malagash, N.S. (July 2018). Interview with Don Brown, Truro, N.S. (May 28, 2018). Interview and follow-up conversations with Lyle Carter, Truro, N.S. (August 8, 2017). Interview with Jack Stallings, Halifax. Telephone conversations and email exchanges with Ted Cumming, Palm Springs, California (September 2017 to present). Interviews with Bob Decker, Zeke Bella, and Gerry Davis at H&D League Reunion, Halifax (June 1989). Interview with Johnny Clark, Halifax, N.S. (November 29, 1989).

Chapter Three: Email correspondence and telephone conversations with Ted Cumming, Palm Springs, California (2017 to present). Interview with Art Ceccarelli, New Haven, Connecticut (April 12, 1994). Interview with Herm Kaplan, Halifax (January 7, 1990).

Chapter Four: Interviews with Johnny Watterson, Keene, New Hampshire (May 18–19, 1990; April 5–6, 1994). Interview with Ed Willis, Keene, New Hampshire (April 7, 1994). Ken Clark interview with John "Twit" Clark, Pictou, N.S. (October 12, 1989). Interview with John "Brother" MacDonald, Stellarton, N.S. (January 20, 1990). Interview with Johnny Clark, Halifax, N.S. (November 29, 1989). Interview with Clary Johnston, Port Charlotte, Florida (March 18, 1994).

Chapter Five: Interview with Bill Brooks, Doc Murphey and Tunney "Toomey" Brooks, Wilmington, North Carolina (April 1–2, 1994). Interview with Kent "Baby" Rogers, Halifax, H&D League Reunion, Halifax, N.S (July 1989). Ken Clare interview with Gair Allie, San Antonio, Texas (1989). Interview with Joe Fulghum, H&D League Reunion, Halifax (July 1989). Interviews with Art Hoch, H&D League Reunion, Halifax (July 1989); Raleigh, North Carolina (March 28, 1994), and follow-up telephone conversations. Interview with Syd Roy, Stellarton, N.S. (October 12, 1989). Conversation with Frank Robinson, *Diamonds in the Desert Conference*, Phoenix, Arizona (March 21, 1998).

Chapter Six: Telephone interview with Paul "Breezer" Brissette, Boca Raton, Florida (March 19, 1994). Interview with Brian Pulsifer, Kentville, N.S. (November 15, 2017), and subsequent emails. Interview with Ron Perry, Worcester, Massachusetts (April 8, 1994). Interview with Bill Thurston and Dave Jauss, Amherst, Massachusetts (April 6, 1994). Interview with Gerry

Levinson, Halifax, N.S., H&D League Reunion (July 1989). Telephone Interview with Ralph Lumenti, Grafton, Massachusetts (April 7, 1994).

Chapter Seven: Interview with Ted Cumming (September 17, 2017). Telephone interview with Art Dorrington, Atlantic City, New Jersey (March 20, 2012). Interview with Darrell Maxwell, Truro, N.S. (August 8, 2017), and subsequent telephone and email correspondence. Telephone interview with Devin Maxwell, Ottawa (August 2, 2019), and subsequent email correspondence. Interview with Willie O'Ree, Saint Mary's University, Halifax, N.S. (October 13, 2017), and subsequent conversations. Interviews with Johnny Mentis, Lyle Carter, Scotty Maxwell and Danny Maxwell, Truro (August 8, 2017). Informal conversations and email correspondence with Bob Dawson, Ottawa. Informal conversations and email correspondence with Frank Mitchell, Oakfield, N.S.

Chapter Eight: None.

Chapter Nine: Interviews with Brian Pulsifer, Kentville (November 15, 2017; May 10, 2019). Telephone Interview with Jack Kubiszyn, Tuscaloosa, Alabama (March 22, 1991).

Chapter Ten: Telephone interview with Grover "Deacon" Jones, Sugarland, Texas (August 4, 2019). Interviews with Johnny Graham, Truro (November 2011; August 8, 2017). Telephone interview with Charlie Wambolt, Dartmouth, N.S. (August 18, 2021). Telephone interview with Ray Looney, Cheshire, Connecticut (April 10, 1994). Interview with Donny Brown, Truro (August 15, 2017). Telephone interview with Bev Frizzle, Antigonish, N.S. (May 30, 2020), and subsequent email correspondence. Interview with Wilson Parsons, Truro (September 1, 1995). Telephone interview with Devin Maxwell, Ottawa (August 2, 2019). Interview with Howie Spears, Enfield, N.S. (May 1, 2014). Interview with Moe Morhardt, Hartford, Connecticut (April 11, 1994).

Chapter Eleven: Interview with John "Jake" Lockhart, Kentville (July 2, 2018). Telephone interview with Bill Saunders, Fredericton (June 20, 2016), and subsequent conversations. Telephone interview with Mike Thomson (January 12, 2021). Dartmouth Informal conversations with a number of former Kentville Cardinals at the 16 September 2018 reunion.

Chapter Twelve: Informal discussions with various members of the 1963 Kentville Cardinals at a team reunion, September 16, 2018, were helpful in writing this chapter.

Chapter Notes

Preface

1. David McGimpsey, *America's Pastime and Popular Culture* (Bloomington: Indiana University Press, 2000), p.131. On Sarandon and the "Church of Baseball," see p. 40.
2. W.P. Kinsella, *Shoeless Joe* (New York: Ballantine, 1982).
3. Richard Ford, *Independence Day* (New York: Alfred A. Knopf, 1996).
4. Canadian Baseball Hall of Fame, Induction Ceremony Program, Bill Harris, 2008; Ronnie Joyner, *Farewell to Flatbush: The 1947 Brooklyn Dodgers* (Jefferson, NC: McFarland, 2022), pp. 197–204, provides a nice overview of Harris' career in the Dodgers organization.
5. Colin D. Howell, "Nova Scotia's Protest Tradition and the Search for a Meaningful Federalism," in David Jay Bercuson, Ed., *Canada and the Burden of Unity* (Toronto: Macmillan of Canada, 1977).
6. Frank Underhill, *The Image of Confederation* (Toronto: University of Toronto Press, 1964), p. 63.
7. Colin D. Howell, *Northern Sandlots: A Social History of Maritime Baseball* (Toronto: University of Toronto Press, 1995).

Chapter One

1. Frank Underhill, *The Image of Confederation* (Toronto: University of Toronto Press, 1964), p. 63.
2. "Elia Swings for the Seats, Rips Fans, Apologizes," *Chicago Tribune*, 30 April 1983, p.17.
3. Paul Scimonelli, *Roy Sievers: The Sweetest Right-Handed Swing in 1950s Baseball* (Jefferson, NC: McFarland, 2017).
4. Samuel Regalado, *Viva Baseball: Latin Major Leaguers and Their Special Hunger* (Urbana: University of Illinois Press, 1998).
5. Charles Bevis, "Norm Gigon," SABR Biography Project. Baseballreference.com.
6. J. Douglas Elgin, "When Baseball Coach Gigon Speaks, Players Listen," *Lafayette Alumni Quarterly* (Spring 1978), p. 32.

Chapter Two

1. Burton L. Russell, *Seven Decades of Nova Scotia Baseball: 1946–2016* (Kentville, N.S.: self-published, 2017), p. 6.
2. Danny Joseph, *Put It on Paper* (Bible Hill, N.S.: self-published, 2021) provides a lively recollection of his family and their continued love affair with baseball.
3. According to USA Baseball President Mike Gaski, "Coach Stallings was not only one of the founding fathers of USA Baseball, but he was perhaps the greatest ambassador for international baseball." "USA Baseball Mourns the Loss of Jack Stallings," *USA Baseball News*, June 22, 2018, usabaseball.com.
4. Burton Russell, *Nova Scotia Baseball Heroics* (Kentville, N.S.: self-published, 1993), p. 71.
5. Quoted in Bob Douglas, *Life Is a Ball: 50 Years of Nova Scotia Sport* (Halifax: Links Publishing, 2000,) p. 112.

6. *Halifax Herald*, June 5, 1946, p. 5.
7. Douglas, *Life Is a Ball*, p. 71.
8. Burton Russell, *Nova Scotia Baseball Heroics* (Kentville, N.S. self-published, 1993), p. 30.
9. *Halifax Herald*, August 20, 1943.
10. Douglas, *Life Is a Ball*, pp. 96–106.
11. *Bridgeport Herald*, August 6, 1950. This newspaper was quite aware of summer baseball leagues in the Maritimes and commented on the number of players from Connecticut who went north of the border. Among them were New Haven natives Gordon Grolms (Truro), Gene Savard (Halifax), Mickey Bonaster (New Waterford), Ed Lewicki (Kentville), and Bill Burteau (Moncton). *Ibid.*, July 23, 1950.
12. Personal correspondence, Gerry Davis to Colin Howell, undated (1994). This letter accompanied a large package including photographs, newspaper clippings and box scores involving his baseball career.
13. *Halifax Herald*, May 9, 1947, p. 5.

Chapter Three

1. *The Sporting News*, September 1, 1948, p. 32; *Ibid.*, March 30, 1949, p. 34.
2. *The Sporting News*, March 2, 1949, p. 18.
3. *Brooklyn Daily Eagle*, August 4, 1948, p. 19.
4. Alan Cohen, "The Hearst Sandlot Classic: More than a Doorway to the Big Leagues," *The Baseball Research Journal*, SABR (Fall 2013), pp. 21–29.
5. *Brooklyn Daily Eagle*, August 5, 1948, p. 16.
6. *Halifax Herald*, August 4, 1948, p. 7.
7. SABR audio interview, Sonny Senerchia.
8. *The Sporting News*, April 6, 1944, pp. 1–2.
9. *Ibid.*, May 24, 1950, p. 2.
10. *Halifax Herald*, May 7, 1947, p. 4.
11. Although Tanner had hoped that the Dodgers would reinstate him and send him once again to Montreal, the Royals had apparently been unimpressed with his mediocre performance in Quebec and Nova Scotia during his blacklisting. He signed instead with the Boston Red Sox, who sent him to the Southern and later the Florida International League. *The Sporting News*, May 24, 1950, p. 22. During the summer of 1947, Dodger scout Jim Ferrante regularly checked on Tanner, but after seeing him get knocked around a few times, Ferrante wondered why Tanner seemed to have lost his effectiveness. *Halifax Herald*, July 21, 1947, p. 6. Fortunately for Tanner, Red Sox scout Maurie DeLoof was imbedded in the Middleton pitching staff and had a more favorable opinion.
12. Birdie Tebbetts and Jim Morrison, *Birdie: Confessions of a Baseball Nomad* (Chicago: Triumph Books, 2002).
13. Fred Lieb, "'Fear Strikes Out' Best Hollywood Job on Game," *The Sporting News*, March 13, 1957, p. 31.
14. *The Sporting News*, October 24, 1951, p. 20.
15. *Burlington Daily News*, June 19, 1949, p. 6.
16. *The Portsmouth Herald*, July 15, 1949, p. 6.
17. *Kentville Advertiser*, June 23, 1949, p. 3.
18. Ace Foley, *The First Fifty Years: The Life and Times of a Sportswriter* (Windsor, N.S.: Lancelot Press, 1970), pp. 24–25.
19. *Halifax Herald*, July 8, 1949, p. 7.
20. Quoted in Jose de Jesus Ortiz, Jr., *Houston Astros: Armed and Dangerous* (Champaign, IL: Sports Publishing, 2006), p. 20.
21. *Fredericton Daily Gleaner*, May 13, 1949.

Chapter Four

1. Dr. J.P. McGrath to Johnny Watterson, April 1, 1950 (author's possession).
2. *The Sporting News*, April 28, 1948, p. 17. "I don't believe I ever had any better time in my life," MacInnis said. "Those coal mining people were crazy about the game and the players, most of whom were boys who worked in the mine all day..., tired and all, and with little previous experience, they did well enough to battle Halifax for the championship."
3. *The Sporting News*, February 27, 1952, p. 2.
4. *Ibid.*, May 7, 1952, p. 27.
5. *Halifax Herald*, July 6, 1951, p. 8.

6. James Myers, "Hard Times—Hard Ball: The Cape Breton Colliery League 1936–1939," (unpublished MA thesis, Saint Mary's University, 1997).
7. Ed Smith, "Cape Breton Review," *Maritime Baseball Pictorial Yearbook*, 1947, pp. 17–18; Pat Connolly, "Cape Breton Review," *Ibid.*, pp. 7, 41; *Ibid.*, 1950, p. 29.

Chapter Five

1. Elizabeth City, *The Daily Advance*, September 2, 1948.
2. *The Sporting News*, June 6, 1951, p. 4.
3. Elizabeth City, *The Daily Advance*, October 3, 1949.
4. *The Sporting News*, April 15, 1953, p. 19.
5. New Glasgow *Evening News*, July 6, 1951.
6. *High Point Enterprise*, May 29, 1952, p. 13.
7. *Halifax Herald*, May 12, 1954, p. 10.
8. *The Sporting News*, March 7, 1956, p. 5.
9. *Ibid.*, July 2, 1952, p. 14.
10. *Ibid.*, March 7, 1956, p. 5.
11. *Ibid.*, February 1, 1956, p. 11.
12. *Ibid.*, March 14, 1956, p. 22. "Very impressive," said manager Birdie Tebbetts when asked about Werber.
13. Terry Sloope, "Curt Flood," SABR Biography Project. BaseballReference.com.
14. David Skelton, "Al Spangler," SABR Biography Project. BaseballReference.com.
15. *The Sporting News*, June 12, 1957, p. 15. Sime initially contemplated signing with a second division club, but "it's the majors or nothing with him." He also thought he could balance medicine and baseball as Bobby Brown had done, but subsequently abandoned his baseball plans in order to pursue his medical career. *Ibid.*, October 9, 1957, p. 29.

Chapter Six

1. Brent Kelly, *Baseball's Bonus Babies: Conversations with 24 High-Priced Ballplayers Signed from 1953 to 1957* (Jefferson, NC: McFarland, 2006).
2. Bill Doyle, "Holy Cross Legend Ron Perry Reflects on Amazing Ride," *Telegram and Gazette* (online), telegram.com (March 22, 2015).
3. Chip Hart, "Ray Fisher," SABR Biography Project. BaseballReference.com.
4. Armand Peterson, "Johnny Gee," SABR Biography Project. BaseballReference.com. Gee played unaffiliated ball in a number of locations between 1947 and 1954, including Homer, New York; Fergus Falls, Minnesota; Blacks Harbour; and Truro. In 1955 he became a high school principal, which ended his peripatetic baseball career.
5. Bill Hass, "1955 Wake Forest Demon Deacons, 'National Champions,'" diamondsinthedust.com, p. 5.
6. Steve Treder, "Cash in the Cradle: The Bonus Babies," *The Hardball Times*, November 1, 2004.
7. Bill Nowlin, "Ron Jackson," SABR Biography Project. BaseballReference.com.
8. *The Sporting News*, February 9, 1955, p. 6.
9. Brent Kelly, Interview with Tom Carroll, SABR Oral History Project, 1991.
10. *The Sporting News*, March 21, 1956, p. 24.
11. *Ibid.*, October 5, 1955, p. 26.
12. *Ibid.*, October 3, 1956, p. 48.
13. *Ibid.*, October 10, 1956, p. 14.
14. *Ibid.*, March 28, 1956, pp. 8, 16.
15. Bill Hass, "1955 Wake Forest Demon Deacons, 'National Champions,'" diamondsinthedust.com.
16. R.J. Lesch, "Moe Drabowsky," SABR Biography Project. *BaseballReference.com*. Lesch estimated Drabowsky's bonus as "anywhere from $40,000 to $80,000."
17. *The Sporting News*, September 11, 1957, p. 14.
18. *Ibid.*
19. *Ibid.*, September 18, 1957, p. 12.
20. *Ibid.*, March 12, 1958, p. 15.

Chapter Seven

1. Graham Reynolds with Wanda Robson, *Viola Desmond. Her Life and Times*

(Halifax, N.S.: Roseway and Fernwood Books, 2018); Russell Bingham, "Viola Desmond," *The Canadian Encyclopedia* (online), thecanadianencyclopedia.ca (January 27, 2013, updated January 28, 2022); *The Clarion*, December 1, Volume 1, No. 1, 1946, p. 1. Archives.novascotia.ca.

2. *The Clarion*, August 1, 1949, p. 2.

3. Colin Howell, "Black Bases/Black Ice: The Multi-Sport Careers of Canadian Black Athletes and the Struggle for Social Justice," *Telling the Stories of Race and Sports in Canada*, https://scholar.uwindsor.ca/racesportsymposium/rscday2/sep28/5. Barry Swanton and Jay-Dell Mah, *Black Baseball Players in Canada, A Biographical Dictionary, 1881–1960* (Jefferson, NC: McFarland, 2009) is an especially useful place to start when uncovering the stories of forgotten black players, but this is an ongoing project. Many of the players in the postwar Maritimes have escaped their attention.

4. *The Clarion*, August 1, 1947, p. 4.

5. Ibid., July 2, 1947, p. 5.

6. Colin Howell, *Northern Sandlots: A Social History of Maritime Baseball* (Toronto: University of Toronto Press, 1995), pp. 183–84.

7. Jules Tygiel, *Baseball's Great Experiment: Jackie Robinson and His Legacy* (New York: Oxford University Press, 1983).

8. Howell, *Northern Sandlots*, pp. 182, 184.

9. Rick Westhead, "The 'Coloured Boy.' Baseball pioneer Manny McIntyre could handle anything other players threw him—anything except their silence," *The New Brunswick Reader*, August 12, 1995, pp. 13–15. One scout told Manny that he was "sure fire to go to the majors."

10. John Lutz and Bill Young, "Manny McIntyre: A Black Canadian Pioneer 1930s–950s," *Telling the Stories of Race and Sports in Canada* 4 (September 29, 2018); John Lutz, "Pioneer on the Diamond, Ace on the Ice: Manny McIntyre," in Arif Khadid and Keith Elman, *In the Shadow of Obscurity: Toiling in a Reluctant Society* (Los Angeles: ENH, 2020); Ron Barry, "Manny McIntyre: A Trailblazer of his Generation," *Saint John Telegraph-Journal*, August 31, 2013.

11. Howell, "Black Bases/Black Ice"; Tom Hawthorn, "Art Dorrington was considered the Jackie Robinson of Hockey," *Globe and Mail*, February 5, 2018.

12. Willie O'Ree, *Willie: The Game-Changing Story of the NHL's First Black Player* (Toronto: Penguin Canada, 2020).

13. Although this story was often repeated by many of my interviewees, I was unable to find corroboration in written sources. I am nonetheless quite certain that this happened although perhaps not with the exact wording in the quotation included above.

14. Merritt Clifton, *Disorganized Baseball: The Provincial League from LaRoque to Les Expos* (Brigham, Quebec: Samisat, 1982), pp. 17–18. Clifton includes Mentis as one of five outstanding players in the Provincial League between World War II and the coming of the Expos. When Clifton asked Johnny why he didn't play professional baseball, Mentis replied: "I had one chance when I was young to sign and go south to play ... but I wasn't ready for that then, where you had to walk in the street while somebody else could walk on the sidewalk."

15. Francis G. Mitchell, *The Boys of '62: Transcending the Racial Divide* (Halifax: New World Publishing, 2008).

Chapter Eight

1. Colin D. Howell, "Baseball, Class and Community in the Maritime Provinces, 1870–1910," *Histoire Sociale [Social History]* 22, no. 4 (November 1989), p. 285.

2. *Spalding's Official Canadian Baseball Guide, 1912* (Montreal: Canadian Sports Publishing, 1912). The Guide was unpaginated but included an eleven-page section on the New Brunswick-Maine League and a lengthy description of the St. John-Lowell series.

3. Will Anderson, *Was Baseball Really Invented in Maine?* (Portland: Will Anderson, 1992) provides a useful overview of Maine's baseball history.

4. Robert Ashe, *Even the Babe Came to Play: Small Town Baseball in the Dirty 30s* (Halifax, N.S.: Nimbus, 1991).

5. Chris Jensen, *Baseball State by State: Major and Negro League Players, Ballparks, Museums and Historical Sites* (Jefferson, NC: McFarland, 2012), p. 127.
6. *The Portsmouth Herald*, May 27, 1954, p. 14.
7. *The Gardner News*, June 26, 1992, p. 7.
8. *Rutland Daily Herald*, June 8, 1951, p. 10.
9. Jim Carter, "Aroostook Sports History," http://history.pilib.org.
10. *Houlton Pioneer Times*, September 22, 1949, p. 6.
11. "N.B.-Maine League," *Maritime Baseball Pictorial Yearbook* (1950), p. 31.
12. *Bangor Daily News*, April 27, 1955, p. 17.

Chapter Nine

1. Francis "Joe" Fulghum, "Obituary," Spicer-Mullikin Funeral Homes and Crematory, Newark, Delaware (May 23, 2020); Hugh Townshend, "Through the 1950s, the best ball ever," Pictou, *The Advocate*, February 4, 2022; Hugh Townshend, "A Popular old Albion Passes Away in U.S.," Pictou, *The Advocate*, February 4, 2022.
2. Colin Howell, *Northern Sandlots: A Social History of Maritime Baseball*, p. 216.
3. *Halifax Herald*, September 7, 1951, p. 10.
4. *Atlanta Constitution*, May 12, 1953, p. 8; *The Sporting News*, May 20, 1953, p. 35.
5. Joe DeMacido "Peabody's Waselchuk Reflects on Pitching Against Hank Aaron," *The Salem News*, August 9, 2013 (e-edition) n.p.
6. The estimated loss reported in the Halifax *Chronicle Herald*, August 31, 1954, p. 23, was substantially less than the actual loss included in the club's financial records.
7. Halifax *Chronicle Herald*, August 31, 1954, p. 23.
8. Unfortunately for the Albions, most clubs seemed to ignore the agreement. Halifax *Chronicle Herald*, August 10, 1955, p. 14.
9. Halifax *Chronicle Herald*, July 22, 1955, p. 10.
10. *Halifax Herald*, August 15, 1955, p. 17.
11. New Glasgow *Evening News*, August 3, 1955.
12. Halifax *Chronicle Herald*, April 15, 1955.
13. Halifax *Chronicle Herald*, May 11, 1956, p. 26.
14. Chester *Daily Times*, September 27, 1958.
15. Jackie Friedman, "Heralded Baseball coach Eddie Lyons, who died Friday, helped mold young players," Newark, NJ, *The Star-Ledger*, November 3, 2011 (online).
16. Andy Sturgill, "John Boozer," SABR Biography Project. BaseballReference.com.
17. Lucy Stallworth Kubiszyn, *When a Star Fell on Alabama: The Jack Kubiszyn Story* (Tuscaloosa: Word Way Press, 2008), pp. 250–54.
18. *Ibid.*, p. 64.

Chapter Ten

1. Mark McCarter, *Never a Bad Game: Fifty Years of the Southern League* (Madison, WI: August, 2014).
2. Larry Colton, *Southern League: A True Story of Baseball, Civil Rights and the Deep South* (New York: Grand Central, 2013).
3. *Chicago Tribune*, 28 March 1967, p. 56.
4. Bob Logan and Pete Cava, *Amazing Tales from the Chicago Cubs Dugout: A Collection of the Greatest Cubs Stories Ever Told* (New York: Simon & Schuster, 2012). Elia recalled that in 1967 he hit a grand-slam homer off Bob Gibson. which made the difference between making the White Sox opening day roster and being sent to the minors. His manager at the time was Eddie Stanky.
5. Pat Jordan, *A False Spring: A Memoir* (New York: Dodd, Mead, 1975).
6. *Chicago Tribune*, April 8, 1962, p. 102.
7. *Chicago Tribune*, April 10, 1962, p. 50.
8. Vern Handrahan (audio interview), *Island Voices*, Prince Edward Island.
9. Nashville, *The Tennessean*, March 29, 1959, p. 53.

10. Kevin Czerwinski, "Stowe Snags Win Without a Pitch. Left-hander left behind by Yankees found quick way to net a 'W,'" May 11, 2007 (online), mlb.com.

11. Burton Russell, *Nova Scotia Baseball Heroics*, p. 181.

12. Roy Terrell, "The Signing of Danny Murphy," *Sports Illustrated*, June 27, 1960. vault.si.com/vault/1960/06/27.

13. Burton Russell, *Seven Decades of Nova Scotia Baseball: 1946–2005* (Kentville, N.S.: Self-published, 2017), p. 88.

Chapter Eleven

1. Charlie Fox, *Fox Tales: Recollections from Moments in Time* (Pictou, N.S.: Advocate Printing and Publishing, 2020), pp. 159–223.

2. Burton Russell, *Seven Decades of Nova Scotia Baseball 1946–2016*, p. 136.

3. John White, "Lyle Carter: Nova Scotia's journeyman goalkeeper, all-star third baseman," *The Nova Scotian*, June 11, 2018.

4. Andrew MacGilligan, "The Ghosts of Baseball Hill," *Edit Magazine* (martimeedit.com), vol. 10 (September 11, 2019).

Chapter Twelve

1. Bill James, "The Quality of Competition Over Time: Presumptive Strength," *Bill James Online*, November 4, 2019.

2. Peter Palmer and John Thorn, eds., *The Hidden Game of Baseball: A Revolutionary Approach* (Chicago: University of Chicago Press, 1984) is an important starting point for those interested in the new analytics. One of the most important metrics to arise from Palmer's early work was OPS, which is a much more comprehensive measurement than batting average since it recognizes both the ability to get on base and raw power. Over the last two decades, the work of sabermetricians has found an important outlet in *By the Numbers: The Newsletter of the Statistical Analysis of the Committee of the Society for American Baseball Research*.

3. *Halifax Herald*, August 27, 1949, p. 12.

4. Tonery returned to the H&D League for three summers and was a run-of-the-mill pitcher-outfielder and .250 hitter after his injuries. When his Central League performance is included, his career batting average in Maritime baseball was slightly over .300.

5. *The Sporting News*, March 2, 1949, p. 18.

6. Cappy Gagnon, *Notre Dame Baseball Greats: From Anson to Yaz* (Charleston, SC: Arcadia, 2004), p. 63.

7. Christian Trudeau, "Punching Above its Weight: The Quebec Provincial League," in Andrew North, ed., with Len Levin, Bill Nowlin, and Carl Reichers, *Our Game Too: Influential Figures and Milestones in Canadian Baseball* (Phoenix: Society for American Baseball Research, 2022), pp. 292–301.

Bibliography

Books

Anderson, Will. *Was Baseball Really Invented in Maine?* Portland, ME: Will Anderson, 1992.
Clifton, Merritt. *Disorganized Baseball: The Provincial League from LaRoque to the Expos.* Richford, VT: Samisdat, 1982.
Colton, Larry. *Southern League: A True Story of Baseball, Civil Rights, and the Deep South's Most Compelling Pennant Race.* New York: Grand Central, 2013.
Douglas, Bob. *Life Is a Ball! 50 Years of Nova Scotia Sport.* Halifax, NS: Links, 2000.
Elliott, Bob. *The Northern Game: Baseball the Canadian Way.* Toronto: Sport Classic, 2005.
Ford, Richard. *Independence Day.* New York: Alfred Knopf, 1995.
Fox, Charles. *Fox Tales II. Recollections from Moments in Time.* Halifax, NS: Advocate, 2020.
Gmelch, George. *Playing with Tigers: A Minor League Chronicle of the Sixties.* Lincoln: University of Nebraska Press, 2016.
Howell, Colin. *Northern Sandlots: A Social History of Maritime Baseball.* Toronto: University of Toronto Press, 1995.
Humber, William. *Diamonds of the North: A Concise History of Baseball in Canada.* New York: Oxford University Press, 1995.
James, Bill, and Rob Neyer. *The Neyer/James Guide to Pitchers.* New York: Fireside, 2004.
Jordan, Pat. *A False Spring: A Memoir.* Lincoln: University of Nebraska Press, 2005. First published 1975 by Dodd, Mead.
Kinsella, W.P. *Shoeless Joe.* New York: Houghton Mifflin, 1982.
Kubiszyn, Lucy Stallworth. *When a Star Fell on Alabama: The Jack Kubiszyn Story.* Tuscaloosa: Lucy Stallworth Kubiszyn, 2009.
Lewis, T.J. *A View from the Mound: My Father's Life in Baseball.* Lulu.com, 2009.
McCarter, Mark. *Never a Bad Game: Fifty-Plus Years of the Southern League.* Middleton, WI: August Publications, 2014.
McGimpsey, David. *Imagining Baseball: America's Pastime and Popular Culture.* Bloomington: Indiana University Press, 2000.
Mitchell, Francis G. *The Boys of '62: Transcending the Racial Divide.* Halifax: New World, 2008.
North, Andrew, ed., with Len Levin, Bill Nowlin and Carl Riechers. *Our Game Too: Influential Figures and Milestones in Canadian Baseball.* Phoenix: Society for American Baseball Research, 2020.
O'Ree, Willie. *Willie: The Game-Changing Story of the NHL's First Black Player.* Toronto: Penguin Canada, 2020.
Palmer, Pete, and John Thorn, eds. *The Hidden Game of Baseball: A Revolutionary*

Approach to Baseball and Its Statistics. Chicago: University of Chicago Press, 2015. First published 1984 by Doubleday.

Peeler, Tim. *The Easter Monday Baseball Game: North Carolina State and Wake Forest on the Diamond, 1899–1956.* Jefferson, NC: McFarland, 2013.

Piersall, Jim, and Al Hirshberg. *Fear Strikes Out: The Jim Piersall Story.* New York: Bantam, 1957.

Russell, Burton. *Nova Scotia Baseball Heroics.* Kentville, NS: Burton Russell, 1993.

_____. *Seven Decades of Nova Scotia Baseball, 1946–2015.* Kentville, NS: Burton Russell, 2017.

Saccoman, John T., Gabriel R. Costa, and Michael Huber. *Practicing Sabermetrics: Putting the Science of Baseball Statistics to Work.* Jefferson, NC: McFarland, 2009.

Swanton, Barry. *The ManDak League: Haven for Former Negro League Ballplayers, 1950–57.* Jefferson, NC: McFarland, 2006.

Swanton, Barry, and Jay-Dell Mah. *Black Baseball Players in Canada: A Biographical Dictionary.* Jefferson, NC: McFarland, 2006.

Tebbetts, Birdie, with James Morrison. *Confessions of a Baseball Nomad.* Chicago: Triumph, 2002.

SABR Biography Project

Subject (Author)

Stan Benjamin (Chris Rainey)
John Boozer (Andy Sturgill)
Ed Connolly, Jr. (Bill Nowlin)
Ike Delock (Ray Birch)
Moe Drabowsky (R.J. Lesch)
Ray Fisher (Chip Hart)
Johnny Gee (Armand Peterson)
Dick Gernert (Don Hyslop)
Norm Gigon (Charles Bevis)
Ron Jackson (Bill Nowlin)
Deacon Jones (Bill Nowlin)
Jack Lamabe (Bill Nowlin)
Charley Lau (Stan Grosshandler)
Bill Lefebvre (Bill Nowlin)
Ray Martin (Jim Gormley)
Stuffy McInnis (Aaron Davis and C. Paul Rogers)
Joe Morgan "Walpole Joe" (Rory Costello)
Danny Murphy (Doug Skipper)
Johnny Murphy (John Vorperian)
Dave Ricketts (Eric Vickery)
Hal Smith (Dick Rosen)
Hal Smith (Tim Flannery)
Al Spangler (David E. Skelton)
Bill Spanswick (Bill Nowlin)

Other Interviews (see also Interview References in "Essay on Sources")

George Alusik (SABR audio)
Tom Carroll (SABR, Lou Kriger chapter audio)
Vern Handrahan (*Island Voices*, PEI)
Jack Kaiser (April Earle, June 12, 2012)
Sonny Senerchia (SABR audio)

Index

Acocella, "Doc" 17, 45, 190
African Zulu Giants 49
Agganis, Harry 115–6, 125
Albemarle League (Carolinas) 58, 63, 70, 73–4
All-Time Maritime All-Star team 185–8
Allard, Jacques 107–8
Allen, Archie 10, 115, 118–9, 196
Allie, Gair 72–4, 167, 184–5, 189, 196, 198, 200
Alusik, George 42, 120
American Baseball Coaches Association (ABCA) All Americans 82, 89–90
Arbucho, Jim 32, 47, 62, 115, 176
Aroostock League 116–7, 120, 207
Atlantic Coast Conference 9, 80, 89
attendance 69, 128–30, 132–4, 136, 154
Atwood, Bob 61
Augusta Millionaires 23, 115, 117, 120, 125
Aylward, Paul 61

Bagwell, Bob 57
Bagwell, Jeff 57
Bailey, Jim 136
Ballestrini, Dick 170
Baltimore Orioles 11, 89, 92–3, 108, 127, 132, 134, 139, 152, 168, 175
Barber, Arlan 123
barnstorming teams 9, 30, 44–5, 50, 52, 110
Barteaux, Frank 159
Barteaux, Walter 25
baseball in Saint John 8, 16, 26, 29–30, 34, 39–42, 45, 51, 66, 68, 84, 99, 103, 110–3, 116, 118, 120, 122, 177, 190
Batts, Matt 49
Beckman, Jim 149, 157
Bella, John "Zeke" 9, 32, 56, 65, 91–2, 165, 167–8, 170, 184–9, 191, 199–200
Benjamin, Stan 115, 132–3, 210

Bentfield, Richard 122, 190
Berardino, Dick 18, 144, 194
Bergeron, Bill 67, 77, 194, 199
Berry, Morton 99
Best, Cal 99, 199
Best, Carrie 98
Birdie Tebbetts Major League All-Stars 8, 50–2, 120, 204–5, 210
Bissonette, Del 112
Blacks Harbour Brunswicks 10, 16, 23, 42–3, 46, 57, 68, 87, 108, 116–23, 172, 205
Blackstone Industrial League 58, 62, 73, 82
Blount, Bruce 53, 115–6, 195
Bobotas, Socrates "Soc" 13–4, 53, 115, 189, 191, 195
Bonus Babies 1, 10, 82, 90–1, 97, 124, 205
Boozer, John 136, 207, 210
Border League 11, 22, 30, 65, 100–3, 114
Boss, Hilton 66
Boss, Len 31, 62, 104
Bossidy, Larry 89, 124, 134, 196
Boston Braves 62, 103, 121
Boston Red Sox 13, 34, 36, 38, 48–9, 60–1, 88, 111, 114, 137, 140, 149, 151, 204
Boston Royal Giants 49
Boudreau, Don 91, 131, 160
Bowers, Charles "Buzz" 18, 62, 83, 149, 176, 199–200
Bowers, Mac 65, 131
Bowes, Jackie 23, 57, 66, 166, 177
Brady, Walt 131, 195
Breen, Joe 45, 47, 57, 101
Brightman, Harry 60
Brissette, Paul "Breezer" 83–4, 194, 199–200
"Brooklyn-Against-the-World" tour 44–5
Brooklyn Junior Dodgers 44–5

211

Brooks, Bill 9–10, 62–3, 69–71, 73–77, 80, 88–9, 115, 119, 122, 128, 130–2, 196, 199–200
Brown, Bobby Lee 129, 132, 177
Brown, Donny 28, 148, 200
Brownell, Cecil 51
Bruce, Carl 30, 48
Buckler, Bev 14, 25, 53–4, 135, 199
Buckler, Reg 14
Buckwalter, Hal 60–1, 168, 170, 185–6, 191, 196
Bujnowski, Tom 147, 193, 195
Bulger, Paul 192
Bunker, Dick 176, 195
Buntain, Bill 159
Burby, Hal 53, 115, 195, 199
Burchell, Bob 150
Burchell, "Red" 39, 65, 67–8
Burden, "Brownie" 31, 62

Camacho, Joe 140, 149–150
Cambridge White Elephants 30
Canadian-American League (Can-Am) 114, 170–1
Cape Breton Colliery League 9, 13, 22, 26, 38–40, 50, 56, 67–8, 83, 93, 100, 112, 133, 157, 168, 183–4, 186, 191, 205
Cape Cod League 135
Carroll, "Muck" 51
Carroll, "Ownie" 46–7
Carroll, Tom 90–3, 190, 195, 205, 210
Carter, Billy 23, 91–2, 104, 131, 149, 190
Carter, Lyle 28, 158, 199–201, 208
Cassell, Tom 67
Catallo, John 120–2, 190, 192
Ceccarelli, Art 42, 53–4, 166, 199–200
Central League 8, 22, 53, 56, 61, 63, 119, 128, 168–9, 171, 176, 183–4, 208
"Chappie" Johnson All-Stars 49
Charlton, Donald "Chic" 41
Cheney, Hal 116–7
Chicago Cubs 11, 79, 87, 90, 108, 123, 144–6, 186, 207
Chicago White Sox 20, 30, 40, 90, 105, 129, 143, 145, 172, 174
Chirurgi, Ray 60
Christoff, Ernie 5
Clapp, Roger 121–2
The Clarion 98, 199, 206
Clark, Johnny "The Westville Flash" 22, 25–6, 34, 37, 56, 64, 66, 91, 184–6, 190, 192, 199–200
Clarke, John "Twit" 47, 61, 65, 199–200
Cline, Ty 4, 6, 80, 90, 138, 166, 171, 184, 186, 189, 194, 198–9

Cline, William 91, 194
Coleman, Joe 51
College World Series (CWS) 1, 10, 13, 68, 72, 80–3, 85, 89
Color Bar Limbo 11, 98, 100, 106, 109
Coluni, Bob 72, 196
Condy, W.A. "Buddy" 23, 26, 28–9, 31, 33, 45, 56, 166–8, 184–6, 189, 191–2
Conick, Ab 37
Connelly, Ed 149, 195, 210
Cormier, Dick 120
Cormier, Joe 53, 101
Cormier, Rheal 12, 161
Cote, Ron 84, 177, 193–4
Craig, Jim 150, 177, 194
Cronin, Bill 43, 61
Cullum, Ken 145, 195
Cumming, Ted 49, 100–1, 199–200
Curran, Jack 60, 195
Czerniakowski, Ed 125, 135–6, 171, 176, 195

Dagres, Angelo 124, 166–8, 174, 185–6, 189, 191
Daly, Tom 41–2, 110, 112
Dartmouth Arrows 4–6, 8–10, 13, 17, 22–4, 26, 39, 45, 56, 64–5, 83–4, 89, 104, 108–9, 128, 130–3, 139, 146–7, 150–4, 158, 170–1, 179, 186, 189–90
Dartmouth Moosehead Dry 158, 160–1
Davis, Bob 9, 91–2, 123, 193–4, 196
Davis, Gerry 33, 40, 199–200, 204
Davis, Robert "Dizzy" 77
Decker, Bob 9, 91–2, 123, 193–4, 199–200
Deitz, Hal 18, 90, 136, 147, 152, 178, 182, 185–6, 194
Desmond, Viola 98, 107, 204–6
Detroit Clowns 49
Detroit Tigers 87–8, 122, 173, 181
Detroit-Windsor Baseball Federation 10, 29; connections to Maritimes 30–1, 40, 86–8
Dickman, Emerson 8, 43, 60
Dickson, Jason 12
Dietz, Emmett 145
DiFrederico, Jim 178
Doroin, Phil 157
Dorrington, Art 11, 23, 37, 99, 103, 106, 201, 206
Dorrington, Frank "Danky" 104, 107
Drabowsky, Moe 11, 33–4, 90, 94–6, 136, 166, 180, 185–6, 193, 196, 199, 205, 210
Duke University Blue Devils 77, 79, 122, 180

Index 213

Dumeah, Jimmy 10, 29, 40, 46, 161
Durkin, Harry 171, 176, 195
Dussault, Norm 35, 102
Dyer, Jim 117, 120

Eaddy, Don 11, 87, 89, 108, 195
Eason, Don 87, 186, 193, 195
Eason, Ron 195
East Coast Athletic Conference (ECAC) 52, 70
Edmundston Republicans 8, 23, 68, 80, 84, 88, 110, 116, 120–4, 172, 185, 187, 190, 192
Edwards, Jim 130–1, 190
Elia, Lee 17, 21, 143–5, 154, 203, 207
Elliott, Bob 5, 209
Erickson, Stu 77, 122, 171, 194

Fahey, Leo 53, 133
Fantuzzi, Al 80, 125, 194
Farino, Jim 125, 147, 193–4
Farrell, Richard "Turk" 5, 42, 115, 166, 178
Ferguson, Bob 24, 199
Ferguson, Philip "Skit" 23, 25, 30, 37, 45, 64, 166, 184–5, 187–8, 199–200
Ferrara, Sal 137, 140, 172, 185–6, 189, 192
Fillmore, Frank 4, 148–9
Fisher, Ray 43, 83, 86, 104, 115, 122–3, 172, 195, 205, 210
Flemming, Fred 23, 57, 76, 116, 122, 185–6, 189
Flynn, Bob 124, 172
Forbes, Wendell 172
Ford, Edward "Whitey" 47, 52
Forizs, John 178
Fortunato, Johnny 27, 37, 194
Fowler, Lawson 31, 62
Fox, Jimmy 23, 34, 57, 122
Francis, Earl 124
Fredericton Capitols 23, 56–7, 67–8, 100, 102, 104, 110–1, 120, 122, 125, 168, 172, 185, 189–91
Fulghum, Joe 31, 72–5, 80, 89, 127, 131, 136, 166–8, 184–6, 189, 191, 196, 199–200, 207

Gastall, Tom 11, 90, 92–3, 116, 122, 190, 195
Gaudet, Alonzo 57
Gaudet, Oscar 157
Gaudet, Pius 57
Gautreau, Walter "Doc" 83, 115
Gee, George 114
Gee, Johnny 57, 86–8, 195, 205, 210

Genthon, Mike 41
Georgia Chain Gang 49
Gernert, Dick 13–4, 29, 31, 42, 47–8, 53, 61, 142, 165–9, 184–6, 189, 191–2, 196, 210
Gigon, Norm 17, 20–1, 143–5, 154, 185–6, 194, 199, 203, 210
Gillis, Bob 158, 199
Gillis, Eddie 13–4, 53, 67, 76, 155, 160
Glynn, Gerry 149, 178, 182, 195
Goldfader, Sid 5, 122, 167, 190, 199
Goucher, Pete 7, 155–6, 160
Graham, Johnny 23, 109, 147, 152, 157, 166, 193, 199, 201
Grand Falls Cataracts 16, 51, 57, 68, 88, 110, 120–5, 127, 175, 190–1
Grant, Dick 123
Gray, Jimmy 34, 41, 45
Greenaway, Harry 66
Griggs, Alvin 108, 123, 172, 196

Hadlock, Ed 121, 193–4
Hafenecker, John 61
Halifax Cardinals 23, 31, 90–2, 175
Halifax Citadels 125, 135–6
Halifax Defense League (HDL) 8, 15, 26, 35, 38, 41, 58
Halifax Red Sox 140, 147, 149–50, 151
Halifax Shipyards 26, 34, 41, 45–6, 55–6, 65, 68, 101, 166, 192
Halpin, Jack 42, 44, 56, 166, 185–6, 188, 193
Handrahan, Vern 23, 146, 166, 177, 207, 210
Hannan, Jim 146, 195
Hannon, Billy 38
Harris, Bill 6, 23, 57, 66, 166, 203
Harris, Richard "Dickie" 77, 147, 172
Harvey, John 23, 30, 51, 123
Harvey, Laurence Scott, Jr. 158
Harvey, Scott 118
Haynam, Bruce 10, 87–8, 195
Hearst Classic 44, 116, 204
Hector, Cyril 30
Heerlein, Charles 179
Heller, George 179
Heller, Jim "Smokey" 56, 91–2, 166, 179, 184, 186, 193
Henrichs, Russ 132, 136
Heximer, Jim 39, 114
Hoch, Art 10, 17, 69–70, 72, 74, 76–8, 80, 82, 89, 95, 122, 139–40, 146–7, 164, 171, 185, 190, 196, 198, 200
Hodgdon, Warren 124, 134
Hodgson, Paul 12, 124, 161
Holt, Lynwood 89, 196

Holy Cross Crusaders 10, 16, 18, 68, 81–6, 112, 123, 134, 147, 174, 176, 194, 205
Horsman, Vince 12, 158
Houlton Collegians 68, 111–2, 117, 120–2, 124, 190, 192
House of David 49, 125

Iceton, Terry 64, 66
Imports and Locals rivalry 9, 12, 63, 125, 127, 134

Jackman, Bill 49
Jackson, Ron 90, 195, 205, 210
James, Bill 76, 163, 182–3, 185, 208
Jay, Joey 115
Jirsa, Ron 193
Johnson, Clarence 22, 26–7, 32, 37, 88, 130, 200
Johnson, Don 57, 122
Johnston, Manly "Shot" 143–4
Jones, Grover "Deacon" 79, 87–8, 104–5, 123, 144, 172, 185–6, 190–1, 196, 199, 201, 210
Jones, Lucius Jeff 48, 66, 84, 87, 103, 105, 145, 153–4, 157, 180
Joseph, Alex 27
Joseph, "Bam" 27
Joseph, Hummit "Hum" 23, 27–8, 37, 57, 64, 104, 159
Joseph, Kemal 27

Kaiser, Jack 10, 13–4, 47, 53, 61–2, 83, 115, 125, 168–9, 173, 190–1, 210
Keany, Walter "Huck" 62, 71, 73, 195, 199
Kearns, Bill 16, 84
Kentville Junior Cardinals 155
Kentville Wildcats 13–4, 18–9, 23, 31, 46, 53, 56, 59, 85, 116, 119, 155, 168–9, 176, 184, 186
Kiley, Dave 23, 51, 57, 190
"King and His Court" 100
Kinsella, William: *Field of Dreams* 2, 203, 209
Korcheck, Steve 84, 166, 173, 184–6, 189, 195, 199
Krakauskas, Joe 39
Krausse, Lew 134–5
Krichell, Paul 78, 91
Krop, Bob 20, 136, 179
Kubiszyn, Jack 136–40, 166, 184–6, 189, 192, 194, 199, 201, 207, 209
Kunkel, Bill 124, 134
Kurty, Jack 62, 122, 127, 185–6, 190–1, 196

Lamonica, Joe 61, 191
Langille, Win 37, 42, 64
Lary, Gene 88, 138, 179
Lau, Charley 5, 86–7, 118, 210
Laurentide League 30, 124
Lay, Joe 114
LeBlanc, "Copie" 33
Lee, Bill "Spaceman" 157, 161
Letteri, Larry 30, 34, 57
Levinson, Gerald 91, 195, 199, 201
Lewis, George 167, 190, 195
Lewis, Joe 77, 122, 180, 194
Lepcio, Ted 115, 125, 196
Linkletter, Tommy "Mountain Boy" 33–4
Liptak, Ron 5, 144, 190, 194
List, Bob 136, 147, 180, 196
Liverpool Larrupers 8, 10, 16, 23, 29–30, 38, 40, 65, 72, 83–4, 90, 92, 94, 96, 112, 116, 121, 123, 128–31, 136–7, 158, 169, 173, 178, 181, 184, 186, 189–90, 193
Lloyd, Harry Lee 77, 147, 190, 194
Lockhart, Johnny 17, 148, 150, 155, 199–201
Loes, Billy 44–5, 115
Loiselle, Dick 158–60
Long, Vance 80, 180
Looney, Ray 137, 139, 167, 173, 190, 194, 199, 201
Luck, Eugene "Bucky" 80, 173, 190
Lumenti, Ralph 90, 94–7, 117, 123–4, 134, 136, 147, 195, 199, 201
Lupien, Tony 50–1, 194
Lyons, Eddie 83, 135–6, 207

MacDonald, Angus "Sonny" 26, 36, 57
MacDonald, Harold "Purv" 34
MacDonald, John "Brother" 24, 63, 67, 100, 199–200
MacFayden, Danny 111
MacKenzie, Ken 5, 139, 180, 182, 196
MacLeod, Don 136, 191, 195
MacVicar, Don 24, 199
MacVicar, Jim "Lefty 24
Maddon, Joe 20
Maglie, Sal 52
Maguire, Fred 67, 83, 115
Mahaney, George "Peanuts" 149
Mahoney, Neil 9, 154
Maine-New Brunswick League 11, 22, 68, 82, 96, 114, 117, 119–25, 134, 164–6, 168–9, 176, 181–2, 185–6
Major League Equivalencies (MLE) 163, 166, 168, 189–90
Marchildon, Phil 39
Marsh, "Bull" 24, 53

Martin, Howie 64, 66
Martin, Ray 49, 210
Marysville Royals 16, 29, 105, 125, 160–1
Massa, Gordon 194
Matheson, Carl 28, 37, 64, 104
Matheson, Glen 28, 155
Maxwell, Stan "Chook" 10–1, 23, 88, 104–6, 108, 130, 148, 153, 190
McConnell, Mickey 46–7
McCracken, Jack 17–20, 147, 199–200
McElroy, Francis 122, 190
McGinley, Jack 89, 136, 190, 193, 196
McGowan, Andy 123, 192, 195
McGowan, Jack 126–7, 196
McInnis, John Phalen "Stuffy" 10, 43, 60–2, 84, 115, 119, 210
McIntyre, Billy 34, 64
McIntyre, Vincent "Manny" 11, 23, 30, 35, 48, 57, 100–2, 206
McLenahan, Roly 23, 57, 102, 122, 166, 168, 185–6, 189, 199
McLeod, Claude "Dingie" 31, 62
McLeod, Herb 23, 31, 48, 104, 185–6, 189, 199
McLeod, Stew 31, 33
McManahan, Ralph 30
McManus, Jim 20
McMullen, Tom 33, 47–8, 53
Mellen, Charley 125, 132, 190, 195
Mentis, John 11, 99, 104, 106–8, 199, 201, 206
Merullo, Lenny 66–7, 93, 95, 146, 154, 195
Middleton Cardinals 29, 34, 46–9, 102, 112, 161, 172
Moncton Cubs 6, 66, 119
Mont, Gordie 37
Montreal Expos 4, 91, 157–8, 160, 173
Montreal Royals 6, 11, 42, 48, 98, 204
Moore, Balor 4
Moore, Curt 57
Moossmann, Art 83–4, 194
Morgan, Harold "Duke" 45, 47
Morgan, Joe 5, 83, 194, 210
Morgan, Tom 90, 136, 173, 176
Mullen, "Moon" 57, 166
Murphey, "Doc" 71–2, 196, 199–200
Murphy, Danny 144, 153–4, 167, 174, 176, 208, 210
Murphy, Johnny 9, 210
Murray, Meredith "Spud" 135, 193
Mustain, Vern "Preacher" 73, 75, 196

"NCAA North" 1, 9–10, 42, 52, 68, 72, 80, 82, 86–7, 108, 119, 126–7, 150, 157, 159, 166, 194–5
Neal, Milton "Bomber" 47, 108

Negro Leagues 9, 11, 49, 101–2, 207, 210
New Brunswick (and Southern NB) Leagues 7, 10, 22, 26, 30, 48, 82, 86–7, 93, 103, 114, 118, 120, 122, 183–4
New England Hoboes 49, 125
New England League 111, 121
New York Black Yankees 49, 101
New York Cubans 11, 101
New York Equitable Life series 9, 49, 55–56
New York Giants 9, 33, 50, 52, 55, 62, 69, 73, 87, 179
New York Yankees 8–10, 12, 18, 31, 34, 37–9, 50–1, 61, 66–7, 72–3, 76, 78, 80, 90–2, 96, 112, 114, 116, 120, 125, 129, 131–3, 135, 144, 147, 150–2, 154, 158, 169–70, 179–81, 187, 208
Noiles, Carman 23, 137, 153, 157
Norskey, Al 116, 190, 199
North Carolina State University 70, 80, 95, 194, 210
Northeastern Borderlands 1–2, 7–8, 12, 86, 110–11, 113–4, 120

O'Brien, Stu 56, 64–5, 150–1, 189
O'Connor, William "Oakie" 8
Odom, John "Blue Moon" 143
O'Donnell, Bob 174, 176
O'Ree, Willie 11, 105–6
Oster, Bill "Wild Bill" 90, 195
Overcash, Ron 18, 150, 194
Owen, George 10, 83, 196

Pankratz, Burt 30
Pare, Albert 47
Parent, Bernie 29–30, 40, 161
Parent, Leo 133, 136, 166–7, 185, 189, 193, 195
Parsons, Eric 147, 157
Parsons, Wilson 22, 66, 150–2, 166, 180, 199, 201
Patula, John 181
Pellagrini, Eddie 50–1
Perranoski, Ron 124, 166, 185, 188, 195
Perry, Ron 84–5, 194, 199–200
Pesaresi, Ed 8
Pesky, Johnny 50, 52, 120
Philadelphia Phillies 8, 12, 18, 20–1, 35, 62, 67, 74, 108, 114, 116, 121, 133, 135–6, 143–5, 150, 171, 173, 176–8
Piersall, Jim 50–1, 142, 210
Pittsburgh Pirates 12, 48, 74, 94, 105, 108–9, 115, 139–40, 157, 172–3
Piurek, "Whitey" 39
player salaries and team expenses 1, 23, 27, 39, 52, 63, 66, 83, 116–7, 130–2

Polli, Lou "Crip" 9, 38, 42
PONY League 103, 114, 137
Porter, Bobby 39
Portland Pilots 113
Presque Isle Indians 23, 68, 96, 112, 116–7, 120–4, 166, 168, 185, 189, 191
Prohovich, Don 82, 84, 90, 116, 123, 174, 176, 190, 194, 199
Proulx, Pat 120–1, 166, 189
Provincial League (Quebec) 26, 30, 34, 40–1, 47, 64–5, 91, 101, 104, 106, 108, 114, 122–3, 135, 150, 177, 183, 198, 206, 208–9
Pulsifer, Brian 14, 16, 76, 84–6, 126–7, 159, 199–201
Pyle, Charlie 57, 67, 99–100

Quality of Competition Index (QUOC) 2, 163–5, 170, 183, 188, 208

Rada, Roger 166, 185–6, 189, 191, 199
Raines, John "Monk" 129–31, 152, 193
Rancourt, Larry 135–6, 174, 191
Raugh, Jim 90, 136, 139, 181, 194
Raymond, Claude 4–5, 7
Raynor, Art 42, 47–8, 53, 115
Reardon, "Puddy" 47
Reddick, Phyllis 99
Reekie, Harry 23, 61–2, 73, 75, 133
Reimer, Don 38, 45–6, 194
Richard, Maurice "the Rocket" 35
Ricketts, Dave 11, 108, 134, 210
Rickey, Branch 11, 44, 74, 108
Ritacco, Bob 137, 159, 195
Roach, Cliff 37, 64
Roarke, Mike 5, 42, 57, 118, 120, 195
Robbins, Dean 190
Roberts, Mike 23, 149, 157
Roberts, Robin 62, 115
Robinson, Frank 79, 200
Rogers, Kent "Baby" 75, 131, 196, 199
Rollins College 80, 194
Ross, Raymond "Nap" 40
Rossmann, Herb 45, 184, 186, 192
Roy, Clyde 23, 26, 34–5, 37, 64, 101
Roy, Syd 62–3, 66, 73, 75, 133, 166, 193, 199–200
Russell, Burton 14, 25–6, 31, 35, 38, 152, 154–6, 184, 199, 203–4, 208, 210
Ruven (Ruvinski), Irving "Peaches" 40–2

Sabermetrics 76, 168–9, 198, 208, 210
Sabourin, Armand "Babe" 17–9, 144, 150, 154, 195, 199–200
Saia, Frank 90

St. John's University Redmen 10, 47, 140, 147, 179, 195
St. Pierre, Marcel 35
St. Stephen Kiwanis 28–9, 110–3, 117–8
Santaniello, Dick 175, 194
Saunders, Bill "Buzzard" 161, 199, 201
Scarborough, Ray 51
Schang, Wally 41
Schiller, Eugene 84, 189, 194
scouts and scouting 2, 8, 22, 24, 26, 31, 35–6, 43–4, 66, 68, 78, 82, 88–9, 95, 105, 116, 119, 124, 143, 146, 154, 159, 161, 164–5
Sczesny, Matt 175
Seale, Oscar 68, 99–100
Seaman, Danny 23, 38–9, 68, 83, 131, 137, 166, 185–6, 190
Seaman, Garneau 23, 38
Senerchia, Emmanuel "Sonny" 42, 47–8, 115, 204, 210
Seymour, Charles 124
Shaulis, Charley 30
Shea, Frank "Spec" 51
Sheldon, Rollie 147, 149, 166, 195
Sime, Dave 77–80, 90, 124, 134, 190, 194, 205
Sires, Leroy 63, 73–4, 194
Smith, Hal W. 42, 93, 118, 210
South Shore League, Nova Scotia 121, 171
Spangler, Al 5, 77–8, 90, 122, 175, 185–6, 190, 194, 205, 210
Spears, Howie 150, 153, 199–200
Springfield College 10, 61–2, 88–9, 118–9, 123, 196
Springhill Fencebusters 16–7, 20, 23, 27, 31–3, 42, 44, 61–2, 64, 68, 70, 83, 112, 118, 137, 153, 166–7, 178, 186
Stafford, Don 175, 194
Stairs, Matt 12, 161
Stallings, Jack 28, 77, 136, 196, 199–200, 203
Staples, Neil "Ozark" 42, 64, 66, 186, 193
Staples, Ron 124, 195
Stebbins, Ray 17, 144
Steitz, Ed 118–9, 196
Stellarton Albions 9, 23–4, 31, 42, 60, 67, 71–2, 74–5, 83, 119, 128–9, 152, 177
Stenhouse, Dave 20, 43, 84, 117, 123, 166, 193–4
Stokoe, John 89, 139, 196
Stowe, Hal 80, 147, 181, 185, 188, 194, 208
Sukeforth, Clyde 22, 199–200
Sullivan, Haywood 125

Index

Susce, Paul 17, 80, 194
Swanson, Art "Red" 90, 92, 94, 194
Swanson, Don 181, 195
Swasey, Hank 8, 13, 53, 195

Tanner, William "Bucky" 46–9, 204
Tarpey, Phil 90–1, 181, 195
Tettelbach, Dick 120
Thomas, Clarence "Sonny" 109
Thomas, Fred 39, 99, 103
Thomson, Mike 153, 158–60, 199–200
Thurston, Bill 88, 124, 134, 195, 199–200
Tippery, Ken 10, 87, 90, 195
Titus, "Aukie" 51, 57
Tominaga, Hank 46, 119, 196
Tonery, Chris 60, 127, 168, 189–91, 195–6, 208
Troke, Gordon 53
Truro Bearcats 10, 22, 25, 32, 37, 41, 48, 60, 63, 66, 75, 100–1, 116, 136, 144, 146, 152, 171
Tuminelli, Joe 35–7
Turney, Jack 131, 147, 190–1, 194

University of Michigan Wolverines 1, 10, 68, 81–2, 86–7, 108, 122, 195
University of North Carolina 10, 70, 80, 122, 181, 194

Valke, Tom 5
Vickers, Dev 38
Vickers, Gus 38
Vogel, Fred 5

Wade, Bill 14, 23, 136, 159, 196
Wake Forest College Deacons 9–10, 28, 68–70, 72–4, 77, 80–2, 89, 122, 129, 136, 140, 172, 176–7, 196, 205, 210
Walsh, Bill 77, 89, 196
Ware, Al 67, 100, 167–8, 185–6, 191
Waselchuck, John 129–31, 207
Washington Senators 19–20, 77, 90, 96, 125, 147, 149, 159, 172, 177
Watterson, Johnny 13, 32, 53, 56, 59–60, 62, 68–71, 73, 115–6, 195, 199–200, 204
Wedin, Bob 90, 137, 195
Weidenhammer, Ron 90, 127
Weinstock, Art "Whitey" 57, 62, 195
Werber, Bill 75, 77–9, 122, 190, 194
West, Art 196
White, Burlin 49
Willey, Carlton 5, 121
Williams, Ted 29, 33, 57, 142, 149
Windsor, Ontario Ryancretes 40
Wingo, Jim 161
Wingo, John 48, 161
Winkin, John 125
Wojtowicz, Clark 44, 169
Woods, Leo 41, 65, 190
Wrinn, Charles 5
Wynn, Early 59

Yarmouth Gateways 29, 112
Yvars, Jack 194
Yvars, John 17, 194

Zash, Tony 149

www.ingramcontent.com/pod-product-compliance
Ingram Content Group UK Ltd.
Pitfield, Milton Keynes, MK11 3LW, UK
UKHW041956140426
5217IPUK00015B/831